WHEN THE REWARDS CAN BE SO GREAT

D1533466

WHEN THE REWARDS CAN BE SO GREAT

ESSAYS ON WRITING & THE WRITING LIFE

KWAME DAWES *editor*

JAIME BRUNTON & DAVID HENSON *assistant editors*

1849
EDITIONS

An Imprint of Pacific University Press
FOREST GROVE, OREGON

Published by

1849 Editions, *an imprint of*

Pacific University Press

2043 College Way

Forest Grove, Oregon 97116

Cover image © 2011 Santiago Cal. *Some Kind* (2011; Collection of Art Museum of the Americas, Washington, D.C.). Used with permission.

Editor photograph © Andre Lambertson

Cover design by Joyce Gabriel & Isaac Gilman

ISBN 978-0-9884827-4-6 (pbk)

ISBN 978-0-9884827-5-3 (epub)

Published in the United States of America.

First Edition

PERMISSIONS

Contents

"THE COURAGE TO SOUND LIKE OURSELVES"
Reflections on the Writing Life

"THE GEOGRAPHY OF THE PAGE"
Reflections on the Writing Process

"SPECIFICITY? YES. BUT ONLY IF IT'S RELEVANT"
Reflections on the Nuts and Bolts of Writing

ACKNOWLEDGEMENTS

Deep gratitude for Isaac Gilman and the team at Pacific University Press for taking on this project as one of its first publications. We hope that this maiden journey will prove to be a good omen for future publications for the press.

Thanks also to Jaime Brunton and David Henson, Graduate Assistants at the University of Nebraska who played a key role as assistant editors in putting together this collection of essays. Finally, I am grateful to all the faculty at Pacific who contributed essays to this anthology—for the generosity of this act and for the way that it speaks to their commitment to the writing community. Thanks also to the University of Nebraska for keeping me fed while doing this work.

Special thanks to Shelley Washburn for her visionary leadership of the program and for her unfailing support for this project.

Finally, thanks to my family for their constant patient support even when they have no idea what I am doing.

KWAME DAWES

PREFACE

THE REST IS NOT OUR BUSINESS . . .

So here I am . . .
Trying to learn to use words, and every attempt
Is a wholly new start, and a different kind of failure . . .

> —T. S. Eliot, *The Four Quartets*

Several simple but significant impulses can be said to have driven the publication of this book of essays. For almost eight years, I have been a faculty member at the Pacific University low residency MFA in Writing program. When I began to teach in the program, I did not expect to be making a statement like "for almost eight years. . . ." Something happens to you when you spend twenty days a year with a bunch of people. Yes, the faces change as students graduate and as faculty members rotate out, but many remain the same, and the rituals that come with educational institutions and communities tend not to change a great deal. Seaside, Oregon, does not change much during the early days of January, and the lazy summer days in Forest Grove, Oregon, are reliably gentle on the body, predictable.

When I was a new faculty member, I was aware that the veterans knew each other and had an ease with one another. I decided to give my time to trying to learn as much as I could about my fellow faculty members. I read as many of their books as I could, and I began a ritual of trying to attend as many craft talks as possible. I assumed that after a few years, this enthusiasm would wane, and I took some solace in the thought that by then I would be so properly and solidly in place that no one would accuse me of slacking off. But the practice became a ritual and then a habit. Craft talks are splendid places for writers to speak about the life of writing and the pleasures of reading and making art, and finally, to offer useful tips and suggestions about how to write better. They are, more often than not, directed at the students in the program, but it becomes clear that the faculty are often talking to each other. Enough people have said to me, "Hey don't come to my talk this time, I gave a similar talk three years ago." I go anyway. Why? More often than not, the new energy in the room, the questions asked and the fact of time passing, changes things and makes the experience for all of us quite different.

I had not been a faculty member for more than a few years when the thought occurred to me that an anthology of these craft talks would be a good idea. Like many good ideas that come to me, I stored it in my closet of good ideas with the knowledge that the right time would come for it to be dusted off and reviewed.

A few years ago, the faculty was in discussion about ways to increase the profile of the program even as we started to consider the possibility of increasing scholarships for our students. In this period of increasing numbers of low-residency MFA programs, the two issues were not unrelated. We tossed around some ideas, including an anthology of the writing of our faculty members, but it became clear that what we offer at Pacific that is particularly distinctive and endearing are these varied, idiosyncratic, and really gifted writers talking about writing.

The craft talk at these residencies is a peculiar genre of thought and pedagogy. For many writers the idea of writing about the process of writing is either annoying or distracting, reactions representative of a somewhat superstition-based taboo against jinxing the writing process by talking about it. Some writers, especially those in the midst of a writing project, feel the least bit qualified to start telling people what they should or should not do as writers. It is one thing to lead a workshop, to give hints, to cross-pollinate ideas one-on-one with students in the rich and intensely rewarding exchange of packets over the course of the semester, and it is another thing entirely to stand in front of a hundred note-taking students along with other fellow faculty members (many of them very accomplished in their own right) and pontificate about the dos and don'ts of writing.

But we do it. And we do it because there is a special circumstance that operates at these residencies. At Pacific, there has been a long tradition among the faculty to remind the students that they, the faculty, are also learning, trying to make things work, and even struggling at the business of creating art. Most of the nightly readings that feature the faculty are distinguished by the willingness of faculty members to read works in progress or recently completed pieces. It is a risky thing, but it is also a generous act that reminds the students that we are in a community of people trying to write well. This spirit of experimentation, art in process, carries over to the craft talks. The effect is quite liberating, and at the same time extremely exciting. It is liberating because the faculty are allowed the space to be speculative, to be deeply introspective, and to speak about things that are important to them. At the same time, the pressure to be completely authoritative is removed. Indeed, the talks have a quality of exploration and venturesomeness. Residency after residency, it becomes clear that a conversation is going on. This fluid, open quality is something that has made the craft talks often quite daring. It is possible to bomb quite badly during a craft talk. It is allowed. And it is allowed because "bombing" is never the same as failure or uselessness. The time spent in question and answer, the long discussions that follow after the talk and even the silences, tend to be part of the process of making sense of the art that we are there to strengthen. This is true even when a talk struggles to be perfect—perhaps *because* the talk struggles a bit.

For all its challenges, the craft talk is, to my mind, a truly important ritual for writers who teach writing. For me, the knowledge that I have to give a craft talk twice a year allows me to slow down and think carefully about what I think is important about writing and about the business of making art. I have to examine myself and ask myself the kinds of challenging questions that, when asked of me by others, I can dismiss with humor or some kind of nimble avoidance. I can even assume the position of a mystic who simply pretends that making art is all quite magical and unknowable. The craft talk, in such moments, can demystify the process, leave us naked, vulnerable, and human. And for those of us who like to pretend that the writing process is all technical matters, all about the details of style and mechanics, the craft talk, by its very existence, almost demands that we at least answer the question, "Why do this?" My point is that as we embark on writing these talks, we are forced to think about our work and our practice and to start to develop the special language of how to make sense of it. Thankfully, what emerges is never uniform, never predictable. What emerges are essays like those collected here that remind us that writers all come to this business in distinct ways. Some of us allow ourselves to get deeply bogged down in mechanics while others flee from mechanics, reaching for larger themes, broader motivations; others, in an effort to bring clarity, find ourselves escaping to the mysterious, the unknowable place of a certain magic, and others of us just laugh. The beauty of this is that each of these acts, these gestures, constitutes a most valuable and honest engagement with the business of writing. I am especially pleased about this quality of the book.

I believe that one of the things that makes this book especially enjoyable and engaging is that at the core of these pieces is a quality of communication that suggests that there is a real audience, a known audience, that is listening to what is being said. That audience has had meals with the author, has had workshops with the author, has shared time with the author at the karaoke nights, and has walked along the boardwalk in the evening chill chatting with the author. The list could go on, but the point is that a semblance of intimacy sits at the basis of these pieces. It is true that each piece has undergone much necessary editing and rewriting to meet the expectations of the print platform. But what I have sought to do in each piece is to retain the energy and fluidity of the original talk, the original presentation. I believe this comes through in each of the essays collected here.

I believe, also, that the overwhelming pressure to communicate that comes with teaching, generous teaching, undergirds the collection. Of course, the writers are not conformists, and in many cases, they resist anything that would suggest conforming to some presumptions about the relationship between the so-called student and teacher, and they also, fully aware of the long history of writing pundits pontificating from on high, are gleeful about undermining any such dynamic with their writing style. As a result, we have a fitting range of essays, and I can think of no better introduction to the faculty at the Pacific University MFA in Writing program than this.

At the end of the day, the book is about rewards. The hope for all of us involved with the MFA program is to ensure that everyone who comes through the program, whether faculty or staff, can leave feeling as if the rewards for the effort are worth it. We struggled with a title for the book until I ran into a line in Dorianne Laux's splendid essay collected here: "[. . .] it's worth the trying when the rewards can be so great." It is an apt title for this collection because it makes no grand promising. In fact, that word "can" carries with it all the complexity of a writer's anxiety, a hint of doubt sandwiched by the grand dreams of success: "rewards" and "so great." It is almost comic, and no doubt this is Laux's intent, as she knows, like all writers do, that without the combination of ambition and hope and doubt and deep insecurity, genuinely meaningful art cannot be created. The business of learning the craft, of apprenticeship, if you will, is the "when" referred to in the title.

Recently, a visiting writer described us as a rag-tag group. Tellingly, this was seen as a tremendous compliment, and for this brilliant insight, the visiting writer was invited to join the faculty! Of course, any quick glance at the resumes of this rag-tag group will assure you that we are dealing here with very accomplished writers. These essays reveal as much. They remind us that these are thinking writers, writers who never take a single thing about the craft for granted. They are as engaged in the technical details of punctuation as they are in the demands of characterization, of musicality, of tradition, of influence, of fear, and of responsibility. They are writers living in this world, and they never lose sight of it. And here and there, we find these gems, these glittering gems of pure delight in the art, and they remind us of why we do this work, why we keep coming back to make this art that we do, why we keep trying. Each of these writers will agree that what we are doing is re-saying what others have said, and perhaps even better than we could say it. But what we bring is our own distinctive history, our own narrative of struggle and triumph in the making of our art, and our satchels full of the wisdom and empathy that other writers have given to us. For as long as writers have sought to write, writers have talked about the challenges of writing. This is part and parcel of what we do. We are in good company, and few could capture the sum of what this book is about as succinctly and with ample portions of the morose and the hopeful, than does T.S. Eliot in his poetic memoir, *The Four Quartets*, who in the section "East Coker," which reflects on his twenty years of "failure" as a writer, understands that at the end of it all, there is "perhaps neither gain nor loss." The measure of a writer cannot be so simple or definitive especially when the writer herself is doing the measuring. Eliot arrives at something both comforting and unsettling in its reliance on providence (some might say fate); he finds comfort in accepting that there is only one sure thing for a writer: that she can try to write. "For us," as he says it, "there is only the trying. The rest is not our business."

KWAME DAWES

"THE COURAGE TO SOUND LIKE OURSELVES"

Reflections on the Writing Life

CAROLYN COMAN

Why I Write for Children

The idea that some lives matter less
is the root of all that is wrong in the world.

—Dr. Paul Farmer

Being asked why I write for children feels a bit like being asked when I stopped beating my wife (or, in my case, husband). Because I *don't, I never did*—write for children. What I do is answer to the material that calls to me and more often than not that material has a child at its center. My tendency is to glom on to a child's perspective in relating what is happening, and that lands me in the territory of "writing for children"—perhaps the only genre that must bear the weight of its audience in its very name.

Both the question and the genre name presuppose that audience determines content and form, when really, at least for me, it's the other way around: What I write about determines how and for whom my books are published and marketed. Certainly children's book publishing and marketing affect how my books are put out and received in the world, and certainly adults and children are drawn to different stories, but those realities are to the side and after the fact of what I do and why I do it. What I do is write.

So let me tweak the question a bit: Why do I write about what I write about—the consciousness and made-up lives and adventures of certain children?

I didn't set out to, consciously, and I find that's usually a pretty trustworthy way to start. It came as news to me that the first novel I wrote—about a 12-year-old girl coming to terms with the loss of her mother, told by a third-person narrator who stays close and true to the protagonist and her 12-year-old heart—was "young adult." (The agent I submitted it to told me so, in horror, adding I could "kiss my career goodbye" if I went that route. The editor I sent it to at Farrar, Straus and Giroux accepted it with glee.) The next novel I wrote stayed true to a little boy scared to death by an act of domestic violence, and the one after that settled in with a 13-year-old girl deeply lost in the woods of an incestuous relationship; the one after that, set in South Africa, tracks an angry teenager's ragged path to reconciliation with her father . . . such were the characters and thematic content that called to me. I may not have consciously set out to write children's books, but left to my own devices and inclinations, that's exactly what I found myself doing, time and time again.

My editor and publisher, Stephen Roxburgh, summed it up best when he observed that I am more interested in discovery than recognition. Yes: first love, first awareness, first killing loss, first mortal wound, first forgiveness, first tectonic shift of consciousness . . . the kinds of discoveries that are so much the stuff of youth and that inevitably lead me to the lives and hearts and minds of children. You could say, I suppose, that I'm drawn to the same thematic material as many of my brother and sister writers of adult fiction, only I prefer my material enacted as opposed to reenacted, experienced rather than reconsidered, analyzed, or interpreted through adult retrospection.

Although I live in the adult world and read and am nurtured by adult books, when it comes to what I want to look into and live with creatively, I gravitate toward the awakening consciousness, savor the connections children make more than the connections adults do. I am more often delighted by and interested in writing the lives of children. Let's face it: We adults are just not as fresh.

I'm also constitutionally drawn to distilling things down. No-thought-unexpressed doesn't really cut it in our genre. In my effort to get to the bottom of things, I try to distill what I'm looking at—not reduce or diminish it—down to its essence, both in terms of language and content, and doing that inevitably leads me to a story simple enough for a child to read. Oscar Wilde said that his fairy tales were intended for "those who have kept the child-like faculties of wonder and joy, and who find in simplicity a subtle strangeness."

Writing for children and young adults is an elastic genre that over the last 25 years has provided me with plenty of room to maneuver and grow. I've written dark, serious, character-driven stories and funny, plot-driven over-the-top romps. True collaboration with artist Rob Shepperson on our graphic storybook, *The Memory Bank*, was my deepest plunge yet into imagination. For the past several years, I've been at work on an adult novel. Does the genre really matter? Are there consequences to writing for children? Sure, there are consequences to everything. Think of Peter Rabbit, who ended up with chamomile tea while his sisters got to have milk and blackberries.

Yes, my grown son always makes air quotes around "book" when he asks what I'm working on. And people occasionally say goofy things to me in response to hearing that I write for children—my personal favorite, said with a little squeal: "Oh, FUN!!!" An adult short story writer once complimented me after a reading, saying, "Hey, you do what *we* do!" The truth is that the age of our audience neither lowers the bar nor makes child's play of the work of writing.

I teach with a terrific bunch of writers in the MFA program at Pacific University. Within every genre—poetry, novel, short story, memoir, essay—children and teenagers abound. Writers are eternally drawn back to childhood and adolescence, forced to grapple with how and from what perspective to portray younger selves. Whether they look back at them from a wise and retrospective distance or stay glued to the young character's emerging consciousness, the work is exacting and the territory rich. Genres are distinct and define our work to a certain extent, but childhood and adolescence flow through them all.

When I mentioned to my collaborator Rob Shepperson that I was pondering the question *Why I Write for Children*, he sent back his own response. Enough said.

JOHN MCNALLY

The Shame, the Necessity, the Discouragement, and the Freedom: Rejection, Failure, and the Bigger Picture

The writer is the person who stays in the room.

—Ron Carlson

Here's an overview of my fiction writing book-writing career so far. This does not include individual stories, essays, nonfiction books, anthologies, or screenplays.

1. Novel. Rejected; never published. Year completed: 1991. 2 years to write.
2. Novel. Rejected; never published. Year completed: 1996. 5 years to write.
3. Story collection. Accepted. Year completed: 1999. 10 years to write.
4. Novel. Rejected; never published. Circulated by agent as a partial manuscript: 2002. 1.5 years to write.
5. Novel-in-Stories. Accepted. Year completed: 2003. 2 years (or more) to write.
6. Novel. Accepted. Year completed: 2005. 2 years to write.
7. Novel. Rejected; never published. Year completed: 2006? 2007? Less than a year to write.
8. Story collection. Accepted. Year completed: 2007. 10 years to write.
9. Novel. Accepted. Year completed: 2009. (Took a break writing Book #10 to write Book #9.) 9 months to write.
10. Novel. Rejected. Year completed: 2013. 2 years to research, then 5 years to write. At the moment, I'm considering a radical rewrite of this novel, but in its present form, it has been rejected by every major publishing house.

Three things for context: First, I earned my MFA in 1989; second, "rejection" means that the book was sent around to many, many publishers/editors by an agent; third, all of the acceptances came with rejections, in some cases many, many rejections.

I should have known I was in for a lifetime of rejection and failure when, in the fifth grade, I sent my friend Frank Scarcellato over to Mary Micek to tell her that I had a crush on her. He came back seconds later limping, tears in his eyes, from where she'd kicked his leg, hard. I was disappointed in Mary's reaction, but as someone who appreciated a good laugh and who may have been more of a sadist than some of my other classmates, I wanted to watch Frank limp back a little more injured each time he went away, so I sent him again and again, and the result was the same: Mary would kick him as hard as she could, and my loyal friend Frank would howl like a wounded animal and then limp back to deliver the news. I had figured out how to turn a negative into a positive, albeit at the expense of my friend's leg.

I won't say that I'm impervious to the feelings that come with rejection and failure. I'm not. But when I see fellow writers, especially those who are in their early years of submitting, posting on Facebook about their rejections, even good-naturedly posting about it, as in "Hey, look, I must be doing something right . . . I've been rejected by twelve magazines this past month," I grow suspicious because it would be like anyone else posting about breathing: "I woke up this morning and took a breath, and I've been breathing all day and into the night." In other words, the words "writer" and "rejection" are inexorably linked. You're not posting something that every other writer who's ever lived has never experienced, which makes me think that the good-natured tone is masking hurt, disappointment, and maybe even a measure of fatalism.

I'll also take a minute to blame the very nature of Facebook here, where friends—some of them, at least—post hourly updates on their successes, from movie rights to the amazingly delicious pan-seared tuna cooked by their beautiful and brilliant spouse who took over cooking duties that morning so that he or she (usually he) could spend the day reading ten novels; annotating seven hundred pages of brilliant student work, amazing and humbling students he or she (usually he) is so grateful to be working with; and going over for the twelfth time the copyedited manuscript of his or her new novel that he or she (usually he) is so thrilled to have made perfect that day, thanks to the lovely spouse and the pan-seared tuna. If you're like me, such posts make you want to drive to Alabama or North Dakota (or wherever) and beat said person over the head with a cast-iron skillet, the very pan, in fact, that seared the very tuna that appeared in the photo that accompanied the status update.

What I'm saying is that Facebook is brilliantly designed to make you feel like shit, day after day. To make you feel like a loser. To make your rejection from a magazine named the *Old Red Kimono* all that much more painful and bitter, even though we all know that our friends' Facebook personas are facades. The pan-seared tuna cooking spouse is no doubt having an affair with, well, anyone, even while she or he (let's say she) is planning to murder her spouse by stuffing the spouse's copyedited manuscript, all 500 brilliant pages of it, down the spouse's throat one night while the spouse is on his back, snoring and farting like a beached whale.

My point here is that we falsely use other people's careers as markers for where we feel we should be, even though we know deep down that this is a logical fallacy. There are thousands of factors other than age and talent that come into play when you assess another writer's life, many of them out of her control, like luck, chance, and serendipity. Writing isn't a competition. It's not. Or it shouldn't be, at least. The only things you should be competing with are the hours in each day. Did you conquer the hours by writing or did the hours win by convincing you that there would be more of them in the day than there are? I used to think that the only person you were in competition with was yourself, but I don't even believe that anymore. It's time: That's our enemy. All the rest of it is ego.

I don't have to tell you that our entire culture is geared toward success, that success is the benchmark for worthiness, and if we don't succeed while others around us (our classmates, strangers, people on Facebook) do succeed, we instantly feel like shit even if we are happy that our classmates, strangers, and people on Facebook have succeeded. We are, most of us, good people, and we like to hit the "like" button, and it makes us feel good to hit the "like" button. If we could, we'd hit a "like" button for having hit the "like" button on a status update about somebody else's success. But then, after hitting "like" a few dozen times, we go to the fridge and eat a gallon of coffee ice cream and wake up with cramps so bad we think, "Why bother writing today? I've got the cramps. I have a coffee ice cream hangover. Besides, no one wants to read my crap anyway."

Let me be honest for a second because I think this is an important point: The world doesn't need another writer. Okay, there. I said it. The world doesn't need another writer. If I were to quit writing tomorrow, there may be a dozen people in this world who will wonder what became of me, and I will likely know all twelve of them. That's a fact. And I'm not being self-pitying. It's the honest to God truth. Okay, so if the world doesn't need another writer, why write?

Ah ha! This is the question you should be asking yourself. If no one out there cares if you put down your pen right now and never pick it up again, why keep doing this thing that you're doing? There's no right answer, obviously. For me, it's partly because it's the only thing I'm even remotely good at. I like to sit around in sweatpants and a t-shirt and listen to music, but that's usually called being a stoner, so I'm not crazy about the stigma that goes along with that. It's bad enough when someone asks me on an airplane what I do and I have to say "writer," although to the benefit of answering "stoner," you're unlikely to spend the next three hours listening to unsolicited story ideas.

But I digress. Why do I do what I do if no one would care if I gave it up? I hate sounding like a cliché, but it really does nourish my soul. Like probably everyone else with a penchant for creativity, I have problems with depression, and when I'm not writing, I easily fall into a depression. Now, of course, when I'm really on a roll with my writing, spending all day at the computer, printing up dozens of new pages a day, I've likely gone manic, but that's another issue.

Everyone's soul needs nourishing, and it's up to you to figure out how to nourish yours. For me, it's writing. It's not publishing. It's not making money. It's not giving readings. It's not signing copies of my books. All of those things are nice, and I'm grateful when opportunities come up in my life that allow those things to happen, but it's the writing that does it. Why does it do that? Because each story I write, each novel, is a journey into my subconscious, and by the journey's end, whether it's a week or a month or several years later, I've learned something about myself. Every narrative I've written, which comes to me much as a dream might come to me, is a collection of disparate images and characters and situations. My first job is to make it all work as a story. My second job is to figure out what its cumulative effect is. Not necessarily to analyze it or even to understand what it all means, but rather to see how those disparate parts work together, either in harmony or not. And that's the satisfying moment for me, when I've connected the dots, when the story finally congeals. Does the story or novel not getting published negate that experience? No. And that's why I don't put all my eggs in the basket of publication. If I'm diligent about putting my work out there, I ultimately have no control over whether something gets published or doesn't, which is why I don't take it personally. It's like letting go of a helium-filled balloon and hoping it touches an airplane. Once you let go of the string, it's no longer in your control.

Here's the one thing I've learned about the people who work in publishing. No one really knows anything. Everyone—agents, editors, publicists, booksellers—may get behind a book that doesn't sell squat. The book disappears after the first week it's out. On the other hand, another book may get roundly rejected by every major publisher in New York only to get taken by a tiny press and then sell copies in the six figures. An anomaly, to be sure, but I've seen it happen, and it reinforces for me that nobody knows anything. This is further reason for you to know why you're doing what you're doing, and why not to use anything external as a benchmark for success or failure.

I'm always having to remind myself of my own lessons, and here's perhaps the most important of those. In 2001, after my first short story collection came out with a university press, I really wanted to jump into the major leagues with a big, smart commercial novel, and so I set out to write what seemed to me a book that might just earn me a big advance and a lot of attention. I showed the first 200 pages to my agent, who said something like, "This is the reason I became an agent," which is the sort of thing that makes you double the amount of the imaginary advance in your head. I've since come to learn that agents always say stuff like that, and my heartbeat goes neither up nor down at those kinds of compliments. But I didn't know that then. I thought, "She knows what she's talking about, by God! She's an industry professional!" She was so stoked over what I had sent her that she wanted to send it around as a partial manuscript, something that rarely happens for a literary writer. And send it out she did, flooding the inboxes of every publishing house in New York. A few weeks later, when the rejections started coming in, two, three, four a day, I experienced the seven stages of grief:

- Shock or disbelief
- Denial
- Anger
- Bargaining
- Guilt
- Depression
- Acceptance and hope

Well, okay, I'm lying. I don't think I ever reached acceptance and hope. I stalled out on depression. But while depressed, I put aside the roundly rejected manuscript and began working on a different book. The new book had grown out of a few new short stories I'd written, and it was shaping up to be a second collection of interlinked short stories. Following up my first book, which was a short story collection, with another collection seemed like career suicide, but so be it. I was having a great time writing these stories, and each time I started a new one, ideas for other stories in that cycle came to me. I had plenty of material for a book. My agent kept telling me to get back to the unfinished book, that several editors wanted to see the entire manuscript when it was done, but I had lost interest in it. This other book, however, was the book I really wanted to write. My agent said, "Yeah, okay, it sounds like a fun book, but . . . I can sell the other one. I don't think I can sell this one."

One day, after she had said this to me for the third time, I fired her. I decided that I didn't want anyone breathing down my neck while I wrote this new book. Rejection gave me the freedom to write whatever the fuck I wanted to write—or, more precisely, to write the book that I wanted to write, regardless of its fate—and firing my agent further cemented the fact that I was writing this book for myself.

Once you give up thinking about a book's fate—and once you accept that its fate may well be that it remains a stack of computer paper—you're free to write any damned book you want to write. Let me repeat that: Once you give up thinking about a book's fate—and once you accept that its fate may well be that it remains a stack of computer paper—you're free to write any damned book you want to write.

Once I finished writing the book, I contacted on a Monday an agent who had emailed me a few years earlier to see if I needed rep-resentation. At the time, I didn't. But I was polite to her, and I told her that I would contact her should I ever need an agent. And now I needed an agent. She read the book on Tuesday, agreed to represent me that night, sent the book out on Wednesday, and secured for me a two-book deal by the following Monday.

The moral of this isn't that if you write the book you really want to write, everything will fall into place. I was lucky. Things happened to fall into place. I have since written another book under similar circumstances, and things didn't fall into place. But the moral, for me, is that I am far more likely to write something that will connect to readers when I write something in which its publication plays no role. My agent had secured for me a two-book contract, and the second book that I turned in, and that was subsequently published, is not a good book, in my opinion. And while I still get emails, eleven years later, about the book I wrote without the hope of publication, no one has written to me about the second book of that contract since the book was first published, and very few people wrote to me about it even then. You would think that having a contract for a book would give you the freedom to, at long last, write the book you've always wanted to write, but the opposite was true for me. That's not to say that someone else wouldn't have been able to seize that opportunity.

This brings me to my next point: learn what your strengths and weaknesses are. My weakness is that I can't write under contract. Or, rather, I'm not good at it. Just as I wasn't good at doing homework as a student. Some people excel under that kind of pressure. I don't. Some people also excel at writing highly commercial novels. I don't. My writing life has been one of trial and error—with lots of error—all in an attempt to learn what I'm good at. The times I've failed, I've given a lot of thought to why I failed, but sometimes it takes years to untangle the reasons. If you look at my list of books published and books not published that begins this essay, you'll see that I have a 50% batting record, which would make me the best baseball player in the history of baseball, but which would be mediocre in just about every other venture. But when I look at the first four of those rejected books, books that have never (and will never) see the light of day, I see pretty clearly why they didn't get published. They're not good. Or I wrote them for the wrong reasons. The other books, the books that did get published with the exception of the book written under contract, are all a little quirky in ways that the others just aren't. I'm reserving judgment on the fifth rejected book because it's still too fresh to comment on. But I will say this about most all of the accepted novels. They grew out of failed projects.

The Book of Ralph, which is written from the first-person reflective point of view and stars an eighth-grader, began its life ten years earlier as a third-person short story from the point of view of a sixty-something-year-old mother of two. *America's Report Card*, a satirical novel about the testing industry, began its life at least six years earlier as a failed essay that I had hoped would expose what I saw as a deeply corrupt industry that I had worked in. *After the Workshop* started its life as a long-forgotten novel fragment twenty years earlier.

For the most part, I had forgotten the origins of these books until long after they had been published, and then I would stumble upon the abandoned earlier version while moving boxes or packing up old papers. What this reinforces for me is that failure is, at times, the byproduct of your unconscious mind unable to properly translate into fiction (or whatever art you work within) whatever it is that's bothering you. Years later, you may now be able to translate it because you're no longer the same person. A failed project one year may be a successful project twenty years later. In this regard, no project is a failed project because it's really just part of a long continuum of revision, even if you're not conscious that you're revising it. I call this the project's *gestation period*. Would I have been compelled to sit down and write *After the Workshop* if I hadn't written a version of it twenty years earlier? Maybe. But I suspect it would have failed or wouldn't have come to me so easily because I wouldn't have had the seed for it planted in my subconscious. When I found the draft of the unfinished novel, written in the summer of 1989—a novel I had entirely forgotten about until I opened a filing cabinet drawer in my basement this past summer—I realized that all of the characters in *After the Workshop* had counterparts in the old manuscript and that some of the characters were nearly identical. Given that I hadn't given the book another conscious thought for twenty years, these similarities suggest that the characters and ideas had been growing in some petri dish stored in my unconscious mind, which makes me wonder what the hell else is in there.

As it turns out, the first version of the novel wasn't a failure at all. It was just a very early draft of something I would pick up two decades later. And so I now have begun to think of all of my writing on some larger, lifelong continuum instead of how I had always thought of it, as a project in and of itself. This is a freeing idea to me. And it suggests that there are no failed projects, that there is an interconnectedness between all the things that I write, and in order to get to the thing that works, I have to slog through things that don't work.

My professor Frank Conroy used to say, "The good work is connected to the bad work," and while I don't care for the terms "good" and "bad," his point is maybe the one lesson in all of my education that I return to daily. When he said this to my class in 1987, I knew it was true—it seemed self-evident to the point of being not worth saying—but now, in 2015, I know more intimately what he meant, and I see how you have to write a certain amount of stuff that doesn't work to get to the stuff that works.

My first teaching job was in 1989 when I returned to my alma mater, Southern Illinois University, to take over the classes my former teacher, Richard Russo, was scheduled to teach while he had a Guggenheim to work on his third novel, *Nobody's Fool*. In the few years that I had known Rick, I had never seen him angry, but one day when I stopped by his house, I saw a man I'd never seen before. His body language, the expression on his face—all of it suggested anger and defeat. His Guggenheim year was about to end, which meant, more than likely, his writing time was about to end as well.

"Is everything all right?" I asked.

"No," he said. "It's not."

He had spent two years working on this new novel, only to real-ize that day that the page he wrote that morning was where the novel needed to begin. In other words, he had spent two years writing back story. He knew, of course, that all of what he'd written was impor-tant to get him to where he was today, but it would have been a hell of a lot easier to have known that two years before. While I stood there listening to him, I remembered something he had told me when I was his student. He had just finished writing his second novel, *The Risk Pool*, and that book had come to him quickly. "It was a gift," he said. But then he laughed and shook his head and said, "But I already know I'm going to pay for it with the next book. You don't get a gift without paying for it down the road." Wisely, I didn't remind Rick of his own grim prophecy. In the end, Rick did the dif-ficult thing and started the book over, and, as it turns out, the book was Rick's first big breakthrough. While tossing the first three hun-dred pages—the first two years of his work on the book—must have seemed like a failure at the time, it was anything but. I have no doubt the book was richer because of it. And Rick, whose instincts were on the money, did the more difficult thing to make the book work rather than resisting.

The problem, to my mind, is to cast these kinds of developments as failure or rejection instead of considering them as what they are: another part of process. It only becomes failure or rejection when it's attached to publication, awards, grades, graduation from an MFA program, or something else that ultimately has little to do with the creative process, no matter how enviable or useful those things may be. When we attach any of these other things to the writing, the writing becomes about what it can yield rather than what it *is*.

This, of course, is the American way. As a culture, we are always seeking the prize at the end of the day's work. We want to be rewarded for what we've done. We want the free Big Mac. We want our Happy Hour. We deserve it, dammit. But I would urge you to let the act of writing be its own reward. The very fact that you can sit down and create a three-dimensional world out of the alphabet's 26 letters is a tremendous gift. While they may provide a sense—sometimes fleeting—of validation, those other things have little or nothing to do with what you do when you sit down to write, but if we invest our emotions in them, if we continuously want validation, we are more inclined to see our writing in terms of successes and failures. And the more we seek validation, the more we want it. It's addictive, which only means that the failures, as we see them, become more excruciating (crushing, even) when we experience them.

The great basketball player Michael Jordan once said, "I've missed more than nine thousand shots in my career. I've lost almost three hundred games. Twenty-six times I've been trusted to take the winning shot and missed. I've failed over and over again in my life. And that is why I succeed."

Whenever I move, as I just did, I'm always stunned when I open a box and find inside entire short stories that I've written, revised extensively, and then set aside and forgotten about. Or a hundred pages of a novel I remember very little about. Or story and novel fragments, hundreds of them, stuffed away. Back when I wrote sporadically, from 1984 to 1995, I invested everything in those stories that I wrote. They *had* to get published, I told myself. I pinned my hopes to them because getting published in magazines would mean getting a book published and getting a job, and keeping the job would require publishing more things in magazines and more books, and . . . okay, you see how this is going. It's a loop. And once you jump onto that ride, you find yourself endlessly strapped in and forever traveling that loop until you feel nauseated. Around 1995, I finally—*finally*—made writing a daily habit. Instead of writing in eight-hour bursts of manic energy that would leave me drained and unable to communicate with other human beings, I would write just a little bit every morning. Some mornings, I would be done by eight a.m. Other times, I might actually work until noon. Just a little bit, every day. The result was that I significantly increased the quantity of what I wrote. That little bit adds up fast. By writing more, I also wrote a lot more stuff that didn't work, but it didn't feel like failure in the way that it did back when I wrote sporadically because now the things I worked on would bleed into other things I worked on, and I would simply set aside the thing that didn't work and pursue the thing that called to me. And that's how I've worked ever since. I work on the thing that calls loudest to me. Sometimes I'll hold out, especially if it's a novel, just to make sure that it's really, actually calling to me, and if indeed it is, I will start writing it with the hope that there's enough there to sustain 300, 400, 500 pages.

But there are always outside forces wanting to disrupt productivity. You sometimes have to shield yourself from other people. My father, who passed away in 2013, couldn't have been more supportive of me on the one hand, but on the other hand, his measure for success was money and fame. The very first recognition I ever got came in the form of placing third in the *Playboy* College Fiction Contest. I was ecstatic. I had finally gotten some recognition. My name would appear in the magazine. They would send me a check and a framed certificate. My mother was also happy for me. She understood that this was a big deal, so much so that she bought me a subscription to *Playboy* for my birthday.

But my father's response was "Too bad you didn't win first." This was in 1987. For the next twenty-five years, until his death, my father's response to whatever I did was pretty much the same. When I published a book with a big commercial publisher and a well-known author mentioned my book on the *Today Show* while talking about the book that he ultimately chose for the *Today Show*'s book club, my father said, "Why the hell didn't he pick yours?" When I published a short story collection with a small press, my father said, "Wouldn't it be great if it made the best-seller list?" "Yeah," I said, "but that's not going to happen, so. . . ." "You never know," my father said. "No," I said, "I do know. It's a short story collection. It's published by a small press. I don't think that a short story collection published by a small press has ever made the best-seller list." "Well," my father said, "it could happen. You don't know that." And on and on it would go. Each time I published a book, he would say, "Wouldn't it be great if Oprah chose it?" "Yes," I would reply, sounding as emotionless as a robot. "It would be."

I hate to admit this, but I quit telling him when I would have a book published. I know he meant well, but he always set the bar too high, and it turned what I did into something else—a failed goal. If Oprah had chosen my book, he would wonder why a film of it wasn't being made. If a film had been made, he'd wonder why it wasn't nominated for an Oscar. I knew that no achievement would ever satisfy him, and that, no matter how many times I explained to him why I did what I did, he would continue to raise the bar to an impossible height. Fucked-up father-son relationships being what they are, I took the things he said more to heart than I should have. And I often, after hanging up from a phone call, felt like shit. I felt like my career, such as it was, was a joke. Every notion about writing that I had learned to resist would come back in full force whenever I spoke to my father.

My father didn't finish high school. He spent his entire adult life as a roofer, and when my mother died, after a long illness, he filed for bankruptcy and lived in poverty for the next several years. So I know that the things he hoped for me were things he valued because of his own lot in life. Still. . . . Still. . . . I had to make a decision whether to tell him about a new book or not, and during the last few years of his life, when nothing made him happy, I decided not to. When he brought up my writing at all, I would steer the subject elsewhere. My father was expert at asking unanswerable questions. Whenever a novel of mine failed to find a publisher, my father would ask, "Why?" "I don't know," I would say. And then he would say, "Well, why? People just didn't like it or what?" And then I would laugh my half-crazed laugh and say, "Yeah. That's why."

My suggestion is to minimize the negativity that comes with talking about your writing with people who don't understand the process or who may not understand why you're doing it, unless, of course, you are setting out to do it for money. This is why I hate reader reviews on Amazon or Goodreads. On the same day that an Amazon reviewer gave a steam cleaner three stars with the subject line "It works!" she gave one of my books one star. "This is a book of dark and twisted stories. I couldn't even finish it." It was the first review of the book to appear on the site, and it was a book that had taken ten years to write, and I sat there reading her review while having fantasies of finding the reviewer and beating her repeatedly with her damned steam cleaner.

Maybe other writers can shrug off dumb reader comments, but I'm not one of those writers, so I keep my distance from them now. I keep my distance for the same reason that I quit telling my father about new books: because it reinforces every false conceit about why I do what I do. And my resistance to the Amazon reviewers of the world isn't because I think my book deserved five stars, but because I'm the sort of person who starts to think maybe the reviewer is right. Maybe the book sucks. That's my personality type, to agree with the negative rather than resist it. And then the negativity that I've internalized poisons the well, making it harder to get up in the morning to write. With my last few books, I finally reached a kind of contentment with the process by telling myself just to enjoy the ride and not to take the publishing of it and its reception too seriously. And part of that contentment was not to pay much attention to what was going on with the book. If someone sent me a good review, sure, I would read it. But if I stumbled on a negative one, I would quit reading as soon as I realized it was heading south. The most important thing was to stay focused about the day's work and to put my energies there instead of in the things that were out of my control.

Maybe all of this is about persistence and how to avoid that which keeps you from pushing on. When I get disappointed, I look back to where I was five years ago and then ten years ago and then twenty years ago. By doing this, I see that I have in fact accomplished more than I think I have since I tend to think that I haven't accomplished much. But clearly I'm hard-headed. I just keep going. One of my childhood heroes was Evel Knievel. Evel would jump fifteen cars on a thousand-pound Harley, crash the motorcycle on the other side of the jump, break half the bones in his body, and then, six months later, get back on the bike and do it again. And he would keep doing it for years. He quit only after seriously injuring someone else when he crashed during a practice jump. Injuring himself was okay; injuring someone else, well, that was something different altogether. If I had quit writing after my first novel was rejected, I wouldn't have had a writing career. If I had quit writing after my second novel was rejected, I wouldn't have had a writing career. And believe me, I thought about quitting all the time in those days, and there were people close to me who probably thought, while not saying so explicitly, that I'd given it a good run and should start thinking about being more pragmatic. But I have always been of the belief that as long as you're not hurting anyone, it's foolish not to pursue the thing you want to pursue, even if you pursue it badly, because it's a hell of a lot harder to pursue it once you're dead.

There are, of course, times in your life when everything you write is garbage, or when you really don't have the time or energy to sustain much of a writing life. Many years ago, I had a one semester teaching gig in Colorado. I had moved there from Chicago for that gig, and it was a shitty paying gig with a ton of students, a heavy course load, and no health insurance. But it was a job. And I anticipated that job lasting a while. In late November of that semester, however, the department chair informed all of the adjuncts that we would not be needed in the spring. In other words, we were fucked. Big time. All of us had moved there from far-flung places. I happened at the time to be reading a book about the writing life by Erskine Caldwell, who wrote *Tobacco Road* and *God's Little Acre*, and how he had moved to a cabin in Maine and hammered out a draft of one of his novels in just a few months. In a flash of foolhardy confidence, I thought, *Hell, I could do that!* And so, in what would prove to be a grim comedy of errors, I moved to an 18-foot camping trailer in southern Illinois that my father owned.

It snowed heavily for several days after I arrived, effectively shutting me in for a week. I tried driving to a store, but I got stuck in the snow and had to walk back to my trailer. The trailer had no running water, save for a garden hose sticking in through the window by the sink. To get electricity, I ran an extension cord to an outlet attached to a wooden pole outside, and to keep warm, I used a kerosene heater. I spent most of my time inside, wondering why I was so damned tired all the time—that is, until I cracked a window and realized that I was probably asphyxiating myself from the kerosene fumes. When the garden hose froze, as it did each morning in January and February, I plugged a hair dryer into the extension cord and stood outside, ankle-deep in snow, blow-drying the hose until the water thawed.

Upon moving in, I took great pains to set up my computer (which, at the time, was one of those monstrous, cheap IBM clones) on the dining table, which looked like a miniature version of a booth you might find at Denny's. Instead of writing, however, I began watching a lot of TV, including morning shows, like *Oprah*, which I had never watched before, and by the end of the month, after being snowed in and eating nothing but crappy food, I had gained so much weight that I could no longer fit inside the little booth where my behemoth of a computer sat.

To make matters worse, the local newspaper ran an article about someone finding a woman's head in nearby Rend Lake. Next to the article was a drawing of the unidentified woman's head. There was no attempt by the artist to recreate what she might have looked like *before* the grisly murder. The drawing was simply that of a head that had been under water for a while. Since my trailer door didn't have a lock—my only security was a bungee cord keeping the door shut—I kept beneath my pillow a 9 millimeter gun that my father had left in one of the cabinets. As the weeks wore on, I spent significant time at the bars in town, more desirable places than my trailer, which was smaller than most jail cells. Many of the women I met were the wives or girlfriends of men who were doing time in the nearby prison. As winter thawed and the temperatures rose, the vinyl ceiling of my trailer began to droop so that every time I stood up, it rested on my head, further driving me insane. By the end of my seven-month stint in the trailer, I'd written a pathetic thirty pages, none of them usable.

What this experience prompted me to do, however, was apply to PhD programs. The PhD program I attended allowed me time to write what became my first published book. If you think of plot as a series of cause-and-effect relationships, you can, with some distance, look back on your own life and see the causation there as well. The reason I was able to write my first book was because I was in a PhD program that gave me time to write, and the reason I was in a PhD program was because I was living in a miserable camping trailer for several months, and the reason I was living in a miserable camping trailer was because I was let go from a shitty job, and so on. It was a series of life failures that led me to something better. But you'll notice that in this series of cause-and-effect scenes from my life, I am on the move. At the start of each new year, I put together a list of things

I would like to work on in my life, broad ideas rather than specific goals, but I always put at the top of the list each year "Stasis is Death."

Stasis is Death. I really believe that. I like to keep changing, ducking, moving. I can't sit still for very long. I fear getting burnt out or, worse, becoming bitter. I won't let that happen. By not remaining static, I don't mean that you have to move across the country. It means that if something isn't working in your life, do something about it. Change it. Shake things up. Sometimes this means less money, periods of instability, maybe even a stretch of depression as you're in flux. But at least it's change. At least it's a catalyst for making something happen.

I'm also an advocate for reinvention. If one aspect of your writing life has stalled out, channel it into another genre, another subject. Figure out how to keep nourishing your soul. I'm fascinated by artists—writers, musicians, filmmakers—who seize opportunities for radical change, and in most careers with any longevity, you'll find creative lulls followed by reinvention. From Fleetwood Mac, who moved from blues to pop, to the crime writers Chester Himes, who began as a writer of social protest novels, and James W. Hall, who began as a poet, you'll see periods of transformation, pivotal moments when a decision is made to move in another direction. Your new direction may not always work out, but even if it doesn't, it may be enough of a catalyst to reenergize you artistically. I think of myself primarily as a fiction writer, but I also write screenplays, personal essays, book reviews, the occasional journalism. By doing so, I learn what I'm good at and what I'm not good at, and all of it has proven useful for fiction writing by forcing me to think of my craft in new ways.

I'm often asked if I'll ever go back to those old unpublished novels and work on them, and my answer is "Fuck no!" I have no interest in it, just as I have no interest in calling up a high school girlfriend and saying, "Hey, so look: I've been mulling over what went wrong

thirty years ago, and I'm thinking I'd like to give it another chance."
It would make absolutely no sense for me to go back to those novels.
The way I look at it, they served their purpose. They were stepping
stones to the next book that *did* work, and to go back to them with
some sort of hope that they might be useful to me again would be an
exercise in futility. I don't ever look at them. Ever. They're in boxes
somewhere in my house among other boxes of my crap. Forge ahead,
I say. Let the past go!

By now, you may be thinking one of two things: Wow,
McNally's really got his shit together. Or: Wow, McNally's really
full of shit. If you chose the latter, that I'm full of shit, you may be
closer to the truth. Because, up until now, I'm giving the illusion that
I can focus on my work, that rejection doesn't bother me, that I have
proper perspective on failure. But all you have to do is look at the
tenth book on that list, the one that took two years to research and
another five years to write, the one that was sent to every publishing
house in New York and was roundly rejected by every publishing house in New York, and then consider this essay, and on closer
inspection, you may very well see an elaborate justification for having lost seven years of my life. As the rejections started coming in for
that particular novel, I decided to take a year off writing altogether.
In truth, it's impossible for me to take time off. I wrote two new
short stories, two essays, and endlessly revised a screenplay, but I did
not write every day as I had, with very few exceptions, since 1995. I
allowed myself the freedom not to write.

As it turned out, this was a good decision because I had some
rather large transitions in my life—the death of my father followed
by a 1,000 mile move across the country and a new job—so my frustration at not being able to keep a writing schedule would only have
depressed me. But now, with the new year, I have better perspective. There's still a possibility that the book will be published with
an independent press, but you see what happened: for this particular

book, I had my heart set on one of the big publishing houses, and I began to equate the book's value—its artistic value—with an acceptance or a rejection from those publishers. I foolishly allowed certain desires—namely, a need for money after a divorce—to impinge on my process. I eventually asked my agent to quit sending it around. I wanted time to think about whether or not the book was any good, and what I decided, seven months later, is that it needs work, a *lot* of work, but that there's still something worth pursuing in it.

In the meantime, I'm about to start writing a new novel, and like the published books that I'm happiest with, it's a novel that I just want to write. And I suspect I'll have fun writing it. I have no idea what's going to happen in it, but I know the basic gist of it—enough, at least, to push ahead on it. Is it commercial? I don't even know what that means anymore. But it's the kind of book that I know how to write—which is to say that I have no idea what the fuck I'm doing. I will wake up and write a little bit on it each day. And that's the kind of book I know how to write, the kind of book that keeps calling me back and is a pleasure to return to.

The books I don't write well are the ones that are a chore, and maybe that's why this last book didn't translate into a published book: because it broke my brain in two. It was the most difficult thing I ever wrote, the longest novel I'd written, with the most characters. Maybe I can't write that book, and maybe the purpose of writing that book was to show me that I don't know how to write that book. Maybe the purpose was to illuminate the kind of book I'm good at writing. I don't know yet. It's all still too fresh.

If you look at my life in the abstract, you're likely to see a history of failure and rejection: two divorces, mountains of debt, weight gained and then lost and then gained again, a childhood replete with more trailer parks and crappy apartments than I ever want to see again. But I don't look at my life in the abstract. I've lived it. And who I am today is because of what I went through yesterday and the day before yesterday and the 50 years before that. I am, like the ending of a short story, the meaningful synthesis of every large and small detail that preceded this moment, and as anyone who knows me knows, I'm always looking at my future in tiers: what do I want to accomplish today, what do I want to accomplish in five years, what do I want to accomplish by the end of this life? I know all of those things because I revise them every few years—sometimes on paper, sometimes in my head—but I don't live my life pursuing those goals. I measure my goals not by a typed page, not by a paragraph, not by a sentence. But by a word. One word. Because I know well enough now that one word will lead me to the next word, and that this is how you get to where you're going. So here's my advice on rejection and failure. Close this book, pick up a pen and paper, and put down a word. And then put down another word. And then another.

MARVIN BELL

32 Statements about Writing Poetry

The habit of analysis has a tendency to wear away the feelings.

—John Stuart Mill

1. Every poet is an experimentalist.
2. Learning to write is a simple process: Read something, then write something; read something else, then write something else. And show in your writing what you have read.
3. There is no one way to write and no right way to write.
4. The good stuff and the bad stuff are all part of the stuff. No good stuff without bad stuff.
5. Learn the rules, break the rules, make up new rules, break the new rules.
6. You do not learn from work like yours as much as you learn from work unlike yours.
7. Originality is a new amalgam of influences.
8. Try to write poems at least one person in the room will hate.
9. The I in the poem is not you but someone who knows a lot about you.
10. Autobiography rots. The life ends, the vision remains.
11. A poem listens to itself as it goes.
12. It's not what one begins with that matters; it's the quality of attention paid to it thereafter.
13. Language is subjective and relative, but it also overlaps; get on with it.
14. Every free verse writer must reinvent free verse.
15. Prose is prose because of what it includes; poetry is poetry because of what it leaves out.
16. A short poem need not be small.
17. Rhyme and meter, too, can be experimental.
18. Poetry has content but is not strictly about its contents. A poem containing a tree may not be about a tree.
19. You need nothing more to write poems than bits of string and thread and some dust from under the bed.
20. At heart, poetic beauty is tautological: it defines its terms and exhausts them.

21. The penalty for education is self-consciousness. But it is too late for ignorance.

22. What they say "there are no words for"—that's what poetry is for. Poetry uses words to go beyond words.

23. One does not learn by having a teacher do the work.

24. The dictionary is beautiful; for some poets, it's enough.

25. Writing poetry is its own reward and needs no certification. Poetry, like water, seeks its own level.

26. A finished poem is also the draft of a later poem.

27. A poet sees the differences between his or her poems but a reader sees the similarities.

28. Poetry is a manifestation of more important things. On the one hand, it's poetry! On the other, it's just poetry.

29. Viewed in perspective, Parnassus is a very short mountain.

30. A good workshop continually signals that we are all in this together, teacher too.

31. This Depression Era jingle could be about writing poetry: Use it up / wear it out / make it do / or do without.

32. Art is a way of life, not a career.

PAM HOUSTON

Corn Maze

Try to be one of the people on whom nothing is lost.

—Henry James

Just before I was to start kindergarten, my father lost his job. We were living in Trenton, New Jersey, at the time, where he had lived most of his life. With no college education, he had worked his way up to the position of controller at a Transamerica-owned manufacturing company called Delavalve. The company restructured itself and dismissed him. My parents decided to use his sudden unemployment as an opportunity to take a vacation, to drive whatever Buick convertible we had at the time from New Jersey to California. My parents loved the sun and the beach more than they loved anything except vodka martinis. They promised to take me to Disneyland. We stopped at Las Vegas on the way.

We stayed at the Sands, where my mother had opened, decades before, as a singing and dancing comedian for Frank Sinatra. I got to swim in the kidney-shaped pool and then we ate a giant slab of prime rib each for a dollar. My mother and I went up to the room to bed, and my father stayed downstairs to gamble. I woke up to my mother standing over my bed and sun streaming into the hotel room window. I was four and a half years old. "Pam," she said, "go downstairs and get your father out of the casino."

I found him sitting at an empty blackjack table, looking a hundred and ten. I took his hand and led him through the hazy cigarette air, up the elevator and down the long hall with the zig-zag carpet to our room. He had, of course, lost everything. The money we were meant to live on until he found another job, the money for the trip to California, the money for the hotel bill. Even the car.

My mother's old boss at the Desert Inn loaned us enough to get the car back, to pay the hotel bill, to take me to Disneyland. A few weeks later my father started a new job in Pennsylvania, and we moved there, though when my mother ran away from Spiceland, Indiana, at age 13 to Manhattan, because she had won the bet with her Aunt Ermie, who raised her, that she *could* get straight Cs, and as a result had, for the first time in her life, fifty whole dollars, she'd vowed she would never live west of the New Jersey border again.

★★★

About five years ago, I was asked to be one of four writers to partici-pate in an evening called "Unveiled" at the Wisconsin Book Festival in Madison. Our assignment was to write something new that had never been tried or tested, and read it aloud to an audience of roughly a thousand. I not only accepted, I took the assignment so literally, I didn't start writing until I was on the plane to Wisconsin. I wrote for the entire plane ride and all evening in my hotel room. I stayed up all night and wrote, and I wrote all day the day of the reading. When I started to panic that I would not have something ready in time for the reading, I told myself what I tell my students when they get stuck: *Write down all of the things out in the world that have arrested your atten-tion lately, that have glimmered at you in some resonant way. Set them next to each other. See what happens.*

By late afternoon I had twelve tiny scenes. I have always, for some reason, thought in twelve's. I don't believe this has anything to do with the apostles. One scene was called Georgetown, Great Exuma. Another was called Ozona, Texas. Another was called Juneau, Alaska. Two hours before I was to read, I looked back at my instructions to make sure I had done everything the assignment asked of me. The only caveat, it said, was that the piece had to mention Wisconsin. I knew nothing about Wisconsin, so I left my hotel room and sat on a street corner downtown and waited for something to happen. In less than thirty minutes, something did, and I went back to my room and wrote it down. When I added Madison, Wisconsin, to the original twelve, I had to take out Mexican Hat, Utah, but that was okay with me.

"Jesus, Pam," Richard Bausch said, after the reading, "Write a hundred of them, and that's your next book." I thought, "No, not a hundred, but possibly a hundred and forty-four."

*

When I went on tour with my first book, a collection of short stories called *Cowboys Are My Weakness*, I was asked, more than any other question, *how much of this really happened to you?* "A lot of it" was my honest answer, night after night, but the audience grew dissatisfied with that answer and seemed, more than anything, to want something quantifiable, so I began saying, also honestly, about 82 percent.

Eight years later, when I published my first "nonfiction" book and went on tour with it I would often be introduced in some version of the following manner: "In the past we have gotten 82 percent Pam, and now we are going to get 100 percent," and I would approach the microphone and feel the need to say, "Well, no, still coming in right about 82."

★★★

Between Davis and Dixon, California, in the heart of the Central Valley, just off the I-80, right under the historic sign where the cow jumps over the moon, is the Guinness Book of World Record's Largest Corn Maze. If you get off the highway and drive to it, you find out that technically speaking, it was the Guinness Book of World Record's Largest Corn Maze in 2007 and not in 2010. But, you figure they figure, once a winner, always a winner.

In the corn maze, as in life, there are rules. No running. No smoking. No strollers. No drugs. No inappropriate language. (The corn has ears too!) No tampering with the signs and the maze markers. If you misbehave, you will be asked to leave, though in a corn maze, you understand, that is not always so straightforward. Surprisingly, dogs are allowed in the corn maze, and there is nothing in the rules prohibiting handguns. Sex in the corn maze is also apparently okay as long as you use appropriate language.

The computer-generated grid that the corn maze sits upon runs from A through QQ and 1 through 52. It contains 2,193 squares. When you enter, they hand you a map. To complete the maze successfully, you will make approximately 189 right turns and 156 left turns, though there are a few places when more than one option will get you out, so your individual numbers may vary.

An ear of corn averages 800 kernels in 16 rows. A pound of corn consists of approximately 1,300 kernels. 100 bushels of corn produces approximately 7,280,000 kernels. In the US, corn leads all other crops in value and volume of production. The corn in this maze *is* as high as an elephant's eye, if we are talking the world's largest elephant, in heels.

I have a painting in my kitchen by my friend Marc Penner-Howell of a giant ear of corn with the word *Hallelujah* written in red letters running vertically up the ear and lots of little ghostly gas pumps in the background. When my boyfriend Greg eats corn on the cob, his lips swell up so much we call him Angelina Jolie.

★★★

The reason I have been afraid, until very recently, to make any kind of general, theoretical, or philosophical statements about women, writers, westerners, environmentalists, academics, western women, western women writers, outdoorswomen who grew up in New Jersey and eventually became academics, women who dreamed of running white water rivers and falling in love with poets and cowboys (though not cowboy poets), women who got on I-80 West on the other side of the George Washington Bridge one day and just kept driving . . . is that I have never felt comfortable speaking for anyone except myself. Maybe I was socialized not to make declarative statements. Maybe I thought you had to be fifty before you knew anything about the world. Maybe I was afraid of misrepresenting someone I thought I understood but didn't. Maybe I was afraid of acting hypocritically. Maybe I have always believed it is more honest, more direct, and ultimately more powerful to tell a story one concrete and particular detail at a time.

So I did. I put my boat into the river, some things happened, and I took it back out on the other side. In time though, I began to suspect that linear narrative was not doing a very good job representing life as I experienced it, but I still tried to stretch the things I originally conceived of as Slinkies into straight lines. I don't mean to suggest that I was unique in this. There are so many of us out there, trying to turn Spyrograph flowers into rocket ships. In time I began to gain confidence in my Spyrograph flowers and Slinkies. Eventually, I began to speculate about where they came from. Just for starters, I never met any of my grandparents. Also, every single one of my relatives (expect a second cousin in Alaska who is oddly afraid of me and his illegitimate son who likes me but lives in Prague) is dead.

Also, when both of your parents are alcoholics, one thing never leads to another. There is no such thing as how it really happened. When both of your parents are alcoholics, the only way to get to a narrative that is *un*-shattered would be to run the tape backwards, like a car accident in reverse where the windshield that is in a million pieces magically mends itself. This is not necessarily the bad news. A mind that moves associatively (as my mind does and probably your mind, too) like a firefly in a grassy yard on a late June evening, has more fun (and other things, too, of course, like static, like trouble) than a mind that moves logically or even chronologically. Just the other day for instance, someone said the word *tennis*, and I saw in my mind's eye a lady in a pig suit with wings.

★★★

Not too long after grad school, I was hired by a magazine to write an article about why women over forty take adventure vacations. I was barely thirty and had no idea why, but I needed the money so I called some power women I knew who had climbed Kilimanjaro or whatever and asked them. They gave flat and predictable answers like "for the challenge," so I made up some smart, funny women who said surprising and subversive things about why they took adventure vacations and wrote the article up.

When the fact checker called me, I said, "You're a what?" like an asshole fresh out of graduate school, "you actually believe in things called facts?"

The fact checker, whose name was Bethany, asked for the phone numbers of the six women I wrote about. I gave her the three that actually existed.

"What about Katherine and Louise and Samantha?" she said.

"Well, Bethany," I said, "I made them up."

There was five seconds of silence, then she said, "Well, I guess we don't have to call them then, do we?"

★★★

In 2010 in Las Vegas, in a gondola in the canal that runs from Barney's New York to Kenneth Cole, upstairs in the mall they call the Palazzo, a very young man is proposing to a very young woman. He is on one knee, and the acne-faced gondolier in his straw hat and red kerchief steadies the wobbling boat. The shoppers pause a minute to look over the railing and watch. The girl is either genuinely surprised or good at pretending. She whispers yes and then shouts it for the small crowd. The twenty-five of us gathered clap and cheer, and the boy stands up and pumps both fists, the same exact gesture he uses, one imagines, when he hears that his fantasy football quarterback has gone 18 for 24 with four TDs and no interceptions. The gondolier turns the boat around with his single long paddle and pushes them back toward Bed Bath and Beyond.

Every day in Vegas is upside down day. Walking along the canal, young men in wife beaters say sentences into their cell phones that, if they were not in Las Vegas, they would never say. "I'll meet you in an hour in St. Mark's Square," or "I applied for a job with the KGB," or "Let's meet up in time to see the volcano erupt." People pay money—a lot of it—to see Donny and Marie Osmond. On the poster for the Garth Brooks show in the Wynn Encore Theater, there is a picture of Garth in his big black hat and a one-word review from the Los Angeles Times: *Genius*.

We are staying at the Golden Nugget downtown, a hotel where, if you want to, you can go down a water slide, which is really more like a water straw, through a 200,000-gallon shark tank. At the guest relations desk, there is a very pretty girl with quarter-inch thick makeup and long blonde hair that has been dyed so many times it is leaning burnt sienna, and the kind of ultra-thick, ultra-blunt square false eyelashes that only drag queens wear, and the whole ensemble makes her look like somebody cross-dressed as herself.

Every time we leave the hotel, the junkies are sitting on the steps of the church across the street shooting up under their toenails. The lady in front of the sign that says Hotel-Wedding-Cuban Buffet looks right through the driver's side window into my eyes and says, "Put a muffler on it, you fucking bitch," right before she sits down in the middle of the street and tries to scratch her own scalp off.

★★★

When it was decided (when was that again, and by whom?) that we were all supposed to choose between fiction and nonfiction, what was not taken into account was that for some of us truth can never be an absolute, that there can (at best) be only less true and more true and sometimes those two collapse inside each other like a Turducken. Given the failure of memory. Given the failure of language to mean. Given metaphor. Given metonymy. Given the ever-shifting junction of code and context. Given the twenty-five people who saw the same car accident. Given our denial. Given our longings.

Who cares really, if she hung herself or slit her wrists when what really matters is that James Frey is secretly afraid that he's the one who killed her. Dear Random House Refund Department: If they were moved, then they got their twenty-four dollars worth.

★★★

Back in the 1990s, a magazine sent me to the Ardèche region of France. They wanted me, among other things, to kayak the Ardèche river canyon, one of the five river canyons the French call the Grand Canyon of France. But they sent me in late October, the days were short and getting shorter, all the kayak rental places were boarded up tight for the year, and it was 36 degrees with freezing rain. So I hiked the canyon of the Ardèche, thinking it would be an acceptable substitute.

When I turned in the article, the editor said, "We really wanted you to kayak the Ardèche."

"I know," I said, "but it was too cold, all the rental places. . . ."

"No," she said, "we really wanted you to kayak the Ardèche. . . ."

"Ah. . . ." I said.

"And while you're at it," she said, "could you make it rain a little less?"

I found her request neither difficult nor surprising. The river had, at that time of year, hardly a riffle on it, and would have been a pretty, if chilly, float. To spice things up, I added a water fight with three Italian kayakers. There was some good-natured flirting across the language barrier. It didn't rain that day at all.

Some years later, the editor of an anthology asked my permission to reprint that essay. He said, "I really liked your story, especially the part about the three Italian kayakers."

"Funny," I said, "I made that part up."

Maybe I should have anticipated the depth of his outrage, but I did not. This was pre-James Frey, of course, and who would have ever anticipated that? The editor called back a few days later and said he had removed the kayak trip from the essay. He had added a scene in which I carry my kayak down to the river's edge, and a fog bank rolls in, and I decide not to go.

"I don't want to be an asshole," I said, which of course, wasn't true either, "But if I can't make up three Italian kayakers, I don't think you can make up fog in my essay."

It is hard, all these decades after *The Things They Carried*, to stand here and say the scene with the three Italian kayakers is the truest thing in the entire essay (though, of course it is) even though it never really happened. Nor would I turn an entirely deaf ear to the complaints of those who actually use travel magazines to plan trips. Not to mention war crimes, genocide, sex offenders, presidents who lie about weapons of mass destruction . . . certainly I do believe that sometimes it is necessary for us all to pretend together that language can really mean.

But if you think about it, the fact that I did not *really* have a flirty exchange with three Italian kayakers doesn't make it any less likely that you might. I might even go so far as to argue that you would be more likely to have such an exchange because of my (non-existent) kayakers, first because they charmed you into going to the Ardèche to begin with, and second, because if you happened to be floating along on a rainless day in your kayak and a sexy, curly-haired guy glided by and splashed water on you, you would now be much more likely to splash him back.

★★★

Due north of Newfoundland, there is a small rocky island in the Labrador Straights called Quirpon (pronounced Kar-poon). The island is roughly ten miles long and three miles across, and on the seaward tip there is a lighthouse and a lighthouse keeper's house—both painted a bright red and white—and no other buildings to speak of. Inside the house, two tough and sweet women named Madonna and Doris fry cod, dry clothes, fix mugs of hot chocolate, and hand out maps to soggy hikers who've come to stay the night.

Marked on the map along with the fox den and the osprey nest is an old town site called L'Anse au Pigeon, and underneath the name in parentheses it says "site of mass murder." When I ask Doris about it, she tells me she isn't much of a storyteller, but when I press, she takes a deep breath to get into what I recognize as the Newfoundlanders' story-telling mode, a half-performance/half-trance state that suggests stories are serious matters, whether they are about mass murders or not.

"And now," she says, "I will tell you the story of the mass murders on Quirpon Island." She brings her hands into her lap and folds them as if she's getting ready to pray. "A long, long time ago," she says, "not in this time, but in the time before this time, there was a settlement—several fishing families, living together on Quirpon Island. And one day the government saw fit to send them a schoolteacher. Now this schoolteacher, mind you, he was a handsome fellow, young and smart, and one of the fisherman's wives fell head over heels in love with him. And the husband was terrible jealous, terrible, terrible, so he decided to trick the schoolteacher into drinking a little bit of the stuff—what is it? I don't know what the stuff is called. . . ."

"Arsenic?"

"No, it's the stuff they use in the lanterns."

"Kerosene?"

"Like kerosene, but different from kerosene."

"White gas?"

"Like white gas, but different from white gas . . . anyway, he gave it to him a little, a little, a little at a time, and finally the poor handsome schoolteacher died."

Doris nods her head as a kind of punctuation, unfolds her hands and stands. "And that is the story of the mass murder on Quirpon Island."

"But Doris," I say, "Why call the death of one schoolteacher a mass murder?"

Doris sighs heavily. She sits back down and brings her hands back into her lap. "A long, long time ago," she begins, "not in this time, but in the time before this time, the fisherman who had given the school-teacher the poison to drink became more and more afraid that the men in the town were getting ready to confront him. There wasn't law back then like we have in these times, so he probably would have gotten away with it, but his guilt made him believe his friends were not his friends. So deep, deep into one dark night he soaked one of the fishing boats with the liquid that goes into the lanterns. . . ."

"The same liquid," I say, "that he gave the schoolteacher to drink?"

"The very same!"

"The white gas?"

"Like white gas. . . ." Doris says, "but different from white gas."

"Didn't they smell it?"

"This is the liquid that has no smell. Anyway, all the men in the town went fishing the next morning and one of 'em struck a match to light his cigarette and the whole lot of them burned up or drowned or died of hypothermia. You can't last long in that iceberg water," she says, nodding her head towards the window. "And that is the story of the mass murder on Quirpon Island."

★★★

I was driving over Slumgullion Pass listening to *Ashes of American Flags* at volume 50. There was three feet of new snow on the ground and I watched a herd of two hundred elk gallop through it. I had spent hours the night before on baby-naming websites trying to find something I could search and replace for Pam in my forthcoming novel of 144 chapters. The book is more or less autobiographical. I have, of course, taken massive liberties with the truth.

In past books I have used Millie, Lucy, and Rae. For the sake of sentence rhythm, I was leaning towards something with one syllable, but it would also be convenient to the book if the replacement name meant something as embarrassing as what the name "Pamela" means: *all honey*. I had considered Melinda, which on some sites means *honey* and could be shortened to Mel. I had considered Samantha, which means *listener* and could be shortened to Sam. But in the car with the elk in the pasture and the snow on the road and Jeff Tweedy in my ears, I was all of a sudden very angry at whoever it was who put all that pressure on Oprah Winfrey. This book was in danger of missing the whole point of itself if my name were not Pam in it. If my name were not Pam in it, who was the organizing consciousness behind these 144 tiny miraculous coincident unrelated things?

★★★

About ten years ago, I was looking for an epigraph for a book of my travel essays. I arranged a lot of my Asian travel in those days with an excellent San Francisco outfit called Geographic Expeditions, a company famous for their catalogues, which are full of heart-stopping photos and quotes from writers like Goethe, Shakespeare, Chatwin, and Plato. That year's catalogue contained a quote from Seamus O'Banion: *Eventually I realized that wanting to go where I hadn't been might be as fruitful as going there, but for the repose of my soul I had to do both.* I found it wise and pleasingly self-effacing, and I shamelessly stole it for my epigraph, without taking time to find the original source.

A season later, I was invited to a cocktail party at the offices of Geographic Expeditions, and since my new book contained essays about trips they had arranged for me, I brought them a copy. "And look," I said, "I thieved my epigram straight from your catalog" and showed them the O'Banion quote.

When they could contain their laughter long enough to explain it, they said, "There's no such person as Seamus O'Banion. We made him up, one late night several catalogues ago, and now we bring him back whenever we need him to say something profound."

★★★

When I told my friend Shannon how rattled I got in Vegas, she twisted up her mouth and said, "Well, it seems to me that Vegas is the distillation of American-style capitalism, where what is desired is a facsimile of Old World decadence (Venice) exchangeable only by complete ignorance of its actual cost (the wasteland at its margins). And that the lower-middle class who go there with their obese children are the real fools, because it's their money that keeps everyone else either rich or poor."

For the first time in my life, I truly understood the difference between a writer and a cultural critic. A cultural critic goes to Vegas and lets it serve as proof of everything she's been trying to say about the world. A writer goes to Vegas, and it makes her want to kill herself.

★★★

It is possible that I will be advised to change the character Pam's name to Melinda. It is also possible, though less so, that I will be advised to change the names I have changed back to the actual names, or that I will be advised, the first time I introduce a character called Rick to say "the man I'll call Rick." It is possible I will be advised to do that with all the characters' names I have changed, which is somewhere in the neighborhood of thirty. In the instances where I have combined two or more real live people into one character and thrown a little something in there to make them blend—a little storyteller's *petit verdot*—or even made a character up all together, this method becomes even more problematic.

The Rick I've put on the page bears only a modest resemblance to the man I love and live with—less and less with every draft. But the point I am trying to make here is that the two wouldn't resemble each other much more than they currently do if I called him by his real name and tried with all my might to make the two characters match. Nor would the Pam on the page resemble me any more or less than she currently does (which is only so much) if I am made to call her Melinda. Except in as much as her name would be Melinda, and my name would still be Pam.

★★★

I understand that it is in bad taste to love Venice, the real version. The city exists, now, more or less for the tourists, who number an astounding seven million a year. None of the employees can afford to live there, and the whole city shuts down by 10:30 each night because the waiters have to run for the last boat/train/bus for the city of Mestre, where there are apartments they can actually afford. Eighty percent of the palazzo windows are dark at night because they are all owned by counts or bankers or corporations, and now, because of the wave action of speedboats, the wood pilings that have stood strong under the town for more than a thousand years are finally rotting, and the whole city is sinking, slowly but surely, into the Adriatic Sea.

And still, leaving the rent-a-car at the San Marco carpark and slipping onto a vaporetto at 8 pm on a foggy January night, leaving the dock and watching the first palazzos come into view, some of them still adorned with Christmas lights, puttering past a gondola, its gondolier ram-rod straight in his slim black coat, passing under the Bridge of Sighs, with the dark water lapping softly against the bow, it is hard not to feel like you have entered the world's single remaining magical kingdom.

And when you tell the Sicilian owner at Beccafico, "we have only one night here, so just make us whatever you think is best," and he brings a whole fish cooked in wine and capers and olives and so fresh it is like the definition of the words *fresh fish* in your mouth, and afterwards, your sweetheart buys you for your birthday a small piece of Venetian glass, various shades of umber, in the shape of a life preserver to wear around your neck, and you drift off to sleep in a room that has had fancy people sleeping in it since at least the 1400s, you think, if the worst thing they ever say about you is that you have an underdeveloped sense of irony, that might be quite alright.

★★★

Did I mention that when James Frey was an undergraduate, I was his creative writing teacher?

★★★

In San Francisco, at Alonzo King's Scheherazade, there was one dancer who was head and shoulders above the others. I mean that literally, he was a giant, and figuratively . . . every time he leapt onto the stage, all of our hearts leapt up, too.

It was a difficult problem, I imagined, for the choreographer to solve, to have one dancer in a troupe who was so outstanding, so lithe and fluid, so perfectly free inside his own body, that he made all the other dancers, who I am sure were very fine dancers, look clunky, boorish, and uncontrovertibly white (even the black ones). And yet, having seen that dancer perform, wasn't it Alonzo King's duty to let us see him, even if he couldn't be on stage the entire time, even if every time he left the stage, we all died a little bit inside?

★★★

I did not actually believe, for example, until I saw the signs with my own eyes, that several places in Vegas offer drive-through windows for weddings.

★★★

It has been five years since my trip to Madison, Wisconsin, and I have 144 chapters. 132 of them are titled with a place name, divided into groups of 12 by 12 single stories that take place no place, on an airplane, 39,000 feet above the ground. I had to make a decision as to whether the airplane stories would count as 12 of the 144, or over and above the 144, but that turned out to be easy. If I stuck to 132 non-airplane stories, I needed just 12 airplane stories to serve as both dividers and bookends. If I wrote 144 non-airplane stories, I would have needed 13, which would have ruined everything.

In the final stages of editing, I sent an email to my editor saying "Is it wrong of me to want to call myself Pam in this book? Should I just change my name to Melinda and be done with it?"

She wrote back saying, "No, I like Pam. I think we want people to think it is both you and not you," and I sat in front of the computer and nearly wept with gratitude.

Six months before my father lost his job and we drove to Las Vegas, he threw me across the room and broke my femur. I think it's possible he meant to kill me, and I spent the rest of my childhood, the rest of his life, really, thinking he probably would. Speaking only for myself now, I cannot see any way that my subsequent wellbeing depends on whether or not or how much you believe what I am telling you—that is to say—on the difference, if there is any, between 82 and 100 percent true. My wellbeing (when and if it exists) resides in the gaps language leaves between myself and the corn maze, myself and the Las Vegas junkies, myself and the elk chest deep in snow. It is there, in that white space of language's limitation that I am allowed to touch everything, and it is in those moments of touching everything that I am some version of free.

When my agent read the first draft of my forthcoming book, she said in dismay, *You haven't taken us anywhere and yet you have taken us everywhere!* I know what she was asking for was more resolution, which she was right to ask for and which I subsequently provided, but I still don't know how to inflect her sentence in a way in which it doesn't sound like praise.

One thing I am sure of, having spent the last five years inside a shattered narrative, is that time is a worthy opponent. It does not give up quietly. It does not give up kicking and screaming. It does not, in fact, give up at all. Time is like when you break a thermometer and all the mercury runs around the table trying like crazy to reconstitute itself. Or like the way PCB can start out in a glass transformer in Alabama and wind up on the island of Svalbard, inside a polar bear cub's brain.

A shattered narrative is still a narrative. We can't escape it, it is what we are.

SCOTT KORB

The Courage to Sound like Ourselves

There are zillions of ideas out there—they stream by like neutrons. What makes somebody pluck forth one thing—a thing you're going to be spending as much as three years with? If I went down a list of all the pieces I ever had in The New Yorker, *upward of ninety percent would relate to things I did when I was a kid.*

—John McPhee

This craft essay has its roots in the exchange of a writing packet with a low-residency MFA student a couple of semesters ago. What I'm about to elaborate on—in trying to explore the relationship among character, self-respect, and voice—came together at first while I responded to some reading commentaries. And it came together there because I'd been teaching Joan Didion's *Slouching Towards Bethlehem* in a graduate writing workshop back home in New York and because I'd recently read a new essay by Zadie Smith on the topic that this particular Pacific University student had been mainly concerned with: the environment and the coming apocalypse.

Now it may come as a surprise, but it should not, that I learn a lot from the teaching I do. I can't possibly be alone in this. We writers who teach get to test our ideas in real time, which means bringing together days of reading and writing and other outside conversations for an audience that will just as often respond with a groan as a scribble in a notebook and the smile of new comprehension. What's more, we writers who teach get paid for this. But anyway—back to the coming apocalypse.

It struck me in reading these commentaries that the writer, in highlighting where certain books about climate change and the environment, loosely defined, let him down or put him off, was sometimes emphasizing problems of technique—too much direct transcription, too much speculation about what a subject might be thinking—where he seemed really to be having trouble with an author's voice. So I said:

> This all leads me to say something that may be perfectly obvious, but that, in these commentaries, you don't seem to notice: We can master all kinds of nonfiction writer techniques, but in the end, we're responsible for developing a voice that readers (*though not all readers*) will find compelling. By pointing out how one writer appeals to you while another one doesn't, you highlight for me the basic requirement of what we do (as narrative nonfiction writers). And if we write

enough, and we develop and come to possess what Joan Didion would describe as "self-respect," we almost can't help doing it—we create a voice. We sound like ourselves on the page because we come to have the courage of character to sound like ourselves.

In this instance during the semester, Joan Didion probably seemed to come out of nowhere. I included in my notes to him a link to the full essay, "On Self-Respect," originally published in *Vogue* in 1961. Still, she was on my mind, and so she appeared in my commentary. I was testing out an idea in real time.

A fuller account of what Didion says about the relationship between self-respect and character reveals a little more:

> Like Jordan Baker, people with self-respect have the courage of their mistakes. They know the price of things. . . . In brief, people with self-respect exhibit a certain toughness, a kind of moral nerve; they display what was once called *character*, a quality which, although approved in the abstract, sometimes loses ground to other more instantly negotiable virtues. . . . Nonetheless, character—the willingness to accept responsibility for one's own life—is the source from which self-respect springs. (*Slouching Towards Bethlehem*, 145)

I don't think I can put any better what Didion says here. But I do think I can talk about it in terms that have more specifically to do with writing, as I started to do with the notes I've just mentioned. Dealing with student writers over the past decade, I've encountered a good number who seem to have a difficult time believing that what they have to say—especially about their own lives—is of much worth. This way of thinking has at least two things wrong with it. I'm going to talk about those two things.

First, for those who find their own lives of little value in terms of writing, I'm not sure they have a full enough perspective on what our lives actually are. It's true that not all of us will be adventurers or make life-saving discoveries. Some of us may never even meet an adventurer or someone who's made a life-saving discovery. Others of us will have to seek these people out if we want to write about them. Some of us may never leave the country. Some people never leave their hometowns. And where we live, I've found, we often trace the same paths, drive the same roads, walk the same streets, shop the same shops, take the same elevators, traipse the same beachfronts. And yet many of those people lead lives that compel them to write. Mine does. Perhaps yours does too.

Which leads me to say this: The essential piece of writing isn't what we do—except—and this is a big except—insofar as writing itself is *something that we do*. The essential piece of writing—and so the always valuable piece of the writer's life—is what we think. Let me repeat that: The essential piece of writing—and so the *always valuable* piece of the writer's life—is what we think. How we come to believe something.

And the profound challenge of putting pen to paper is, in Flannery O'Connor's words, making that belief believable.

Consider the opening of Zadie Smith's recent essay "Man vs. Corpse" (this is not the one about the coming apocalypse):

> One September night, running home from dinner to meet a babysitter, I took off my heels and hopped barefoot—it was raining—up Crosby Street, and so home. *Hepatitis*, I thought. Hep-a-ti-tis. I reached my building bedraggled, looking like death. The doorman—who'd complimented me on my way out—blushed and looked down at his smart phone. In the lobby, on a side table, sat a forlorn little hardbacked book. *The World's Masterpieces: Italian Painting.* Published in 1939, not quite thirty pages long, with cheap marbled endpapers and a fond inscription in German: *Meinem lieben Schuler. . . .* Someone gave this book to someone else in Mount Carmel (the Israeli mountains? the school in the Bronx?) on March 2, 1946.

The handwriting suggested old age. Whoever wrote this inscription was dead now.

Here's an essay that begins on the streets of New York, where people supposedly "do things"—but these are the worn streets of this woman's life, the streets she walks to relieve the babysitter. What does Zadie Smith do with her life? On this day she goes to dinner, drinks vodka, comes home bedraggled, pays a babysitter, and sends the sitter home. Sounds like a good evening. And it sounds a lot like a lot of our lives. A lot like mine.

But what does Zadie Smith do with this life? Here's where the lesson comes, I think. Here's the great value of any of our lives as writers. She thinks about her life. And her thoughts bend toward taking stock, taking responsibility for it in a very specific way. Coming home, she half-worries about contracting hepatitis. She tells us she looks like death, which is a thought, not a description. The book she finds was inscribed by someone that she knows—another thought—is now dead. More thoughts come. Because before long, realizing that for months, like the doorman, she'd been spending most of her nights scrolling through email on her own smartphone, she decides to take it home with her in the elevator. "Email or Italian masterpieces?" the book seems to ask. The essay answers: "As I squinted through a scrim of vodka, a stately historical process passed me by."

The book accuses her. (Another thought.) And it contains more than any scroll of email. (This she already believes.) And facing the accusation, she admits her mistakes—she'd rather be thumbing her iPhone, like she'd been doing for months, and presumably paying the price. Then, through that "vodka scrim," she flips through the book armed, I think, with a kind of moral toughness we might call character.

One of the pieces she encounters is *Man Carrying Corpse on His Shoulders* by Luca Signorelli. "Man is naked," she writes,

> with a hand on his left hip, and an ideal back in which every muscle is delineated. His buttocks are vigorous, monumental,

like Michelangelo's *David*. . . . He walks forcefully, leading with his left foot, and over his shoulders hangs a corpse—male or female, it's not clear. . . . He is carrying this corpse off somewhere, away from the viewer; they are about to march clean out the frame. I stared at this drawing, attempting a thought experiment, failing. Then I picked up a pen and wrote, in the margins of the page, most of what you have read up to this point. A simple experiment—more of a challenge, really. I tried to identify with the corpse.

For Zadie Smith, the thought experiment alone fails. Thinking is not enough. She needs to do something. And so, what's important for us to consider—especially those who don't think our lives are worth much to us as writers—is that the other thing she says she does is to pick up a pen and write. She hands her thoughts over to her voice, and the result is a fabulous essay, as much about aesthetics as it is about politics and technologies' claims on us. And in this essay, she concludes, making some reference to her own night out: "Still, a life filled with practically nothing, if you are fully present in and mindful of it, can be a beautiful struggle." By the end of her day, and the end of her writing, she believes this. And I, for one, find this belief believable.

I said before that any way of thinking that leads us—writers or not—to undervalue our lives has at least a couple things wrong with it. And Zadie Smith underscores the first reason I think this is true for writers. Each of our lives can be a beautiful struggle if we put our minds and then our writing voices to making them so.

Another reason I think we're wrong to undervalue our own lives is that, as writers, it's a basic fact that subjects ostensibly outside our own everyday experiences have to pass through our minds in order to get to the page. Now, if you take the first point—that thinking is as much a part of your life, and just as beautiful and difficult, as anything else—then even if you're writing about adventurers or live-savers, climate scientists or Walt Whitman, you must come to respect your own mind's ability to reckon with the world outside yourself. Maybe this is obvious, but when you write about Walt Whitman and democracy, *you* are writing about Walt Whitman and Democracy. This is your life.

Or, on the matters of Whitman and democracy, just for instance, let's consider the lives of Marilynne Robinson and Francine Prose. In the preface to her essay collection *When I Was a Child I Read Books*—a title that reminds us that another thing we DO with a life, of course, is read—Marilynne Robinson directs our attention to Whitman through the lens, in her words, of a lifetime spent studying American history and literature. She is a Christian, too, and she writes as one. "Whitman," she writes,

> was a Quaker and he wrote as one: "I say the real and permanent grandeur of these States must be their religion, / Otherwise there is just no real and permanent grandeur; / (nor character not life worthy the name without religion. . .)." This is from *Leaves of Grass*, and so is this: "All parts away for the progress of souls, / All religion, all solid things, arts, governments, all that was or is / apparent upon this globe or any globe, / falls into niches or corners / before the procession of souls along / the grand roads of the universe." The vision of the soul, all souls, realizing itself in the course of transforming everything that has constrained it and them, finds expression in the writers of the period, prominent among them Emerson, Melville, and Dickinson, and in later writers such as William James and Wallace Stevens. For all of them creeds fall away and consciousness has the character of revelation. (xiii-xiv)

No one else can write like this. And no one else can write like you. For Robinson, just a dip into Whitman contains multitudes: all of Emerson, Melville, Dickinson, James, Stevens, come to mind—as probably does the work of Robinson herself. Poems and essays and novels and stories. And what they all think—what their consciousnesses all contained and produced: those poems and essays and novels and stories—has for Robinson the quality of divine truth. And in this preface, she's gathered up all these consciousnesses to argue about the "corrosive influence" of the "economics of the moment, and of the last several decades" (xv). Her voice is as political as it is religious.

So that is what happens when Marilynne Robinson thinks about a moment from *Leaves of Grass*. What happens when Francine Prose does? In 2011, she wrote of an experience reading Whitman for a website called *Occupy Writers*:

> As far as I can understand it myself, here's why I burst into tears at the Occupy Wall Street camp. I was moved, first of all, by what everyone notices first: the variety of people involved, the range of ages, races, classes, colors, cultures. In other words, the 99 percent. . . . In Zuccotti Park I felt a kind of lightening of a weight, a lessening of the awful isolation and powerlessness of knowing we're being lied to and robbed on a daily basis and that everyone knows it and keeps quiet and endures it; the terror of thinking that my own grandchildren will suffer for whatever has been paralyzing us until just now. I kept feeling these intense surges of emotion—until I saw a placard with a quote from Walt Whitman's "Song of Myself": "I am large, I contain multitudes." And that was when I just lost it and stood there and wept. (401-402)

Here, Prose's experience of Occupy Wall Street is contained in a snippet from Whitman. She's confronted with a crowd and a line of poetry says it all. While much of what she experienced is something some of us can identify with—that dread, the fear of falling off a cliff (not a real cliff, mind you, but that mental one of our own imagining), the isolation and powerlessness of being robbed, the terror of a coming apocalypse—this is Occupy Wall Street as seen and felt by Francine Prose.

We identify with her only insofar as she can voice, even after admitting she might not completely understand, why she broke down and cried. And there's a clear moment of recognition that

Prose, like Zadie Smith with her hypnotic scroll of email, hasn't always accepted responsibility for her own life. We know we're being lied to, robbed, and our grandchildren will suffer as a result of our paralysis. Until now, she says, and she weeps—perhaps because she understands the price of things. That's what Didion would call moral nerve. That's character.

Prose's opening, I think, is special and instructive in terms of understanding the unique relationship—it's truly unique—between our thinking and our voice, between our lives and our writing. Again, she starts: "As far as I can understand it myself, here's why I burst into tears at the Occupy Wall Street camp."

This could be a formula for the opening of just about anything we might want to write. What Prose makes explicit—"here's why"—we typically leave unsaid. But it's always there:

- For Marilynne Robinson: As far as I can understand it myself, here's why I turn to Whitman for revelations about democracy.
- For Cheryl Strayed: As far as I can understand it myself, here's why I set out to hike the Pacific Crest Trail.
- For Rebecca Skloot: As far as I can understand it myself, here's why we must know what happened when George Otto Gey cultured the cells of Henrietta Lacks to create the first known human immortal cell line.
- For Zora Neale Hurston: As far as I can understand it myself, here's why I traveled the South and experienced a hoodoo initiation.
- For Leslie Jamison: As far as I can understand it myself, here's why "intellect swells around hurt" (73).
- For Joan Didion: As far as I can understand it myself, here's why "Life changes fast" (*The Year of Magical Thinking*, 3).

In that self-respect essay, Didion explains, I think, what's going on when someone really sets herself to do this: to go far, *really far*, to understand for oneself why we feel and think what we do. Why do we believe what we believe? This is what writing affords—and requires of—us. Didion writes:

> Although to be driven back upon oneself is an uneasy affair at best, rather like trying to cross a border with borrowed credentials, it seems to me now the one condition necessary to the beginnings of real self-respect. (*Slouching Towards Bethlehem*, 143)

And as with any uneasy affair, our own journey to real self-respect—the self-respect that will lead to your voice and the good writing that depends on it—takes courage. As much as I've tried to emphasize the essential value of your own mind, you always have to face the world. And Didion makes clear that what drives you back on yourself are typically things outside of your control—accusations, if you will, sometimes in the form of an iPhone.

In Didion's case, in "On Self-Respect," what drove her back upon herself was simply being rejected from Phi Beta Kappa; this made her lose "the conviction that lights would always turn green" for her (*Slouching Towards Bethlehem*, 142-143); in *The Year of Magical Thinking*, it was the death of her husband. With Strayed, it was the death of her mother, among other things. Leslie Jamison faced violence, a broken nose after being punched while traveling in Nicaragua, and returning home, the sense "that no matter how [she] talked about the incident [she] would be somehow 'making too big a deal' of it" (Sparks). "This shame," she has said, "runs through the whole collection [*The Empathy Exams*]" (Sparks). And of course, Zadie Smith confronts her iPhone and a drawing of a corpse.

We all have iPhones or art books. We've all lost someone important to us or we will. We've all been rejected by Phi Beta Kappa or another club we'd like to belong to. We've all been punched or we've felt like we have. We've all been accused. In fact, and here comes the apocalypse again, let me accuse you all now. Maybe this will give you something to write about.

Here, again, is the inimitable voice—and we shouldn't try—of Zadie Smith, and the end of the essay, "Elegy for a Country's Seasons," that started all of this.

> Sing an elegy for the washed away! For the cycles of life, for the saltwater marshes, the houses, the humans—whole islands of humans. Going, going, gone! . . .
>
> *Oh, what have we done!* It's a biblical question, and we do not seem able to pull ourselves out of its familiar—essentially religious—cycle of shame, denial, and self-flagellation. This is why (I shall tell my granddaughter) the apocalyptic scenarios did not help—the terrible truth is that we had a profound, historical attraction to apocalypse. In the end, the only thing that could create the necessary traction in our minds was the intimate loss of the things we loved. Like when the seasons changed in our beloved little island, or when the lights went out on the fifteenth floor, or the day I went into an Italian garden in early July, with its owner, a woman in her eighties, and upon seeing the scorched yellow earth and withered roses, and hearing what only the really old people will confess—*in all my years I've never seen anything like it*—I found my mind finally beginning to turn from the elegiac *what have we done* to the practical *what can we do?*

Seriously—what can we do?

Well, lots, I hope. By the end of her own elegy, Smith suggests we stop elegizing so much. How's that for having the courage of your mistakes? But for our purposes, let's get back to those reading commentaries. Or reading and generally listening to more voices.

What has helped Zadie Smith—and we see this in all the writers I've referred to, but perhaps most obviously in what we've seen from Robinson and Prose and Didion—is a deep and thorough commitment to reading. There may be better ways for us to deal practically with the climate disaster we've created, or, just for instance, what the legal scholar Michelle Alexander calls the "New Jim Crow" of this nation's mass incarceration. Or in whatever other large and small ways the world accuses you. But we writers know that even our most practical activities—recycling, bodies-on-the-street protests, getting a babysitter, carrying away and burying our dead—are shaped by our own minds and the thinking and writing of generations of writers before us. But only those writers we've read. Only those voices we've encountered before.

The apocalypse Smith writes about, and Robinson's revelations too, mean a lot more if you know the Book of Revelation or the prophecies of Isaiah, Whitman, or Dickinson. Smith's essay is better, too—and you enjoy it more, play more a part—if, when she says "Maybe we will get used to this new England" (her homeland of biblical floods in April), both Billy Bragg and the book of Genesis flash in your mind. For her, the phrase "Dickensian delusion"—contained in the same paragraph!—calls to mind all the Dickens she's read in her life.

So yes, Didion's better—or you're more prepared for Didion—if Jordan Baker already lives in your mind. You're better prepared for Leslie Jamison if you've listened to Björk, seen *Carrie*, considered the paintings and read the diary of Frida Kahlo, and if you've read Marilynne Robinson and Joan Didion.

What can we do? Lots, I hope. Maybe vote. Or protest. Make love. Drink vodka. Pay your babysitters well. *But read—be sure to read.* Lots. And write about it. And remember, if you're reading well, all of what you read will accuse you of something. All of it will drive you back on yourself. And if you believe, as I do, that self-respect comes from actually reckoning, in your mind, with the world's accusations—an iPhone, a corpse, adultery, Whitman, our prisons, a punch in the face—and if you have both the courage of your mistakes and the courage of your convictions, you'll develop your voice, you'll sound like yourself, and you'll write better.

BENJAMIN PERCY

Get a Job: The Importance of Work in Prose and Poetry

If you wait until you got time to write a novel, or time to write a story, or time to read the hundred thousands of books you should have already read—if you wait for the time, you'll never do it. 'Cause there ain't no time; world don't want you to do that. World wants you to go to the zoo and eat cotton candy, preferably seven days a week.

—Harry Crews

I married into a farm family. For four generations, in the northwest corner of Wisconsin, outside the wooded hamlet of Elk Mound—where the Packers rule and cheese is never far from the hand and the blasting white winters weaken you into something half-alive—the Dummers have risen at 4:30 every morning to milk their seventy-five Holsteins and to disc and plant and harvest their thousand acres of corn and soybeans.

Every few months, my wife and I make the five-hour trek from Iowa to visit; the last time was in May. After we heaved our suitcases inside and collapsed in a travel-weary daze at the kitchen table, my father-in-law came in from the barn, shook my hand, and said, "Corn up?" He wanted to know where he stood compared to Iowa farmers. He wanted to know whether the spring rain had let up, whether the tractors had grumbled through the fields, whether the first green shoots were springing from the furrows. I could say with certainty, "Yeah, corn's up, ankle-high," because I had looked. Because I knew he would ask. Just as I know he will ask in July, "Tasseled out yet?" and in September or October, "Harvesting?"

He's a dangerous driver; as we putter around Elk Mound, his attention flits so often from the road to the fields that we'll frequently find ourselves straddling the yellow line or skirting a ditch. With one hand on the wheel, he'll list off who owns what land, who needs a new combine, who's selling out to a developer ready to hammer together a subdivision. He'll brake along the shoulder to ogle a new manure spreader.

I admit to feeling puzzled when I first met him, when he asked me whether anyone in my family farmed, when every conversation somehow cycled back to chores or machinery or crop yield. It took me a few years to get used to his way of seeing the world. Now I anticipate it—and think of him every time I pass an implement dealer or gaze out over a rust-colored spread of soybeans after an autumn freeze.

And this is what so many beginning writers fail to realize—the same thing I failed to realize when I first met my in-laws—that your way of seeing the world bends around your work.

We spend the majority of our adult lives hunched over a desk in a hive of cubicles, or fitting together auto parts in a factory assembly line, or scraping charred burger off a grill as a line cook, or stuck in traffic limbo somewhere between the boardroom table and the La-Z-Boy recliner. And yet in most of the student stories I read, work is mentioned only in passing or is absent altogether.

Whether we like it or not, work defines us. Work dominates our lives. And we have an obligation, in our prose and poetry, in the interest of realism, and in the service of point of view, voice, setting, metaphor, and story, to try to incorporate credibly and richly the working lives of our characters.

Point of view, as you well know, is the filter through which a reader observes the story. Any number of things will influence the perspective—whether a character was beaten or coddled by his parents—whether a character comes from Libya or Canada or Uzbekistan—whether a character can rack two hundred pounds on the bench or barely hoist a gallon of milk—whether a character has loved or grieved or betrayed or killed—whether a character lives in a time of war or a time of peace—whether a character is a rosy-cheeked seventeen-year-old or a gray-haired, glazed-eyed eighty—but chief among them is a character's job.

Let's say our character is a fashion model. Call her Georgiana. Forget making her complicated and three-dimensional. For the moment, we'll happily wallow in stereotype. Georgiana walks into a room. What does she see? Every reflective surface? A mirror, a window, a knife? Anything she might use to check her hair, her lipstick? Or maybe she accounts for the lighting, standing far from the chandelier that drags shadows across her face but close to a table lamp that gives off a soft glow. Maybe she inventories the designer labels.

Maybe she eyes up the competition—determining who is skinnier, who is prettier. Maybe she clacks her high heels across the hardwood floor to make certain everyone turns to look when she first walks through the door.

The introduction to the Showtime series *Dexter* is similarly exaggerated. As the opening credits roll, the titular character (a serial killer played by Michael C. Hall) goes through his morning routine: a razor nicks his neck, an egg cracks like a skull, ketchup bloodily spots his plate, a tie nooses around his neck. The possibility of violence is everywhere. Will Ferrell is no less a caricature in *Stranger than Fiction*. He plays Harold Crick, an IRS auditor of infinite calculations, who is hardwired to notice numbers, to formulate—calculating the number of steps it takes to get from his apartment to the bus, determining the most precise and efficient way to knot a tie, load a dishwasher.

There are many versions of Harold Crick in Joshua Ferris's white-collar novel *Then We Came to the End*. The characters work in a Chicago advertising firm, and every day everyone wears some variation of the power suit or the long-sleeve button-down with ironed chinos. The characters are assigned to cubicles and glass-walled offices. They carry out the same actions over and over and over again, filling out spreadsheets, calculating earnings, sitting through endless PowerPoint presentations. And their story is told in first-person plural:

> We were fractious and overpaid. Our mornings lacked promise. At least those of us who smoked had something to look forward to at ten-fifteen. Most of us liked most everyone, a few of us hated specific individuals, one or two people loved everyone and everything. Those who loved everyone were unanimously reviled. We loved free bagels in the morning. They happened all too infrequently. Our benefits were astonishing in comprehensiveness and quality of care. Sometimes we questioned whether they were worth it. We thought moving to India might be better, or going back to nursing school. Doing something with the handicapped or working

with our hands. No one ever acted on these impulses, despite their daily, sometimes hourly contractions. Instead we met in conference rooms to discuss the issues of the day. (3-4)

This point of view might come across as gimmicky if not for the circumstances: The work destroys individual identity and the employees become part of a capitalist collective, a conformist hive. Boardroom rhetoric infects the voice: "benefits astonishing in comprehensiveness and quality of care," "printing errors, transposed numbers," "call now and order today." This is what too many meetings and instruction manuals and water-cooler conversations will do to you.

Every now and then a character will break away from the "we," and every now and then the sentences will buck their slow, formal cadence with a "fuck" or a "damn," and every now and then the characters will yearn for something else, something brighter than the harsh glow of the fluorescents overhead. But only for a moment. The voice is as buttoned-down as an Oxford pinstripe.

Compare that to the untrammeled voice and frayed-edge blue-collar perspective of Kevin McIlvoy's "The People Who Own Pianos":

> We never can find their fuckin houses.
>
> We get a set of shit directions there, a different set of shit directions back. Okay, we've got an attitude about the goddamn load no matter what we're told it is—grand, baby, standup, damaged, used, good used, or good—fifth or first floor, basement, attic, narrow or wide staircase—the kit or the whole coffin—it's the same to A.D. Moving.
>
> We carry it out into the light beyond the lighted, decorated, dimwit room we rearrange, rip, gouge, and nick all we want on our way out. Make way, we say, make way—words that give us rights greater any day than the owners', am I right? (345-346)

The piano mover encounters setting as a series of tight hallways, narrow staircases—and as economic indicator. The world is broken down according to the haves and the have-nots. The people who own pianos are the people who have hot tubs, stainless-steel ovens, top-shelf scotch in the liquor cabinet, oxblood wingback leather chairs with gold buttons. Like Ferris, McIlvoy uses the first-person plural. However, in this case, the "we" is there to distinguish the *us* from the *them*. The people who move pianos are not the people who own pianos. And like Ferris, McIlvoy supplies us with plenty of insider jargon—when he describes a grand versus a baby, the kit or the whole coffin, mummifying the sound, amputating the legs—making us trust the author, the credibility of the story.

But unlike Ferris, McIlvoy strips away all formality from the voice, the sentences laden with profanity, comma splices, and paratactic speech patterns meant to capture the rough-edged everyday chatter of somebody who might drag up a stool next to you at the bar. In the texture of the voice, I hear boots clomping up and down stairs, a heavy load gouging plaster—and there is music in this, like a country song writ large.

Sometimes I like to think of myself as a referee—dressed in my black-and-white stripes, whistle dangling around my neck—racing up and down the sides of student manuscripts. Every now and then, I will make a series of complicated hand gestures, screech my whistle, and say, "Point-of-view violation!" This is because the writer, after establishing a first-person or close-third point of view, has violated the constrictions of that perspective. In the first few sentences of a story, you establish a contract with your reader. You have violated that contract if you, say, leap from the gaze of a beachside sunbather to that of a pilot in a plane streaking overhead.

Nor, tonally, can you build baroque sentences when the mind of your character is empty, his life unadorned. Her voice cannot sound like white lace and gold trim when her home reeks of cheap whiskey and wood smoke. The trucker does not have a laugh like a booming bassoon. The trucker laughs like a hot tire ripping apart at eighty-five mph. The kindergarten teacher has Crayola blue eyes, *not* gunmetal blue eyes. Unless, of course, the title of the story is "Mrs. Snodgrass Finally Snaps." Point of view corrals description and metaphor—and the job determines point of view.

Consider Brian Turner's poem "At Lowe's Home Improvement Center":

> Standing in aisle 16, the hammer and anchor aisle,
> I bust a 50 pound box of double-headed nails
> open by accident, their oily bright shanks
> and diamond points like firing pins
> from M-4s and M-16s.

The soldier hovers between two worlds, not at peace and not at war, not a marine and not a citizen, not a part of the United States and not a part of Iraq. A fan reminds him of the rotorwash of a Blackhawk, a cash register drawer has the rattle of a chain gun, a dropped pallet booms like a mortar, paint pools in the aisles like blood. He cannot separate himself from his work. It is there, at every turn, imprisoning him.

A job too sets story in motion.

It is a job in Walter Kirn's *Up in the Air* that leads Ryan Bingham to the woman who will make him crave something more substantial and authentic than his single-serving lifestyle.

It is a job in Philip Levine's poem "You Can Have It" that yellows the hands and hunches the backs and shortens the breath and the life of two brothers who spend their lives sliding ice blocks down chutes, stacking crates into boxcars.

It is a job in Susan Orlean's *The Orchid Thief* that sends her into the swamps of Florida and a plant-poaching underworld in which she glimpses passion for the first time.

It is a job in Margaret Atwood's *The Handmaid's Tale* that punishes Offred, a concubine, and makes her ultimately join a resistance faction that challenges the male dictatorship of her country.

It is a job that frames and sets into motion every element of your story or essay or poem—and it is *your* job to do the required research that will bring the language and tasks and schedule and perspective of your character's work to life. Google can only do so much for you. The library can only do so much for you. You need to write from the trenches.

One way to approach this is to channel your past. The age-old writing maxim is, after all, write what you know. That's what Mike Magnuson did with his novel *The Right Man for the Job*, drawing upon his time working as a repo man in Columbus, Ohio. That's what Pam Houston did with her memoir *A Rough Guide to the Heart*, writing about her experience as a river and hunting guide. The job doesn't have to be extreme—doesn't have to be romantic or dangerous or grotesque—to be compelling. You could do the same with your time making swirly cones at Dairy Queen or nannying for two snot-smeared little trolls or folding skinny jeans into perfect sharp-edged piles at American Eagle.

So you could write what you know. The problem is, of course, that some people don't know shit. In which case, flip the rule on its head and know what you write. Tom Wolfe never walked on the moon, but that didn't stop him from publishing *The Right Stuff*, a book he spent years researching—interviewing astronauts and visiting Cape Canaveral, making sure he secured every detail about the manned space program. I've never worked as a taxidermist, but a few years ago, I wrote a short story about one called "The Killing." I visited a taxidermy studio, stroked my hand along the polyurethane forms, clacked the glass eyeballs around in my palm, and sniffed the formaldehyde. I spent several days working with the employees, eavesdropping on their conversations, taking notes on the peculiar insider lingo you can never glean from Wikipedia.

Writing is an act of empathy. You are occupying and understanding a point of view that might be alien to your own—and work is often the keyhole through which you peer. Before I met my wife, before I heard my father-in-law's alarm blare at 4:30, before I saw him wax a tractor and peel a cowl off a birthed calf and shrug off an oil-stained set of coveralls and combine corn until midnight and toss straw bales into a barn loft and tear through pasture in a mud-splattered ATV, a barn was nothing but a red blur out my car window. Now, after observing him and helping him work—the two of us scraping manure from the barn floor, picking rock in the fields—I understand the greater ways in which our work defines our character.

Get a job.

"THE GEOGRAPHY OF THE PAGE"

Reflections on the Writing Process

CLAIRE DAVIS

The Created World: Setting and Mystery

You have to be smart. The smartest person you can be every moment on the page. I'm not saying profound or anything like that. But smart. Smart.

—William Kittredge

The year is 1972, and I am 24 years old. It is mid-January, 4:30 in the morning, and I am walking down the long driveway of my home in Pewaukee, Wisconsin, heading for the small barn at the far end of the property on which my still-new husband and I house two horses, one dog, a gaggle of geese, a now dormant hive of bees, and two barn cats. All about me is that aching quiet that comes in the heart of winter. I'm wearing my six-foot-four husband's old army coat, the warmest thing in the house, though the stiffened canvas hem whacks my shins and in the overlong arms my hands hole up like small animals gone to den.

The dark is deep—hours yet until the first light of morning. Halfway down the quarter-mile trek, I look up into the wide dome of sky, and the stars, *oh the stars*, their light so fierce, they hard-fire the land, illuminate the snow in banks of indigo, drifts of cobalt blue. I pick up the empty buckets at the barn and walk past the stalls, inside which I hear the first stirring of the horses, and I step back outside and into the orchard. Overhead, through the stubble of apple branches, even the stars wince in the cold.

I work my way to the center of the orchard, where, like a secret in the dark, sits the well housing with its cap of black iron buried in snow. I kick at the cover until it breaks loose its icy grip, and then I kneel and throw back the lid from the bunker. Inside, a 100-watt bulb keeps the pipes from freezing—and the light released is so bright, so sudden that the tree shadows fling up at right angles, and my hands and coat and face, the trunks and underside of branches all about me burn amber in the blue dark. I wait for my eyes to adjust, then lean in, crank the spigot and fill the empty buckets, and when finished, I clamp the iron cap closed before slogging my way back through my own footprints, the shimmering buckets laying a trail of ice behind me.

The nickering of horses is in earnest now, but I pause outside a moment longer to look up the drive to where my still darkened home sits, and all of a sudden it seems miles away, and I am alone in the over-sized coat, adrift in a sea of blue. Up there, within, is the husband still half-stranger to me, perhaps just now turning over to pull the last of the night's dreams like a blanket over him. I look across the narrow lot to the neighboring house that sits uncomfortably close to ours, given the expanse of farmlands all about. A young couple like ourselves, they've just moved in, and I wish I felt better about it. I'm not sure what it is that disturbs me—there's been the occasional beer passed across the fence, rare but polite conversation. I stare a long moment at the house with its black-capped roof nearly seamless in the dark. I turn away, crack the door open on the barn and enter to the horses' welcoming snorts. I exchange buckets of fresh water for near empty ones and toss fragrant leaves of timothy and alfalfa into the mangers. I finish with an offering of oats, then stand in their generous warmth, bury my frosty hands in the mare's mane to let the thaw begin.

★★★

When we talk about setting, we're addressing physical space. But as in the piece above, in addition to the physical, I'm also addressing time frame as setting—the 1970s and, in my case, the back-to-earth movement. It is pre-dawn and winter, with all the associated miseries of that solitary cold juxtaposed against the beauty of the landscape. Because there are barns, we might assume we're exploring rural issues in terms of space: land usage, property, livestock. In this instance, the structures within the expanse provide additional settings within setting—the barns, the well housing, and, of course, the distant houses side by side in all that emptiness, each establishing boundaries that delineate purpose, levels of intimacy, and property rights.

In general, this setting's pretty ordinary stuff, save for it being the dead of night, the surprise of cracking open the well housing with its sudden blinding light. That bright image followed by the introspection of the house next door—its image merging into the dark—while providing contrast also suggests a secret life as contained within the home's walls as surely as the light within the well housing. That's all it takes and we are primed for story—understanding that at some future that cover, too, will be lifted and the truth revealed. The whole scene, in fact, is aimed at the moment that illuminates the dark, just before tamping it shut once again and allowing mystery back in.

For that's what stories are about—the struggle to prize free the greater truths concealed within the heart of mystery.

But, as if by default, in trying to unravel mystery, beginning writers tend to focus almost exclusively on character. They dip in to heads, formulate questions; their characters talk, obfuscate, confess, all in an attempt to pry truth out of their unwitting subjects. But to crack that most elusive of nuts, it helps to have more tools in hand, and one of the more often overlooked tools is setting.

Now, frankly I dislike the word *setting*, in part because it tends to minimize its role in story, relegates it to some stuffy furniture in a backdrop on a stage. Something we move in and out of, rearrange as fast as we can in order to get it out of way for the next "set." Setting as I prefer to consider it—that space in which our characters live lives, define themselves and their relationships to others and the world, defend, invade, get lost in, or find salvation through—*that* setting consists of the greater landscapes of not just room size or even exterior "plains or mountains" but spaces that create opportunity for the character to explore essential mysteries in less "directed" ways within personal psychology, or relationships, culture, history, whatever. It's the space—physical or temporal—that emphasizes or acts as a reflection of, or foil to, character traits and psychology. It is the space that not merely affords the opportunity for action but may, in fact, provoke action. In these kinds of "settings," *shit happens*, or perhaps shit is even *made* to happen.

One way to think about setting is in the construction of boundaries. And it helps to understand the differences in boundaries, the immutable ones—the rock cliff at your back—versus the abstraction of, say, state lines. There are arbitrary boundaries of personal psychology that become the cracks you can't step on, or boundaries drawn within communities in the name of order—law that becomes the line drawn in the sand. Or there are the even more ephemeral and fluid boundaries of time.

Maybe I'm a bit more tuned in to this idea of boundaries because fences have such a long history of conflict in the place where I live, the West. The concept of *free range* is a holdover from the West before the encroachment of farming in which lands were set aside, put off bounds, reserved for tilling and seeding, the movement growing stronger over the years with the advancement of towns and industry and subdivisions until free range became relegated to remote pockets here and there. The free-for-all West is a bygone era, but the *psychology* of it remains alive and well.

It's this psychology of a space that I like to first consider when I'm choosing setting—asking questions both of situation and of character. What's necessary at this point of the story, in terms of moving it forward, in terms of revelation of character, in terms of tension, in terms of generally keeping the work interesting to me, foremost, and to the reader as a secondary matter. Because really, if you're bored with a place or if the story's just not taking flight, it's probably because you've forgotten to put the plane in the air.

In Brady Udall's short story "Midnight Raid" from his collection *Letting Loose the Hounds*, the use of boundaries is central to the heart of the story—transgression in the name of love:

Roy growls and gives me the evil eye from inside his doghouse. He's flustered; I'm fairly certain this is the first time in his life a six-foot-three Apache Indian holding a goat has walked into his backyard in the middle of the night. Roy, there under the comfort of his own roof, seems to be trying to come to a decision. He doesn't know whether to raise hell or to make friends with me. I slowly take a step closer—no sudden moves—and ask him, as sincerely as possible, not to make any undue racket. He pokes his head out of his house and yaps, causing the goat I'm holding to let loose a thin stream of piss down my leg. (13)

A little further into the opening scene, we come to see that the dog is in the yard of a two-story stucco mansion occupied by his ex-wife and her new husband:

[. . .] This is Scottsdale, Arizona, close to midnight and not too many degrees shy of a hundred. I would be untruthful if I didn't say I was a little drunk. I have dead grass in my hair and my belly feels like it's full of sharp sticks. Small, silvery fish are swimming around in my head, flashing behind my eyes like coins.

I'm positive that what I'm doing is the correct, the honorable thing. In that earnest, heartbreaking penmanship of his, my boy has written me at least half a dozen times asking for his pet goat, and no matter what my wife has to throw at me, the injunctions and restraining orders and so forth I'm going to get it to him.

"Roy," I say, looking up at this pink stuccoed mansion that's big enough for two zip codes, "where's Tate?" (14)

The two major boundaries here are property and propriety. But in fact, the scene starts out with a boundary within a boundary: "Roy, there under the comfort of his own roof, seems to be trying to come to a decision. He doesn't know whether to raise hell or to make friends with me." In this initiating moment, the dog, within his doghouse, becomes the "owner" of the yard. In this dynamic, the choices are simple enough: friend or enemy? Does the dog defend or invite? Meanwhile, the dog's owner is sleeping in the two-story mansion unaware, thinking himself safe—believing in the sanctity of *his* property—the circumscribed yard bought and paid for, and bound by the physical delineation of fence, dog.

But inherent in this brief setting, there are additional boundaries that are not just of a physical nature—the measure of the lawn or walls of a home—but also conceptual boundaries such as personal space—the new family composed of son, mother, and stepfather that excludes him—as well as boundaries drawn by the greater arm of the law, up to and including restraining orders. It's the triple threat: physical obstacles, personal space, and the law. There's also the conflict of cultural boundaries here that calls into question the understanding of property—how one culture might question the ability to "own" land at all, blurring lines between what is private and public. The introduction of a goat into the civilized space of a two-story stucco home steps over yet another boundary, that which is acceptable in urban space—dogs—versus rural space—the goat. It's a lovely setting in which, with the lightest of touches, historical boundaries come into play as well: the white man's dog that's never before seen an Apache. This is, of course, ironic, as the localized setting of the yard is Scottsdale, Arizona—the land in which the native Apache has become the intruder. And I haven't even addressed the temporal setting—the time of night yet another boundary—an unstated understanding that clearly separates what is appropriate versus transgressive.

By erecting such boundaries within a setting and then having the character transgress each one of them, we get not only a satisfying introduction of tension to the story but an understanding of the situation and its inherent conflicts *through the setting*. The character doesn't have to say he doesn't belong, that he's being excluded, or that historically and culturally he sees these boundaries as, frankly, arbitrary and absurd—"the house large enough for two zip codes." It's all in there—the insights into the psychology and heart of the man as we come to understand this is not a standard B & E, but a story about love, and a man's willingness to break all the rules in the name of love, even though such action underscores the tragic flaws of the man and will inevitably result in additional trauma and conflict in the boy's life.

Personally? I like to imagine Udall sitting in his chair and laughing, enjoying the hell out of the setting he's just put on the page: the dog, the night, the Indian and the goat, the ex-wife with her new husband in the stucco mansion. How could he not write a terrific story given those first steps? Those first choices he has made in placing the opening of the story in the place and time that he did. The quirkiness of the setting—space and time—invites dynamics, encourages action.

I often get stories from students about domestic situations. And that's not the problem. Stories of ordinary life are important ones, containing some of the deepest mysteries relevant to the greatest majority of us. How do relationships work? How do we sustain them? How do they transform us? Or if they fail, in what manner? And if they fail, how do we survive that?

But stories of domestic life too often end up in a room that's . . . comfortable and ordinary and cozy and there's not an ounce of tension in it. As a result, the writer, who intuits that something here's just not gripping enough, has the character agonize over an imagined conflict or fall into immediate back story in an effort to do something. Anything. It's a paradox, because these most intimate spaces of our lives hold the most potential if we consider what's at stake within the private rooms of homes.

Jhumpa Lahiri's short story, "A Temporary Matter," from her collection *Interpreter of Maladies,* employs, for most of the story, a single setting: the kitchen. The story is about a couple who have lost their baby, a miscarriage at nearly full term, and this loss has shifted the landscape of their lives dramatically. They've become remote from each other. Contrary to their formerly more traditional roles, the husband has become the "domestic" of the pair, while the woman is now keeping herself more and more in the work world and away from the house. During this time, the power company informs the neighborhood they are going to cut the power each night at 8 o'clock for the period of a week:

> It struck him as odd that there were no real candles in the house. That Shoba hadn't prepared for such an ordinary emergency. He looked now for something to put the birthday candles in and settled on the soil of a potted ivy that normally sat on the windowsill over the sink. Even though the plant was inches from the tap, the soil was so dry that he had to water it first before the candles would stand straight. He pushed aside the things on the kitchen table, the piles of mail, the unread library books. He remembered their first meals there, when they were so thrilled to be married, to be living together in the same house at last, that they would just reach for each other foolishly, more eager to make love than to eat. He put down two embroidered place mats, a wedding gift from an uncle in Lucknow, and set out the plates and wineglasses they usually saved for guests. He put the ivy in the middle, the white-edged, star-shaped leaves girded by ten little candles. He switched on the digital clock radio and tuned it to a jazz station. (9)

The setting here is not just the generalized house but the kitchen in particular, the distressed heart of the home. Within are the necessary details: ivy that's left un-watered though it sits alongside the kitchen sink, the mail and library books cluttering the kitchen table, and finally, the birthday candles as the only emergency lighting on hand that resonates with their unpreparedness to deal with the greater catastrophe that has struck their lives.

But amidst the disorder and neglect, there are also the embroidered placemats, signifying not just their wedding and better days but an ongoing desire, at least on the part of the husband, to reconnect to that happier state of their relationship. It remains an ordinary room in the house, but it is now potent with images that demonstrate their distress. Then, the really brilliant move in this story? The enforced dark, that brings with it the forced dinners together around a table, and in this particular scene the birthday candles that burn down so fast, that in the total dark the couple resorts to a game:

> "Let's do that," she said suddenly.
> "Do what?"
> "Say something to each other in the dark."
> "Like what? I don't know any jokes."
> "No, no jokes." She thought for a minute. "How about telling each other something we've never told before."
> "I used to play this game in high school," Shukumar recalled. "When I got drunk."
> "You're thinking of truth or dare. This is different. Okay, I'll start." (12)

They agree to tell each other secrets, and each consecutive night, they sit across from one another at the table, in the dark, and the secrets gain more power and scope until the final evening when the truths are told that will make or break this couple.

This is the *ordinary* transformed, wherein the couple's kitchen becomes a confessional and the dark becomes the vehicle for acknowledging what this couple cannot bear to face in the ordinary light of their home. That Lahiri keeps them in the house, specifically in the kitchen, the center, the heart of the home, is smart. For in its confines they are held within the boundaries of not just its walls but within its associations, such as past happier dinners and the remnants of a marriage contract. Within the small space they are closed in with their grief as well: her abandonment, his last-ditch effort to nurture. Paired to the succession of days in which Lahiri keeps the couple coming back to that same room, that space becomes a kind of pressure cooker, keeping the tension intact and the couple on task—their struggle with and against each other—but with the introduction of the dark and the slow release of the ongoing game over subsequent days, it's as if the valve is opened this least bit, allowing just enough psychological release for this couple to credibly face what they cannot face otherwise—each other's truths. And for the reader? We play the game along with them, the tension drawing finer even as the truths grow bolder until we are given that heart-breaking insight into their individual loss, and a better understanding of the way we withhold and deny our darkest selves in order to protect ourselves, and, in so doing, hurt each other.

In his essay "Origin of the Work of Art," German philosopher Martin Heidegger defines what a *work of art* is: "To be a work means to set up a world" (43). He's talking about a "created world" that is of the earth and that uses the earth as we know it, as a touchstone, but that is free and separate from it as well. Using Vincent Van Gogh's painting "The Shoes," Heidegger demonstrates that the canvas is artifact and the process of painting is the *work*; even the brushwork, mixing of paints is of the craft. But *art* is in the ephemeral, inherent in the way the viewer enters into a world that is and is not of this world. The softened leather of the shoe gives the viewer the peasant himself, the feel and shape of his feet and flesh. But within the shape—the soft folds of tongue and heel—is also the weariness of his labors, his steadfast work, and, in that viewed experience, the truth of one man's connection to the soil, as seen in the dirt ground into the soles of his shoes. All of this and more is the "created" world infused within the image.

The visual artist, the musician, the filmmaker, the poet, the storyteller does not just copy, or "represent," the world but rather creates a separate world of its own. In Lahiri's story, the kitchen becomes the entire world, and the dark, the struggling ivy, the birthday candles give it the physicality in which these people are caught in the perpetual struggle for the truth of their lives, both individually and as a couple.

And that's the other part of Heidegger's theory on the *origins* of art. He suggests it is the artist's prying apart the constant conflict of concealment—denial, refusal, or dissembling—that creates an opening in which we are given brief glimpses into truth, what he calls the "Open," or the "Lighting" (52).

THE CREATED WORLD

Robert Olen Butler's short story "Jealous Husband Returns in Form of Parrot" contains one of my favorite created worlds. In it, he is using setting to construct a world that is both familiar and alien to the reader. A jealous man dies while spying on his wife and in karmic retribution is reborn as a parrot that his widow buys in a pet shop. He must thereafter serve his penance watching her as she starts her life once again with other men. The world of this parrot is, of course, not just the home surrounding him, but the cage that is home within the home, and within that the cage of his body—the human contained by the limitations of parrot. Maximum boundaries—walls within walls within walls. All obstacles he must struggle against, work from within, and transcend:

> But I got my giant cage and I guess I'm happy enough about that. I can pace as much as I want. I can hang upside down. It's full of bird toys. That dangling thing over there with knots and strips of rawhide and a bell at the bottom needs a good thrashing a couple of times a day and I'm the bird to do it. I look at the very dangle of it and the thing is rough, the rawhide and the knotted rope, and I get this restlessness back in my tail, a burning thrashing feeling, and it's like all the times when I was sure there was a man naked with my wife. Then I go to this thing that feels so familiar and I bite and bite and it's very good. (73)

And a little later on:

> My cage sits in the den. My pool table is gone and the cage is sitting in that space and I come all the way down to one end of my perch. I can see through the door and down the back hallway to the master bedroom. When she keeps the bedroom door open I can see the space at the foot of the bed but not the bed itself. That I can sense to the left, just out of sight. I watch the men go in and I hear the sounds but I can't quite see. And they drive me crazy.
>
> I flap my wings and I squawk and I fluff up and I slick down and I throw seed and I attack that dangly toy as if it was the guy's balls, but it does no good. It never did any good in the other life either, the thrashing around I did by myself. (75)

Herein, a character is forced to see the truth of his self through setting. The man is not only bound by the room's walls, or the cage walls, but in a parallel construct of mind and body—the walls of his bird mind, the limitations of what he can do as bird even as some part of him remains human and still plagued with the jealousy that sent him plummeting to his death. Within the physical setting of cage, Butler sets up an obstacle course, complete with bars and toys with which the parrot expends his anger. Even the length of the bird's perch is important with its view limited to the end of the hall, to the end of the bed, just enough to stir the imagination. But beyond the confines of the cage is the larger space that has eliminated his human history with its banished pool table. The tension is ramped to the maximum for this frail creature, and it is the work of this setting to not only reflect the truth of what he was as man but to pressure him in the present to transcend the boundaries of both bird and man.

We can see how if we have a character that is in some way bound by her body—lost within it, or prisoner to it, or coming out of her skin with nervous energy—closing that person within walls may compound the tension in a way that will force the character to act or change or reveal something of herself.

That is not to say putting that person in, say, an unbounded space will necessarily deflate tension. No. For perhaps this particular person—lost within himself—will feel even more lost in the unbound world. Or become more a prisoner of his body for lack of mobility. There's no one way to create tension, or create opportunity, or encourage action; rather it's a matter of choosing what's the best possible prompt/setting for *this* character, given the situation and psychology at this particular moment in the story.

★★★

1976. March. I am 7 months pregnant, and the sleet has just stopped falling outside. My husband is working overtime this weekend. And me? I'm on pregnancy leave, standing watch at the window while in the one spot under the silver maple tree that is not snow-covered or fully iced over yet, two pigs tear up our front lawn. I am confounded by the discipline of their destruction, the speed with which they create a wallow where once a lawn thrived. For the third time in a week and a half, the neighbor's pigs have forged their way under the lot line fence, punching out wood slats with blunt foreheads, pink noses like shovels scooping dirt and turf. Scooping. Scooping. Relentless. And the neighbors? Conveniently not home. No. It's just me. The sleet. And the pigs.

I grab a broom, the old-fashioned sort with woven straw on the business end and hefty oak handle, throw on a coat that, in my condition, is two sizes too small around the belly. I hesitate at the door to consider the icy terrain, the wide open acreage the pigs might run for—the barns, the orchard—and weigh what damage they will do against the risk of a fall to me, to my baby. And thinking about it, I feel the baby stretch and kick, a solid one-two punch, like *go get em*, like *let's go kick their asses*. I straighten my back, button the last remaining button available, and step out. I am young, foolhardy, never one to back away from a battle.

They are young as well, this pair, but stout, and like bullies, I'm convinced, they take a certain pleasure in the game. We circle the tree, scooting over the icy turf, slipping, sliding to my knees at one point, rising, teetering, grass breaking beneath my feet like glass. I cannot imagine what this must look like, perhaps a child's game—ring around the tree and we all fall down?

In the morning's light, the little beasts are a pearly shade of flesh, their dainty hooves skittering every which way each time they hit a broader patch of ice. About fifteen minutes into the chase, they've stopped trotting and are running full out—running circles around the tree, around me, around each other, snorting, ears flopping, tails wrung tight to their asses. And it's then the broom swings full into the nose of one upright little porker, and it sends him flailing and squealing and turning tail, whereupon his consort scampers off across the remnant ice to where they burrowed under the fence, the pair of them squealing back to the make-shift pen on the far side of the neighbor's yard.

It takes me another hour to shore up the fence, to restore order, and when I finish, I stand eyeing them from the fence line, broom in hand just daring them to return. But the little porkers have snugged butt to cheek with each other and are blameless in their repose. I look over at the house, thinking of the young couple whom we care to know less and less of the longer they live there—the wife who shutters herself behind drawn curtains, the lanky husband who slouches in from his work and disappears into the dark recesses with her. Beer cans litter the back of his pickup. His backwoods friends drive beaters, line seven deep in the driveway on weekends and give *us* the stink-eye. Us, the hippy couple next door where the benign smell of pot drifts out windows along with refrains of Chicago, or the Beatles, or the Stones. When *the neighbors* party, they party booze hard—country music booming from trucks or in-house stereo until the sound of guitars twang in my teeth. But for the greater part of the weeks, the months, I have to admit they're a solitary pair, as reluctant as we to mix it up.

I find I am glad he is not home. To face down. The neighbor man.

The pigs have settled, and so has the babe in my belly after the morning's antics. I skate my way back to the house, and for the rest of the day, I avoid looking out the kitchen windows, figuring what I don't see I don't have to fight.

Here we have the great out of doors, the challenge of weather—the sleet—the added complication of pregnancy, and the internecine war carried on by the pigs in the name of their owners. The boundaries are the wide open spaces pitted against one failing fence line. The boundaries between civilization and nature are drawn hard and fast with the animals pitted against the domestic, seriously nesting, mother-to-be. In this broader landscape, it's easy to see how things can happen. Physically. Action is just waiting in the wings. The stranger (or in this case, the pig) comes to town. And once you open the setting up in this way, Lord only knows what's coming next as in Stuart Dybek's short story "We Didn't." In this scene a young couple on a lake shore is contemplating sex for the first time:

> Swimsuits at our ankles, we kicked like swimmers to free our legs, almost expecting a tide to wash over us the way the tide rushes in on Burt Lancaster and Deborah Kerr in *From Here to Eternity*—a love scene so famous that although neither of us had seen the movie, our bodies assumed the exact position of movie stars on the sand and you whispered to me softly, "I'm afraid of getting pregnant," and I whispered back, "Don't worry, I have protection," then, still kissing you, felt for my discarded cutoffs and the wallet in which for the last several months I had carried a Trojan as if it was a talisman. Still kissing, I tore its flattened, dried-out wrapper, and it sprang through my fingers like a spring from a clock and dropped to the sand between our legs. My hands were shaking. In a panic, I groped for it, found it, tried to dust it off, tried as Burt Lancaster never had to, to slip it on without breaking the mood, felt the grains of sand inside it, a

throb of lightning, and the Great Lake behind us became for all practical purposes, the Pacific, and your skin tasted of salt and to the insistent question that my hips were asking, your body answered *yes*, your thighs opened like wings from my waist as we surfaced panting from a kiss that left you pleading *Oh, Christ yes*, a *yes* gasped sharply as a cry of pain so that for a moment I thought that we were already doing it and that somehow I had missed the instant when I entered you, entered you in the bloodless way in which a young man discards his own virginity, entered you as if passing through a gateway into the rest of my life, into a life as I wanted it to be lived, *yes*, but *Oh* then I realized that we were still floundering unconnected in the slick between us and there was sand in the Trojan as we slammed together still feeling for that perfect fit, still in the Here groping for an Eternity that was only a fine adjustment away, just a millimeter to the left or a fraction of an inch farther south though with all the adjusting the sandy Trojan was slipping off and then it was gone but *yes*, you kept repeating although your head was shaking *no-not-quite-almost* and our hearts were going like mad and you said *Yes. Yes wait . . . Stop!* (235)

In this setting, the "greater" world, we get to play with, say, the effects of weather—lightning that throbs becomes the throb of sand in a condom signaling both heat and imminent danger. The shore caught between water and land becomes metaphor for the transitional stage they are in between teen and adult, between virginal and sexual. The setting also taps into the cultural milieu of that time, referencing the popular film *From Here to Eternity*. It's a collision of worlds, of psychologies (the young boy's needs pitted against the girl's caution), romantic ideals against the hard-grit reality, the safety of beach against the lake's grim secrets. This space, which initially provides comic relief, is equally primed for tragedy, and because this couple sets out to explore the most intimate of acts in a boundless space, a space full of the illusion of privacy, it is ripe for incursion.

"What?" I asked, still futilely thrusting as if I hadn't quite heard you.

"Oh God!" you gasped pushing yourself up. "What's coming?"

. . . All around us lights were coming, speeding across the sand. Blinking blindness away, I rolled from your body to my knees, feeling utterly defenseless in the way that only nakedness can leave one feeling. Headlights bounded toward us, spotlights crisscrossing, blue dome lights revolving as squad cars converged. I could see other lovers, caught in the beams, fleeing bare-assed through the litter of garbage that daytime hordes had left behind and that night had deceptively concealed. You were crying, clutching the Navajo blanket to your breasts with one hand and clawing for your bikini with the other, and I was trying to calm your terror with reassuring phrases such as "Holy shit! I don't fucking believe this!" (236)

Once we get past the comic and come to understand that more is at stake here than a midnight raid on a lover's spot, we see the genuine tragedy at hand, the thing that will change this couple's future. Instead of the romanticized ideal of Burt Lancaster and Deborah Kerr, they are faced with a real world horror: a pregnant woman washed up on the beach, dead of suicide:

Their flashlight beams explored her body, causing its whiteness to gleam. Her breasts were floppy; her nipples looked shriveled. Her belly appeared inflated by gallons of water. For a moment, a beam focused on her mound of pubic hair, which was overlapped by the swell of her belly, and then moved almost shyly away down her legs, and the cops all glanced at us—at you especially—above their lights, and you hugged your blanket closer as if they might confiscate it as evidence or to use as a shroud.

When the ambulance pulled up, one of the black attendants immediately put a stethoscope to the drowned woman's swollen belly and announced, "Drowned the baby, too." (238)

This is a story that inhabits both of the central tenets of all story: "you go on a journey," and "a stranger comes to town." In this instance, instead of, say, sequestering the pair in a motel room or in the back of a car or some other enclosed space, the setting itself provides the "arena" in which the extremely intimate becomes public, in which the young woman's greatest fears can be made manifest. They are situated on the "shore" of a world in which any manner of things can wash up or intrude, and it is their rashness, the false belief in the privacy of the dark that sets up boundaries as fast as it knocks them down—the sudden lights of squad cars, flashlights on the scores of fleeing lovers, the couple's romanticized illusions stripped bare like "the litter of garbage that daytime hordes had left behind and that night had deceptively concealed" (236). So, unlike a story wherein the situation demands a kind of pressure cooker in terms of psychological or situational sense, this story plays shifting boundaries—the shore as transitional boundary between water and land—and that inconstant boundary framed against with the boundless dark.

Another example of story that requires the boundless as an element of setting is *The Old Man and the Sea* by Ernest Hemingway.

> The old man knew he was going far out and he left the smell of the land behind and rowed out into the clean early morning smell of the ocean. He saw the phosphorescence of the Gulf weed in the water as he rowed over the part of the ocean that the fishermen called the great well because there was a sudden deep of seven hundred fathoms where all sorts of fish congregated because of the swirl the current made against the steep walls of the floor of the ocean. Here there were concentrations of shrimp and bait fish and sometimes schools of squid in the deepest holes and these rose close to the surface at night where all the wandering fish fed on them. (28)

Here's a landscape that tests, that encourages and necessitates things to happen in that testing. It is the lack of boundaries—the ocean and its denizens within pitted against the limitations of an elderly man. What boundaries exist are the solitude of the boat, the singularity of the aged man. Foil to these frailest of structures is the sea with its great depths beneath and the unbounded sky above. His is a struggle to bring in the greatest catch of his life, but the truth explored is that man's attempt to come to terms with the sum of his own life and, in the midst of that struggle, to war against the sharks relentlessly lining up to take the last of what he sees as his.

So when we consider settings, part of it is like marking off the perimeter of a stage so to speak, but it also involves larger abstractions as well, like psychology. Or culture, say. Or . . . history, as in Philip Roth's scene from *Portnoy's Complaint* in which a man takes his son for the first time to the Jewish bath house, a kind of coming-of-age ritual that steeps the boy and reader in what it means to be Jewish and male:

> The moment he pushes open the door, the place speaks to me of prehistoric times, earlier even than the era of the cavemen and the lake dwellers that I have studied in school, a time when above the oozing bog that was the earth swirling white gases choked out the sunlight, and aeons passed while the planet was drained for Man. I lose touch instantaneously with that ass-licking little boy who runs home after school with his A's in hand, the little over-earnest innocent endlessly in search of the key to that unfathomable mystery, his mother's approbation, and am back in some sloppy watery time before there were families such as we know them, before there were toilets and tragedies such as we know them, a time of amphibious creatures, plunging brainless hulking things with wet meaty flanks and steaming torsos. It is as though all the Jewish men ducking beneath the cold dribble of shower off in the corner of the steam room, then lumbering back for more of the thick dense suffocating vapors, it is as though they have ridden the time-machine back to an age when they existed as some herd of Jewish animals, whose only utterance is oy, oy . . . for

this is the sound they make as they drag themselves from the shower into the heavy gush of fumes. They appear at last, my father and his fellow sufferers, to have returned to the habitat in which they can be natural. A place without goyim and women. (48)

The effect of this scene is curious, because, even though the door to the bath opens on to a room, it does not close us in but rather opens into a kind of temporal time warp in which we walk into a primordial past. Yet in the next step, we move into a much more recent period of Jewish history when he shows the men as "fellow sufferers" ducking beneath the cold dribble of a shower in the corner of the steam room before "lumbering back for more of the thick dense suffocating vapors, as though they have ridden the time-machine back when they existed as some herd of Jewish animals. . . ." Even with the primordial view, there's also a simultaneous vision of people herded like animals into rail cars, rushed under showers of saran gas, the "thick suffocating vapors." Instead of the room tightening down as a pressure cooker would or a space racing boundless to the horizon, within this more "open pot" is the stew of present, past, and distant past, of culture and race and history and gender, all of it boiling and bubbling and producing an interesting mix of tensions, both comfort and terror. The specificity of this setting creates not just the immediate world, but other worlds as well, breaches the broader boundaries of culture and history. Yes, this room *contains*, but it also opens *out*.

★★★

1979. Early summer. Our son Brian is propped in front of me atop my mare. We are walking quiet circles out in the pasture. This will be one of my last rides on the mare—her new owner is coming to claim her the next day. I look over at the house next door, swallow my resentment.

It started with the pigs. No. It started with the woman and

her husband. No. It started with the nature of the properties, long and narrow, the homes side by each, the single line of fence running the length of the long driveways. But it ends here. We have sold our home and bought another. Farther out. Ten acres, meadow and woods. Nearest neighbor? A half mile away across heavily wooded acreage. We are, in plainest words, escaping this place I have loved. This life we've built. Stripping down. The geese long gone, the hives dismantled, barn cats given away, the horses sold. I blame it on the neighbors. An easy target that doesn't altogether explain the tension that has been stewing in my own home. My husband's unhappiness with the restrictions of fatherhood, more time at home, less time partying, or out with friends. He's discontent with the house that's grown smaller with the three of us. But he *is* genuinely pissed off with the neighbor who after a confrontation across the fence grudgingly agreed to take down the trap line that killed one of our cats.

I walk the horse out of the pasture and we head down the long driveway to where my husband is working in the orchard. Brian holds onto the mane and the horse, my sweet mare, a Tennessee Walker, carries the two of us with grace. In the near distance, the neighbor is walking the length of his driveway, parallel to ours, coming in my direction. Though walk is hardly the right word, I think. Patrol is more in keeping—the army camo he wears, the firmness with which he plants each step. Though his hair is strictly non-compliant, long and brittle with neglect. The beard is new as well. But the skittish look in his eyes? That's been there a while now. Unless I turn the horse aside, there is no avoiding him on this narrow two-way trek. Arm around my son, I set my bare heels and urge the mare forward.

As he nears, I see a new complication, for now there's a handgun strapped to his thigh, his hand resting on the grip as if he's preparing for a show-down, high noon on a Wisconsin prairie. Shit. We near, and I'm too close to head back now. With all this wide land about me, it would be easy enough to turn the horse away, head out over the garden we didn't plant this year, head for the neighboring fields, but even as I contemplate that, I know it is too late. Turning my back now feels as dangerous as facing him head on. Instead, I pull the horse to a full halt and he stops as well, stares as if he doesn't fully recognize me at first. Looks down at his boots, his feet, at the gravel beneath them, and then back to me.

"You talked to her, didn't you," he says. His voice is rough as if he's forgotten how to speak to people.

He's talking about his wife. No doubt about that. I shake my head. "We're not friends," I say.

He mulls it over. "Doesn't matter," he says. "I know you talked to her." He glares at me, and then his jaw works. "She left."

I nod. I'd been fairly certain of that. Her car hasn't been there for weeks, and their yard that had been slowly slipping into disarray has tilted over into chaos. The man along with it.

He's looking over at our house now. "You're leaving too."

I nod.

"Can't be soon enough, huh?"

I catch myself nodding again, then shaking my head, then just sitting there foolishly.

But he's already stepping away, and I'm left wondering what just went down.

And I already know. He's not willing to believe his part in it all. The disquiet of that house, the thing I'd sensed in the dark so many years earlier has, over time, been made apparent. The abusive man. The wife who had finally had enough. I set my mare into a walk and aim for the orchard, holding my son to me, not daring to look back, and for the first time genuinely relieved to be leaving this place after all, leaving the mad man next door and all the drama behind. I actually believe that. But that is only because I am not yet ready to face my own life unraveling about me. It will take years and the power of retrospection to see this initial dismantling in the name of a neighbor is really just the beginning of what I will come to know as an end.

★★★

Each of the three scenes of my story were exterior settings—in part because at the heart of this piece is the conflict of the physical boundaries, the wide open fields with the two homes set too close together, side by each, the thin fence running down the center. And that physical space also delineates the differences in the culture of the two couples—hippy and redneck.

The man patrolling the lot line with a gun strapped to his thigh is the ultimate transgression, even though he never once steps foot across the boundary as his pigs had. Instead it is the psychological intimidation that counts here. And as the lots present a parallel in physical space, curiously enough, for all the extreme differences in the two couples, each comes to a parting of ways in a similar story of slow dismantling.

Three scenes in the "same setting" but each with its own specific gravity. The opening setting in the heart of winter, the new home, the new neighbors, the dark, the secret that is planted in the scene. The second set with the pigs, late winter/early spring works as escalating tension and comic relief. We see the dynamic of the two couples being acted out in the ridiculous chase around the tree, and the frustration of the woman who knows this is not the end of it. The final scene, the showdown, brings the stranger into town, gun on hip, and Wisconsin or not, it might as well be the old West. Three scenes, same setting, and yet each one different in what they must address and the ways in which they are manipulated to incorporate situation, the psychology of the individual as well as of the pairs, culture, connection or disconnection from the natural world, and the role of personal property versus law.

However we tackle setting in our work, it comes down to making intelligent decisions—there is no default in setting. We choose it. And that entails knowing what space will best reflect or engage the psychology of the character. What space will encourage action? Con-flict? Revelation? What space will provide opportunity for transgres-sion, within the character or from without? What space will kick you, as a writer, into more deeply imagining your character while providing you the joy of discovery that is the best and dearest gift of this art? Finally, whether poetry, nonfiction, or fiction, our art is one art: the created world that evokes what confounds and compels us in our exploration of the mystery and truths within our lives.

A Match Flaring Up in a Dark Universe

Is there any good in saying everything?

—Matsuo Basho

A tree several hundred feet above the cabin shivers when I come near it. The path into the wilderness goes up and over a little rise past a heartwood post on which a horse skull glows. The leaves start up and I look at the skull and a fence that no longer keeps anything in or out—just barbed wire cutting into pine—and wonder what makes the leaves that remain on a dead tree tremble so.

"One need not be a Chamber," wrote Emily Dickinson, "to be Haunted." I sneak up on that tree the same way one might approach a poem to watch its dark characters shake to life. W.S. Merwin describes such a process around the translation of Hadrian's "Little Soul," a poem that remained with him from his time at Princeton, only to be translated decades later after Merwin came upon it while reading Marguerite Yourcenar's novel, *Memoirs of Hadrian* (2005).

Hadrian haunted Yourcenar as well, as she crossed America in a train during the 1940s "closed inside [her] compartment as if in a cubicle of an Egyptian tomb" writing her novel in "controlled delirium." Yourcenar, like many writers, believed her characters actually existed, and Hadrian rode within her as she wrote. The meaty Latin vowels of "Little Soul" might draw any reader close. They appear as beautiful on the blank page as they do carved in marble.

> Animula, vagula, blandula,
> Hospes comeque corporis
> Quae nunc abibis in loca
> Pallidula, rigida, nudula,
> Nec ut soles dabis jocos.

"Poems have come to me," writes Merwin in his translator's note, "arising from events that recalled the familiar Latin phrases too, and one day I realized that I knew, suddenly, how I would like to hear them in English—if they could exist in English—and the words of the translation, as they occurred to me, seemed to be as literal as they could possibly be" (*Poetry*, April 2006).

Written by a dying Roman emperor in his villa beside the Bay of Naples in 138 CE, "Little Soul" haunted centuries of writers before Yourcenar or Merwin. Pope translated it in 1712 ("Ah fleeting Spirit! wand'ring fire/"), Byron ("Ah! gentle, fleeting, wav'ring sprite") in 1806. Christina Rossetti ("Soul rudderless, unbraced") in 1876 and recently David Malouf and Jean Valentine.

Serendipitously, "Little Soul" came to haunt me.

It was one of the last poems that friend and teacher Patricia Goedicke read as she lay on a hospital bed in Missoula, Montana. Chris Dombrowski, poet and former student of both Patricia's and mine, shared this story in an email: "I marveled at her vitality: between chemo treatments, she revised poems, read Dante, shook her fist at politicians in the news. We talked of where to find the season's first morels; of the afternoon light, which took the color of the good glass of chardonnay she craved; of grocery store tulips—and then she grew almost instantly serious, intent on sharing a poem with me. "'Little soul little stray/' she recited, quoting Merwin's version of Hadrian's deathbed poem. Silly me, sane me, I thought it was the treatments talking; but it was something she wanted me to have, last of many gifts, something she thought might help."

It's eerie the way that a poem, even in translation, can draw us to it. Jean Valentine, in her version, addressed the stray as "uncanny other." Though far from a soul mate, Patricia Goedicke herself was an *uncanny other* to me. We were the odd couple, one composite, dashing over the page, swirling wild-skirted, breathless as Loretta Young, in and out of conversations, and the other isolate. I thought if I waited, we would one day find a place where spirit came together, and because of the repetition of that ancient poem recited to another student and friend, and a small note she left behind, we did. Among the hundred banker boxes of notes, quotations, random written thoughts, plans and descriptions in Patricia Goedicke's papers, now housed at the University of Montana, one can read the following:

to anyone "who might get drowned in the sludge of my psychic and physical pains. Please be sure to speak of my utter joy—inexpressible—but experienced . . . walking barefoot over the grass around the house looking up at the stars and talking to the in-and-out cats in the shadows . . . walking on the same bare-foot grass in the early mornings . . . waking in my sweet bed with the breezes blowing over and no troubles during the night . . . Such pleasures. . . . " (*Missoulian*, July 23, 2006)

> Little soul little stray
> Little drifter
> now where will you stay
> all pale and all alone
> after the way
> you used to make fun of things
>
> (translated by W.S. Merwin)

★★★

"The religion of the short poem, in every age and in every literature, has a single commandment: Less is always more. The short poem rejects preamble and summary. It's about all and everything, the metaphysics of a few words surrounded by much silence," writes Charles Simic in his introduction to Serbian poet Novica Tadić's collection, *Night Mail* (1992).

"Epics grow unreadable, empires collapse, languages and cultures die, but there are short, anonymous Egyptian poems, for instance, that have been around almost as long as the pyramids, and that are still full of life today. Their impact," he writes, "is like a match flaring up in a dark universe."

★★★

So how does one begin to capture this phosphor? Li Ho, 8th-century Chinese poet, composed poems by jotting down single lines on small slips of paper while on horseback, dropping the slips into an embroidered black bag, and assembling a finished poem each evening.

To Mary Oliver, one word might be enough. For over thirty years she has carried a 3x5 inch hand-sewn notebook in her back pocket where she jots her observations randomly, thusly: "6/8/92 woof where on this day, and with this very doggy sound, I first came upon coyotes in the Provincelands. Both the shorthand and the written phrase are intended to return me to the moment and place of the entry." She shares journal entries and articulates her writing process in "Pen and Paper and a Breath of Air" within her collection *Blue Pastures* (1995).

Franz Wright, poet and son of James Wright, said to Alice Quinn in a July 9, 2001 *New Yorker* interview, "My father helped me very early with this kind of thing. When I was about fifteen, I got up one morning and took a walk, and, bam, suddenly a poem was there. I was very excited about it, and I started sending him some of these early poems, which were horrible, but to me they seemed like poems. At this time, I was in California and he was in New York. The first letter he wrote to me about this started with the phrase 'I'll be damned. You're a poet. Welcome to hell.' Then he made a suggestion: 'Try, no matter what—no matter what sort of maelstrom of distraction you find yourself in at any given time—try to write one single clear line in a notebook every day. If you manage to do that, over time, when a certain mood of inspiration does come to you, when you're feeling happy and things are going well, and you want to write, you have this store of material, and it's as if the lines start to bond together, or something starts to crystallize around a particular line.'"

"In fact, I love the fragments so much," said Wright, "that I really don't, for a long time, even want to make a complete poem out of them." One gets that point in reading the opening lines of his poem "Translations": "Death is nature's way/of telling you to be quiet."

What more is there to say?

Einstein likened this moment of capture, of lucidity, to a chicken laying an egg: "Kieks—auf einmal ist es da." Cheep—and all at once there it is.

★★★

I want to branch now, to speak beyond the necessity of the notebook, beyond the process of capturing at least one line a day, to a deeper understanding of a poetic that might allow one to weave warp and weft of disparate lines together, leaving a space, an absence in which a reader might enter, to seize and apprehend meaning from a writer's design.

In Greece, one can still hear porters shouting *Metaphoray! Metaphoray!* offering to carry baggage in small, four-wheeled wagons. A visitor might travel across Athens by public transit called Metaphor, gathering meaning from the trip, as a name accrues a scent in this anonymous Egyptian poem translated by A.M. Blackman in Philip Wheelwright's *Metaphor and Reality* (1962): "Behold my name stinks/More than the odor of fishermen/And the shores of the pools where they have fished."

This type of metaphor is called *epiphor* and describes a metaphor that sums up by transferring something known (the smell of fish) to something less well known (a name).

But with the transit of Eastern aesthetics to the West and the birth of Modernism, we begin to witness a shift from epiphoric metaphor (*epi*/upon *phora*/move) to diaphoric metaphor (*dia*/through *phora*/move) in which new meaning is produced in the latter by juxtaposition.

Ezra Pound describes how he came to understand diaphoric metaphor in his book on French sculptor Gaudier-Brzeska, entitled *Gaudier-Brzeska: A Memoir,* published in 1916:

Three years ago in Paris I got out of a "metro" train at La

Concorde, and saw suddenly a beautiful face, and then another and another, and then a beautiful child's face, and then another beautiful woman, and I tried all that day to find words for what this had meant to me, and I could not find any words that seemed to me worthy, or as lovely as that sudden emotion. And that evening, as I went home along the Rue Raynouard, I was still trying and I found, suddenly, the expression. I do not mean that I found words, but there came an equation . . . not in speech, but in little splotches of colour. It was just that—a "pattern," or hardly a pattern, if by "pattern" you mean something with a "repeat" in it. But it was a word, the beginning, for me, of a language in colour. . . . I wrote a thirty-line poem, and destroyed it because it was what we call work "of second intensity." Six months later I made a poem half that length; a year later I made the following *hokku*-like sentence: "The apparition of these faces in the crowd;/Petals on a wet, black bough." (100, 103)

Of course the hokku or one-breath poem (5-7-5) came to him from Japan where haiku was first a literature of laughter.

For a short course on how this influence grew, visit Yale's Beinecke Rare Book and Manuscript Library installation (http://brbl-archive.library.yale.edu/exhibitions/orient/intro.htm). The origins of literary Modernism and even Postmodernism in Europe and America began with the dissemination of far more ancient civilizations and world views. The Beinecke installation explores how the opening of Japan to the West by Commodore Perry in the 1850s profoundly affected the American (and I would add—the European) imagination.

Pound's intimidating challenge to poets to *make it new* came from an inscription on an 18th-century BCE wash basin that belonged to the first ruler of the Shang Dynasty. It is merely a transposition of the word Buddha itself: *wake up*. With emphasis on the elevated and the base, within a moment, the reader is reminded not only to wake up but that happiness lies in being able to relax into one's state of being in a world that is fluid.

There were many currents feeding Pound at that time. He had not yet received the translations of Chinese and Japanese from Ernest Fenellosa's widow that would cause him to publish the essay "The Chinese Written Character as a Medium for Poetry" or his versions of Fenellosa's translation that became his collection *Cathay*. But he had befriended in Paris the sculptor Brancusi: Brancusi, who walked from his home in Romania to settle in Paris in 1904; who, unlike Rilke, had turned away from Rodin to search for more elemental form; who sought to distill the world down to one simple ovoid—an egg. Pound thought Brancusi a saint.

And like another poet whose writing would be influenced by classical Asian poetry, Anna Akhmatova, Pound was aware of *Le Japonisme* that swept through the art world as well as the literary world. Surely he was familiar with translations of Chinese and Japanese poetry into French in the 1860s and 1870s, as well as the translations of Friedrich Max Müller of Oxford University that brought the major literary and religious treasures of the ancient East into English.

Early in the 20th century, the Imagists, like the Acmeists Akhmatova, Mandelstam, and others in Russia, offered a counterpoise to the more nuanced *Symbolistes*, poets who sought not to name but to evoke a thing's atmosphere through tone, color, and rhythm. *Le Japonisme* became *L'Imagisme*. An image, defined by Pound as that which presents an intellectual and emotional complex in an instant of time, is powerful because of its innate potential to be translated and understood across centuries and civilizations.

★★★

What does this have to do with contemporary American writers? The shift in metaphor that reflects the shift in reality corresponds with our postmodern creation of random access literature for a random access world, and it brings us into close proximity with the nouveau Dickinsonians, American hybridists, minimalists, elliptical poets, and lyric essayists.

"The reality that can be conceptualized is not the essential reality," wrote 6th-century BCE philosopher and poet Lao Tzu:

> from the *Tao Te Ching*
>
> We put thirty spokes together and call it a wheel;
> But it is on the space where there is nothing that
>   the usefulness of the wheel depends.
> We turn clay to make a vessel;
> But it is on the space where there is nothing that
>   the usefulness of the vessel depends.
> We pierce doors and windows to make a house;
> And it is on these spaces where there is nothing
>   that the usefulness of the house depends.
> Therefore just as we take advantage of what is,
>   we should recognize the usefulness of what is not.
>
> (translated from Chinese by Arthur Waley)

Although Lao Tzu was philosophizing about the meaning of reality, his idea might be applied to poetry as well. "What is not" is actually a useful absence that creates breathing room between disparate observations where a reader is invited to participate, to experience privately the lightning strike that causes the poem to cohere. It is the space between the dark and the phosphor, the phosphor being the synaptic ignition in the mind of both poet and reader. It is what Polish poet Adam Zagajewski referred to in the poem "Don't Allow the Lucid Moment to Dissolve." Zagajewski offers a gentle imperative voice command in the poem, translated by Renata Gorczynski in *Without End* (2002): "Let the radiant thought last in stillness. . .//What passes doesn't fall into a void/A stoker is still feeding coal into the fire."

In diaphoric metaphor, the reader makes a leap between two

ideas or images and, in making that leap, discovers the lucid moment. One can follow that leap in the tanka-like sequences of Lorine Niedecker's " Paean to Place," where she writes of her deaf mother:

> I mourn her not hearing canvasbacks
> their blast-off rise
> > from the water
> > > Not hearing sora
> rails's sweet
>
> spoon-tapped waterglass-
> descending scale-
> > tear-drop-tittle
> > > Did she giggle
> as a girl?

(from *Collected Works*, 2002)

Niedecker called "Paean to Place" her *different* poem, her *life long poem* of over two hundred lines, her *marsh poem*, written before and after the assassination of Robert Kennedy and encircled by the violence of Vietnam; it tells the story of a family on an isolated fishing peninsula in Wisconsin and locates an individual lyric voice in the larger theater of the world.

In "Getting to Know Lorine Niedecker," Gail Roub, a neighbor and friend on Black Hawk Island, shared a 1967 letter from Niedecker that signaled a shift in her poetics:

> Much taken up with how to define a way of writing poetry which is not Imagist nor Objectivist fundamentally nor Surrealism alone. . . . I loosely called it "reflections" or as I think it over now, reflective, maybe. The basis is direct and clear—what has been seen or heard—but something gets in, overlays all that to make a state of consciousness. . . . The visual form is there in the background and the words convey what the visual form gives off after it's felt in the mind. A heat

that is generated and takes in the whole world of the poem.
A light, a motion, inherent in the whole. (*Wisconsin Academy
Review,* 1986)

This type of disjunctive leap exists, of course, in rhetorical tropes
other than diaphoric metaphor. For instance, consider the
metonymic revelation of the wrong glove in Anna Akhmatova's
"Last Meeting":

> I was helpless, my breasts were freezing.
> I walked one foot on tiptoe,
> I put my left glove on
> my right hand, like an idiot.
>
> There seemed to be so many steps then
> but I knew there were only three.
> Autumn whispered through the maples
> "Die, like me:"
>
> (translated by Stephen Berg, 1981)

A poet uses metonymy to gesture the unsaid. The brain follows a
metonym the way the eye follows contiguous ripples in a pond, and
so the broken gait, the mistaken glove, and the endless staircase all
come to represent, by association, the awkwardness of parting. Of
the revealing image of the gloves, her contemporary Marina Tsvetaeva wrote in "Poets with History and Poets without History":

Through a patent and even penetrating precision of detail,
something bigger than an emotional state is affirmed and
symbolized—a whole structure of the mind. (A poet lets go
the pen, a lover lets go her lover's hand and immediately they
can't tell the left hand from the right.) In brief, from these two
lines of Akhmatova's, a broad and abundant flow of associations comes into being, associations which spread like circles
from a flung pebble. The whole woman, the whole poet is in
these two lines; the whole Akhmatova, unique, unrepeatable,

inimitable. Before Akhmatova none of us portrayed a gesture like this. And no one did after her. (*Tsvetaeva: Art in the Light of Conscience,* trans. Angela Livingstone, 1992)

While one might describe a poem's seduction as phosphor or lightning, an electrical charge in the center of absence, Jane Hirshfield in her essay on brevity, "Skipping Stones," like Tsvetaeva, gives absence a more material presence: "Like an actual pebble, cold until warmed by an exterior heat source; like an actual pebble, unwavering in outlook and replete in simple thusness" (75-6). She examines the way that good poems move at their core and the way various arrangements of image and statement—and image as statement—work to make that movement happen. The syllogistic poem that follows by Jane Hirshfield appears in *Come, Thief* (2013).

Green-Striped Melons

They lie
under stars in a field
They lie under rain in a field
Under sun.

Some people
are like this as well—
like a painting
hidden beneath another painting.

An unexpected weight
the sign of their ripeness.

In three stanzas, a reader discovers how melons, like people, weather and grow heavy; the unexpected gravity of each signals its ripeness. All three poets—Lorine Niedecker, Anna Akhmatova, and Jane Hirshfield—either translated or were deeply informed by Asian poetics, and the influence of their study is visible in the architecture of many of their poems. Brevity in writing, whether evidenced in a short poem or a series of tankas like Niedecker's " Paean to Place," condenses many of writing's tropes into a few stanzas with enough absence between each stanza for a reader to participate with the writer in a discovery. It is the surprise within the poem that causes readers to lean in for centuries, finding again and again what absence or presence haunts it on the universe of the page; like that tree trembling on the edge of a wilderness, or the poem of a dying Roman emperor, or the song of a last meeting, these words by 17th-century Japanese poet Matsuo Basho written to a friend who has confided too much continue to haunt. To that friend, Basho responds:

"Is there any good in saying everything?"

(*Matsuo Basho,* Makoto Ueda, 1970)

VALERIE LAKEN

The Geography of the Page

We think we tell stories, but stories often tell us, tell us to love or to hate, to see or to be blind. Often, too often, stories saddle us, ride us, whip us onward, tell us what to do, and we do it without questioning. The task of learning to be free requires learning to hear them, to question them, to pause and hear silence, to name them, and then to become the storyteller.

—Rebecca Solnit

A book is not made of sentences laid end to end, but of sentences built, if an image helps, into arcades and domes.

—Virginia Woolf, *A Room of One's Own*

1. SPACE

In every written story, two spatial systems interact: the internal, imagined space where the narrated events *take place*, and the external, material space the words *take up* on the page. The real or fictional places in a story can be charted on maps, but the arrangement of the story across the pages is rarely mapped out or noticed by readers. In fact, it is rarely even mapped out or noticed by writers.

Most fiction writers can tell you which house in their novel is largest, where it's located and how it is furnished. But they would be hard pressed to remember how many paragraphs a given section contains or which chapter is longest. Poets, on the other hand, have a long history of engaging fairly meticulously with the shape of their poems. We can tell on sight, even in a foreign language, whether something is a sonnet or a villanelle, and we can even guess whether it was written by Dickinson or Ginsberg. One of the conventions of poetry is that the words are arranged in distinctive visual shapes, because poets understand that the physical arrangement of the words on the page affects the poem's sound, its speed, its mood. Ginsberg's

"angelheaded hipsters burning for the ancient heavenly connection to the starry dynamo in the machinery of night," ("Howl" 3)

is undeniably different from this:

angel-headed
                    hipsters
        burning

> for the ancient
>   heavenly
>   connection   to the
> starry   dynamo
>   in
>   the machinery
>   of   night.

The fact that many poems can be viewed in their entirety on a single page accommodates poetry's conventions of spatial arrangement. Most prose narratives, of course, span many pages, which, because of a book's binding, can never be viewed all at once. How odd it is even to contemplate the vast surface area a novel's pages would consume. It often seems that the number of pages, or the thickness of the book, is the only significant physical aspect of a book that fiction writers consciously shape—the cover, design, and typesetting being usually out of their control.

Fiction readers can tell you whether a story or novel was extremely long, unusually short, or somewhere in between. And those with highly visual memories can sometimes recall that a particular phrase or image they liked was located in a big fat paragraph toward the bottom of a right-hand page. But that's about the extent of our attention to the spatial arrangement of most prose narratives.

When you open them up, most novels look pretty much the same. This is no accident. In many ways, it is intentional; in other ways, it has been enforced. While poets savor the physical appearance of a poem, what fiction writers seek to create is an all-encompassing, throbbing, seamless dream that so fully absorbs the reader that she forgets she's holding a book in her hands at all.

By following the same bland formal conventions of all other novels, a text can achieve a kind of transparency. By breaking with those formal conventions—say, by using unusual fonts or images, or unconventional arrangements of the text—the author risks distracting the reader, jostling him out of the dream. Narratives that do adopt unconventional typographical arrangements tend to do so in moments of self-reference, to deliberately startle the reader out of the dream and dismantle the funhouse built of words.

This is all well and good, but it's worth noting that over the past few decades, colorful, flashy, image-laden texts have become the norm in almost every other type of reading experience. Aside from narratives and scholarly texts, it is becoming hard to find 500 words printed anywhere in a single, wide, uninterrupted column. From tax forms to websites to instruction manuals, our words come cleverly packaged by graphic design teams. And graphic designers are taught this maxim expressed by Ellen Lupton: "one of design's most humane functions is, in actuality, to help readers avoid reading."

Open any K-12 textbook and you'll see the paragraphs squeezed out by photos, sidebars, pull-quotes, and more. We are training our children to read (or avoid reading) this way. And then we wonder why they don't seem to want to read novels.

I'm not saying we need to bedazzle the pages of our novels to fight for the attention of reluctant readers, although I do think cover art could use a giant kick in the pants. I, for one, am sick of the pull quotes dropped like bombs into otherwise engrossing magazine stories, and if there were a way to eradicate the blinking sidebar ad, I think we would all live better.

What I am saying is, that aside from a few exciting exceptions that I'll discuss later, fiction writers and publishers and reviewers have largely avoided or even denigrated the use of unconventional typographical techniques in fiction, which suggests they are either ignoring or combating these new and increasingly pervasive methods of reading. And maybe we ought to be combating them. But it's possible we are missing out on something important. It's possible that our ways of reading may be changing. And if so, as writers, as the curators of language, we should be taking more notice. So I want to discuss what I'll call the *geography of the page*—by which I mean the ways our eyes travel across the page, and whether and how those journeys might be changing in our time.

2. TIME

If I ask how far you commute to work, odds are your response will mention minutes rather than miles. Our sense of space is tangled with, and sometimes eclipsed by, our sense of time.

In his book, *The Condition of Postmodernity,* the geographer David Harvey talks about how the accelerated pace of postmodern life has altered our relationship to space. From 1500 to 1840, our speediest means of transportation—horse-drawn coach and sailing ship—could carry us only about 10 miles an hour. By the middle of the 19th century, locomotives sped us up to 65 miles an hour. Since the 1960s, at 500-700 miles per hour, jets have been flying people halfway around the world in one long day. In recent years we've gained the option of space tourism and sent rovers to Mars. The universe grows smaller—and more within reach—with each acceleration.

Of course it's not just our modes of transportation that have sped up. We've been doing just about everything faster and faster. A few years ago I was content to wait 3-4 minutes for dial-up to deliver me emails from *across the globe!* Now, if a YouTube video shows a time stamp of more than two minutes, I wonder *Do I really have time for this?*

In the 21st century, we count every second. As Graham Swift writes, "We have developed a wealth of technologies that are supposed to save us time for leisurely pursuits, but for some this has only made such pursuits seem ponderous and archaic. 'Saving time' has made us slaves to speed."

The complaint I hear more than any other from friends is that there isn't enough time for everything. Maybe that's because, by accelerating the delivery and retrieval of stuff and information, we really do mean *everything*. For the right price, almost anything can be delivered to our door—or we to it—by the end of the week, and nearly every idea is accessible by computer *right this second*. Of course we don't have enough time to process *everything*.

Because the thing we haven't sped up is our brains. We can access information in seconds, but we can't absorb or commit it to memory any faster than we could before. In fact, studies show that our mental capacities are diminished by the incessant multi-tasking encouraged by all the flashing things on our desks and desktops.

Novels don't flash.

Novels are, or can be, a break from 21st-century life, a *time-out*. And clearly, for the people who adore novels, it is a welcome time-out, one that offers necessary and increasingly rare modes of stimulus, concentration, and joy in our hyperactive age. When we find time for it.

But Proust said it was the job of writers to tell the truth about time. My question is: Are we telling the truth about *our* time if we keep adhering to the focused, unidirectional, slow-seeming textual conventions of previous eras?

3. SPACE-TIME

In his essay "The Genre Artist," fiction writer Ben Marcus defines fiction readers as "consumer[s] of artificial time" and claims that story-telling means "creat[ing] time where there was none." Non-narrative texts consist primarily of comingling ideas, but narratives consist of a series of events, each of which *takes* time and is sequenced *across* time. The amount of time the events of the story consume and the amount of time the reader will need to read the words is rarely in a 1:1 correlation. So a significant part of the challenge and artistry of writing a narrative lies in the structuring and manipulation of time.

An 800-page novel can, through the fancy footwork of James

Joyce, present events that took only a day to occur. And a twenty-page short story, in the hands of Alice Munro, can span decades or generations. Both treatments can feel dynamic and complete, although the first stretches time out for the reader and the second compresses it radically. Temporal distortions is a fundamental feature of narrative.

Obviously, fiction writers manipulate time when they choose which moments from their characters' lives to include and exclude. They also stop time at key moments to create suspense, adjust the mood, or supply explanation. But temporal manipulation is largely achieved through the arrangement of the text on the page. Paradoxically, the longest periods of story time are often conveyed in the smallest possible page space. Writers compress nonessential periods of time through brief, summarizing lines like, "He stayed inside for two weeks." And the longest time periods of all are frequently conveyed with no words whatsoever—through the white space of section or chapter breaks. Although our eyes can speed past white spaces, by convention white space denotes the passage of significant chunks of (insignificant) time. It also, perhaps through the influence of poetry's conventions, invites readers to pause, to *take time* to reflect. But a standard, relatively undistorted depiction of an instantaneous action often takes up much more space: "She slammed her little fist on to the kitchen table, sending the salt and pepper flying, to collide spectacularly with each other in the air" (Zadie Smith, *White Teeth* 51). This sentence takes a lot longer to read than the action would. In passages like this you see just what fiction writers are up against when we try to depict physical action—and speed—with words.

Dialogue, of course, is the one point where story time and reading time come closest to a 1:1 correlation. In this passage from Bonnie Jo Campbell's short story, "The Yard Man," notice how the length, rhythm, and placement of tag lines and descriptive passages reflect and modulate the passage of time:

"Can we cut a hole in your floor or wall," the beekeeper asked, "if we need to?"

"Sure," Jerry said, although, as he climbed the stairs, he felt less than sure. He was glad his wife hadn't shown up. He should have poisoned the bees, no doubt. What had he been thinking? That the bees could be lured out one by one and their hive and queen, too, without destroying anything?

"You got a beer?" the beekeeper asked.

"For catching the bees?"

"For drinking. I don't drink at home, so I like to have a beer when I go out."

Jerry went back downstairs and retrieved two from the refrigerator, although it was only eleven in the morning.

"I need to watch and see where they go," the beekeeper said. They sat on Jerry's unmade bed. Good thing his wife wasn't there. She'd have hated having this man with the greasy Carhartt overalls sitting on the edge of her sheets. The bees followed one another under the bedside stand. Without speaking, the two men moved the bed and nightstand and sat there in silence, drinking their beers, watching until they were sure where the line of bees was entering, through a gap under the baseboard.

"Right around here," the beekeeper said. He moved his hand over the wall. "You can feel the heat in this spot." (17)

The phrase, "the beekeeper asked" suggests the man's brief hesitation at asking to do something as radical as cutting a hole in the wall. When Campbell wants to show comments flowing in quick succession, she minimizes or eliminates tag lines. When she wants to evoke the long, quiet minutes when the men awkwardly wait on the bed for the bees to gather, she fills a long paragraph with description and introspection, rather than presenting more idle chit chat, which—because of the short (i.e., fast) paragraphs dialogue usually comes in—would make time appear to pass more quickly and easily. Even a scene that looks very simply constructed is still moving us through time in complex ways that we rarely discuss.

In addition to temporal compression, we also have the option of temporal expansion, which tends to feel more striking as it is less common. Authors create a slow-motion effect by giving so much page space to an event that the reading time becomes much longer than the action time. Tobias Wolff's story, "Bullet in the Brain," begins with a standard, almost 1:1 time correlation scene in which a man named Anders waits in line at a bank, annoyed and grumbling about everything around him. Some bank robbers appear, he mouths off to them, and they abruptly shoot him in the head. This happens at almost exactly the halfway point in the story, and at this pivotal moment Wolff stops time and describes at great length the bullet's path through the brain, even reversing and replaying that movement as if it were a sports highlight repeatedly shown in slow motion. First, we see the bullet move "into the cerebral cortex, the corpus callosum, back toward the basal ganglia, and down into the thalamus." Next, we learn that "before all this occurred," the "appearance of the bullet in the cerebrum set off a crackling chain of ion transports. . . ." Finally, the bullet comes under "the mediation of brain time, which gave Anders plenty of leisure to contemplate" a scene from his past that takes up almost as much page space as the opening scene did (204).

This is nothing new or particularly radical; Ambrose Bierce did something similar in his 1890 story, "An Occurrence at Owl Creek Bridge." We are subject to temporal distortions almost constantly while reading fiction, but we only fully notice or discuss them when the difference between story time and reading time is very large, or when our "natural" experience of time is radically disrupted. Stories like these provide great reminders that among the things we can set in counterpoint in our stories—like contrasts in characters or places or events—we can also set up dynamic contrasts in the movement of time.

Perhaps the most common distortion of time occurs when an author arranges events out of chronological order. The tactic can modulate dramatic effect, build momentum and suspense, and create different points of discovery for the reader. It can also reflect the ways in which a character (or narrator or even *author*) feels uncomfortable, or *unwilling to stay* in the confines of their current moment. There is another moment that haunts or entices them, so the story travels back or forth in time, all rules be damned. Fiction readers, first and foremost, are time travelers.

When asked to give a plot synopsis of a non-linear (i.e., non-chronological) story they've just read, my students sometimes recount the story's events in the order they were presented on the page. Other times they reconstruct the story chronologically. As they listen to and discuss one another's synopses, they rarely seem to notice the difference. While a story is still fresh in their memories, careful readers are generally *capable* of remembering the nonlinear sequence in which a story's events were presented, but oddly that act seems to require more effort than reconstructing the story into its "natural" chronological order. The physical structure of the text asks us to read it one way, but the habits of our brains push against that request.

The next time a friend tells you a story in casual conversation, count the number of times he or she flashes back or forward. Try, yourself, to tell a meaningful, interesting story in pure chronological order. I dare you. In fact, it is so difficult and unusual for humans to tell stories in absolute chronological order that professional interrogators have established through research that when someone tells his story in perfect chronological order, it is more likely that he is lying.

The idea that strict chronology is natural may be true in real time, but it is not true in story time because stories occur in the mind, and the mind—unlike real time—moves in many directions at once. Especially these days.

4. ARRANGEMENT

What I'm trying to point out here is that while conventional prose narratives may not look as dynamically designed as web pages, they *do* use typographical arrangement to create and structure not just time but other aspects of the reader's experience. I want to highlight first some conventional and then some unconventional tactics of typographical arrangement in the geography of the page. I hope that by putting some of these authorial choices under a microscope, I can help you become more attuned to tactics that tend to get overlooked or left to instinct.

I believe that the choice to begin a paragraph with "*Tuesday. Rain. Lake of the Rains*" (Vladimir Nabokov, *Lolita* 43) or with "At the start of the winter came the permanent rain and with the rain came the cholera" (Ernest Hemingway, *A Farewell to Arms* 4) is a physical, structural choice on a micro-scale—one that, though far less conspicuous, is in the same category as Joyce's decision to fill the last 30 pages of *Ulysses* with a single unpunctuated sentence. By cutting out all non-essential words and hacking his sentences into fragments, Nabokov simulates the brusque frustration caused by the incessant rain. Hemingway's languid, uninterrupted single sentence omits the requisite comma before *and* to reveal a mind so deadened by the war and rain that it only barely notices the cholera in the end. Both sentences repeat the word *rain* unnecessarily—another choice of arrangement on a very micro-level.

Spatial arrangement can also modulate a story's mood and its dramatic impact. It can manipulate a reader's interest or energy level and transmit messages about what to expect in the pages to come. Michael Cunningham's short story, "White Angel," which is also the third chapter of his novel, *A Home at the End of the World*, contains a striking line at the start of the third paragraph: "Here is Carlton several months before his death, in an hour so alive with snow that earth and sky are identically white" (21). This line ends up being pretty important. Carlton, the narrator's beloved older brother, dies in spectacular fashion at the story's climax: Drunk and drugged, he comes racing into the house, where his parents and friends are gathered for a big party. Not realizing that the sliding glass doors are closed, he smashes through them, piercing his jugular. Lying in his girlfriend's arms, he bleeds out within seconds.

This is a pretty horrific, or at least highly dramatic, climax. It's the kind of sudden, out-of-nowhere violence that can make a lesser story collapse into unbelievability. How does Cunningham get away with it? By warning us with that early line. Now, my eighth-grade English teacher would boil this down to simple *foreshadowing*, and of course that's what it is. The author has made choices of spatial arrangement that prepare the reader for the shocking climax and, in so doing, has modulated—tamped down, in this case—the level of that shock. So we get a little dramatic shock at the beginning of the third paragraph, and it siphons some of the shock off the scene of his death. We swipe drama from a scene that has too much and move it into a calmer—or potentially more boring—part of the story.

That choice of arrangement affects not just the dramatic energy but the mood of the story. There are a lot of very funny moments in the story, so if we're going to *buy* that horrible death scene, we're going to need to be prepared for it. We're going to need to know, off the bat, that this is a story in which dark things will happen.

The most important thing to remember about choices of spatial arrangement is that information placed before or after white space—in other words, beginnings and endings—will receive the most attention. The impressions left at the beginnings and endings—of stories, sections, paragraphs, sentences—will stick in a reader's mind more than anything else.

I have taught this story to at least a dozen classes, and each time, no matter how carefully my students read, there are always a few students in the room who *forget* that line about Carlton's death and are shocked to see him die in the end. I sympathize with those students because I too forgot this line the first time I read the story. And I flipped back to this page and said, *Whoa, it's right here.* At the beginning of a paragraph, no less. How could I have missed it?

Even though it's at the beginning of a paragraph, the line *is*, as it turns out, a little bit buried in the landscape of the page. It follows a long and complicated exposition and precedes an intense and arresting first scene. It is placed at a pivot point, technically serving the role not of information but of transition. Had Cunningham put a period after "his death," I think we would be less likely to forget this sentence. But Cunningham's choice works because we *need* to forget Carlton's impending doom just enough so that when it arrives, we are surprised—but not shocked into disbelief. Our minds spool back and remember, *Oh, he did warn us.*

Choices of textual arrangement can also send a message to readers about what kind of text or voice it is they are reading. When I open a book by Henry James and see those monolithic paragraphs, I feel something different than when I open a book by Raymond Carver and see all that dialogue and white space. The Henry James—at least to me—sends a message that my reading experience may be just a little more challenging. The pace may be slower, the voice or consciousness at the helm may be more languid or contemplative or even, maybe . . . *neurotic.* The Raymond Carver looks more like easy reading. It's a proletariat sort of text, built for the masses, who are busy.

What strikes me in comparing these two is that there is actually a lot of dialogue mixed into those Henry James paragraphs. He just chooses not to break the paragraph after each quote. I am tempted to chalk this up to different formatting conventions of his time; these appear to be the sustained, complex thoughts of a more focused era. But of course, writers from our own era use these kinds of paragraphs too. One thing large blocks of narration do is create the impression that the story is more explicitly controlled and mediated by the narrator's consciousness. The narrator insists on standing in between the reader and the action. Dialogue without or with very little commentary, on the other hand, appears to be unmediated, as if no one has tampered with the story.

Part of the pleasure of stories with very little narration—like Hemingway's "Hills Like White Elephants," a story told almost exclusively in dialogue—is that the reader feels closer to the action, like an eavesdropper. And part of the pleasure of stories that insulate the action and dialogue with long blocks of narration is that the reader feels he has opened a door to the narrator's mind and has the rare privilege of viewing the world through another person's consciousness.

In any case, just by looking at the appearance of a page, many of us make quick, maybe subconscious judgments about what it will *feel like* to read that page—and how much time it will take. I can't be the only person who, in the midst of an onerous college reading assignment, delighted at the arrival of some unexpected white space or illustration. A break! A half-page *off!* But I also remember how thrilling it was, as a child, to move from picture books to chapter books to actual adult books *with small print*. The arrangement of text, white space, and graphics sends all kinds of messages about what *kind* of book this is, and what kind of reader we are if we value it. I often wonder if critics' sometimes dismissive responses to typographically charged texts like Mark Danielewski's *House of Leaves* stem from a conscious or subconscious sensation that books with pictures look a little childish. But more on that later.

One place we most often see writers adopting unconventional typographical techniques is in stories that take on borrowed forms: the list, the email exchange, the diary. David Foster Wallace's story, "Datum Centurio," takes the form of a series of dictionary entries, complete with pronunciation guides and etymologies. Visually, it's a slightly intimidating story because it masquerades as the type of text we *refer to* rather than read straight through. In this sense, dictionaries resemble some of the more utilitarian, graphically designed texts we encounter in the world at large: web pages, maps, product packaging. Such texts don't guide the eye by the set convention of left to right and top to bottom; instead they use visual cues to help the reader quickly locate only the information that's most important to her. Narratives, on the other hand, draw us inexorably along one line of text that snakes all the way from the first word to the last. And so, because Wallace's fictional dictionary appears in a collection of stories, we understand that in *this* case, we should read it from start to finish. Even a narrative that appears chaotic or nonlinear—such as Robert Coover's "The Babysitter," a long collection of fragmented episodes that bounce through time and even contradict one another—is presented in one set order and read accordingly.

Over the past several decades, makers of electronic narratives, such as Shelley Jackson, Tim Wright, Stuart Moulthrop, and many others, have experimented with these strict reading conventions, presenting readers with a variety of choices of which part of the story to read next. The result is the sensation of a story that exists as a web that might go on forever rather than as a chain of events with a start and a finish. I am always thrilled by the look and concept of these works, and by their apparent attempts to capture the chaos and overwhelming sensation of postmodern life. Yet as a reader, I confess that such stories sometimes fill me with the dread and anxiety that John Barth's Ambrose feels when he discovers he may never find a path out of the funhouse. It is probably not accidental that these narratives frequently adopt a central spatial metaphor (the body, a deck of cards, a garden) that provides an organizational framework and suggests where the *edges*, if not the ending, may be found.

Aside from a few notable exceptions like Robert Coover and Jennifer Egan, literary fiction writers have made very few forays into these kinds of electronic narratives. More often, electronic narratives are written by those trained in art, graphic design, and computer technology. The literary world has not yet taken electronic literature very seriously. In part, this may be because the prose itself is sometimes lackluster, with thin characterizations and flimsy or meandering plots. It is very hard, after all, to write a satisfying story that can be read in any direction, because stories by definition rely on causality, which is a close cousin to sequence. But these works are worth studying closely, and it's high time serious fiction writers and teachers brought their talents to this arena.

Increasingly, however, serious fiction writers are crafting stories and novels for print that adopt conspicuously unconventional typographical components. This is, after all, not entirely new, as Lawrence Sterne used such techniques 250 years ago in his wildly popular *The Life and Opinions of Tristram Shandy*.

Mark Danielewski's novel, *House of Leaves*, developed an enormous cult following of fans who fetishized the object of the book itself, following and charting out all the variations in the different printings of the book. The book masquerades as an artifact, a series of mysterious found texts that try to explain the fantastical, ever-expanding house at the core of the story. The reader becomes the researcher or detective sifting through documents that may or may not be useful but that are arranged on the page in visually stunning ways and are charged with the residue of *authenticity, of evidence*. Nearly every page of *House of Leaves* looks different and requires the reader to continually adapt to new modes of reading. This is anything but a childish book, and in fact for many fans the challenge of reading it seemed to be part of its attraction.

More recently, the novel *S*, by J.J. Abrams and Doug Dorst, adopted similar visual techniques, including footnotes and multiple narrators who leave hand-written, color-coded notes in the margins. This book *about* a book, about a mysterious, endangered author, even includes several found texts (postcards, newspaper clippings, code breakers) that have been slipped in between the pages and fall out when the reader turns to them. Once again, the book has a strong mystery at its core that the reader—along with the literary scholar and the librarian who write their notes in the margins—tries to decipher and solve. As an object alone, the book is beautiful to behold, and it captures both in its content and form the intense attachment serious book lovers have toward books and reading and authors. As Abrams said in the *New York Times*, "In a digital age, it's a distinctly analog object. It felt romantic to me." In other words, while these books might have required the aid of graphic designers to execute, they do not use design techniques merely to attract attention or to help readers *avoid* reading. They use these techniques in service of an elaborate, artful, and distinctly literary mission. These are stories that could not be told in conventional forms.

Interestingly, some of the recent authors of graphically enhanced texts, like Reif Larsen and Leanne Shapton, have had entire careers in graphic design and illustration.

J.J. Abrams, of course, has a career in film and television. It may be—don't shoot me—that in the future all writers will have to take a class in graphic design. Although as graphic design and illustration programs become easier and cheaper, classes seem less and less necessary, and there seem to be fewer and fewer reasons not to use these programs.

Shapton's novel, *Important Artifacts and Personal Property from the Collection of Lenore Doolan and Harold Morris, Including Books, Street Fashion, and Jewelry*, takes typographic enhancement to the extreme. The book takes the form of an auction catalogue displaying photographs of all the items involved in a fictional couple's romance. The only written text is found in the terse, formal captions describing these items for sale, and, occasionally, in the letters and notes the lovers wrote to one another. Shapton hired models to pose for these photos, and the book is so true to its borrowed form that Shapton's name is not even listed on the cover. A catalogue of items for sale is typically thumbed through in any order and rarely read in full. A reader can get plenty of amusement thumbing through Shapton's book in this way. But read in its entirety, start to finish, the book comes together as a complete and resonant and very moving novel.

Books like this clearly invite us to engage with the text not as a transparent window to the fictional world but as a material object, lovely and fascinating to behold and even fetishize. The book becomes an artifact sent from the fictional world to us. Indeed, Shapton's book rests on the implied promise that we can actually *buy* the true artifacts of this fictional romance, further connecting us to and validating the reality of the fictional story.

This is, by the way, highly reminiscent of the ways 18th-century readers interacted with the early—and wildly popular—English novels, like *Clarissa* and *Pamela* and *Tristram Shandy*. The title page of *Robinson Crusoe* did not contain Daniel Dafoe's name. Readers were encouraged to believe—and *did* often believe—that the stories were true and the characters were real people. Lawrence Sterne was so frequently confused with his narrator, Tristram Shandy, that he once bet a friend on the continent that he could mail a letter addressed merely to "Tristram Shandy, England," and it would reach him. It did. It seems clear to me that these techniques are not new but are being used more frequently and to much more interesting effect. It also seems to me that they will soon take up a larger and larger portion of our literature. And why shouldn't they?

But there is still a fair degree of resistance to these texts. For one thing, look at the submission guidelines to most literary journals and contests: 12-point font, 1-inch margins, reasonable file size, and nothing else. Anyone who goes through an MFA program is taught that to so much as change the font of the title is to single oneself out as a silly rookie.

5. ENFORCEMENT

Here's another dare for you: Write a narrative that uses unconventional typographical techniques and count how many minutes pass before the word *gimmick* enters the critical reaction to your story. When narratives use conspicuous typographical devices, critics have been very quick to pounce on them. Even a novel like *House of Leaves,* which was widely praised by major critics as ingenious, still came under fire for its typographical devices, even from those who gave it positive reviews. In *The Guardian*, Peter Beaumont wrote that the book's "typographical oddities [. . .] leave one wondering [. . .] where to place Danielewski." Emily Barton, in *The Village Voice*, was frustrated by the book's "typographical experiments, [which] often seem random, requiring the reader to flip the book over and over to follow the narrative thread."

Jonathan Safran Foer's *Extremely Loud and Incredibly Close* suffered similar attacks; his typographical devices became the central focus of the book's reviews, and very few critics enjoyed them. In *The New York Times,* Michiko Kakutani accused Foer of using "razzle-dazzle narrative techniques: playful typography, blank pages, [and. . .] images of everything from doorknobs to mating turtles." John Updike, in *The New Yorker*, described these as "picto-/typographical antics" that "interrupted" the text and created a "hyperactive visual surface." Michel Faber, in *The Guardian,* referred to the book as a "Tower of Babel" and highlighted the "dozens of otiose photographs, rainbow colours and typographical devices, whose net effect is to distract the reader (and Foer) from harsh truths." Tom Barbash, in the *San Francisco Chronicle*, claimed that the book was "positively weighted down with extras."

Reif Larsen's *The Selected Works of T.S. Spivet* was similarly slammed by critics for the use of such devices. Everyone acknowledged it was a beautiful *looking* book, but many were disappointed when they stopped looking and started *reading*. In *The New York*

Times, Gina Bellafante described the novel as "burdened by device" and lamented, "Following some of the marginalia requires repositioning the book, turning it around and sideways, making it something for neither the formalist nor the arthritic."

The words *trick, distraction,* and *gimmick* are all over the place in reviews of books like these. In literary conversations, as in supermarket ones, the word *gimmick* carries an unmistakably derogatory connotation. Gimmicks are the tricks seedy salesmen use to get you to buy a shoddy, overpriced product that you don't need—or perhaps to get people to read in an age when supposedly no one wants to? So authors using these techniques are relegated to the status of *cheaters.* Never mind the fact that these techniques are still damned difficult to employ.

In any case, what strikes me is that most of these reviews seem to operate on the assumption that books should be and have always been laid out in regular, uninterrupted columns of text. But of course the world's history of illuminated manuscripts proves otherwise, and illuminated manuscripts have been some of the world's most valued and sacred texts. Keep in mind that the illuminations were not merely adornments prettying up the margins. In many cases, the illuminations conveyed key information, even separate narratives that interacted with the main body of text in complex and even subversive ways. Sure, the Gutenberg press put an end to all that, but why shouldn't the affordable, easy options of web and desktop publishing revive these techniques?

We cannot read two things simultaneously. And yet more and more of the *non-literary* texts of our era—CNN screens, websites, billboards—pressure us to do so. We may not like them, these tickers and ads, these annoying graphic enticements. But they are multiplying daily. They are not going away.

We can quarantine literary fiction, or we can accept what Jay McInerney wrote in his *New York Times* review of Mark Haddon's typographically charged novel, *The Curious Incident of the Dog in the Night-Time*: "The difference between literature and its imitations might be defined in any number of ways, but let's be reckless, even elitist, and propose that a literary novel requires new reading skills and teaches them within its pages. . . ." I will continue to treasure books composed in conventional, engrossing, uninterrupted blocks of text. But I'm also hoping that more books come along that reshape and acknowledge the ways we really read, and I'm hoping that readers and critics will embrace them. Because the truth about time in our time may have to be told through a book that looks unlike any we have seen so far. And that's exciting.

MIKE MAGNUSON

First, You Tell: Exposition, Statements of Fact, and Using Prima Facie Evidence to Establish Yonder Discursive Fields

Take care of the sentence, and the sentence will take care of you.

—Dale Ray Phillips

Let's run an experiment in narration, shall we? The idea here will be to see if we can generate a narrative from a series of statements, and in order to do this, boys and girls, we will have to use the most important tool in our creative writing toolbox, our imaginations. Ready?

Pretend you're a naughty boy in a fifth-grade classroom on Show and Tell Day—in the last desk in the back of the room, naturally, near the coat racks and everybody's winter boots and Mrs. Johnson's poster of a Bald Eagle with the word *EXCELLENCE* written under it. Pretend you think that poster is stupid. The Bald Eagle squints and looks like your grandpa when he has to take a crap and can't take a crap: What's so excellent about that? You think Mrs. Johnson is stupid, too: with her county-wide smile for the students who kiss her butt and with her frown for you and from the constant corner of her eye, watching you, waiting to catch you, because she knows you're always up to *something*.

She is correct. In your note-taking hand, instead of a *real* Bic Pen, you have the *shell* of a Bic Pen locked and loaded with a plump, juicy spit wad. If you have the chance, you will launch that spit wad blowgun-style at Boy Genius, Mrs. Johnson's favorite pupil, the kid sitting at the front, in the first desk, with a shaft of sunlight on him and a halo glowing over the point on the top of his head.

The Bic Pen spit-wad blowgun is an extremely accurate weapon—from close range all the way to about twenty-five feet—but you'll never be able to use it because of Mrs. Johnson's all-seeing eyes. You can feel them on you. You can feel them penetrating your brain and washing your skull out with soap. But she won't catch you today. You're the kind of boy who will only cross Mrs. Johnson's rules if there is a zero chance of her pinning the infraction on you, which is too bad, because Boy Genius is an extremely deserving target.

Look at him, with his perfect posture and butt-kissing smile, and next to his desk sits a long rectangular black case exactly the same as your older sister's bass clarinet case. This does not bode well. Every time your sister plays bass clarinet, she sounds like Gollum, when the orcs had him in Mordor and tortured him till he gave up the whereabouts of the one ring. "Baggins! Shire!" That's what a bass clarinet sounds like. Maybe worse than that. And Boy Genius has one.

Mrs. Johnson says, "Boy Genius, would you like to begin show and tell for us today?"

"Why, yes," Boy Genius says and rises from his seat like he's in church coming forward to take over for the priest—*I got this, Father: sit down, relax, and enjoy the flight*—and he carries his bass clarinet case to the front of the room and bends to it and opens it—and for a second, you think this might be awesome. Maybe he's got a Supersoaker or a Nerf Crossbow!—and he lifts a ventriloquist's dummy from the case and sets it upright on his knee and places a hand behind the dummy's back.

The dummy looks exactly like a small Boy Genius. Boy Genius looks exactly like a large dummy: perfect posture, tucked-in polo shirt, perfect hair, pointy head, halo.

Boy Genius says, "Everyone, this is Dummy. Dummy, say hello to the class!"

Dummy says, "Hello, class. Hello, Mrs. Johnson."

You can see Boy Genius's lips move when Dummy talks. Right? The whole act is a *hoax*! But hey, at least he's not playing the bass clarinet.

Okay. Enough with that nonsense. There surely isn't much of a story there.

A kid takes a ventriloquist's dummy to the front of the room, and that's it. That's the entire action of the story. Wow. I guess we won't be optioning the film rights for that one! But let's be serious and try to make the best of what we've got.

First, let's shift the terms a bit. Let's call stories *narratives*, because that way, we can apply the following ideas not only to fiction but to nonfiction and to narrative poetry and to standing around the back-yard grill with our friends and telling lies about our fabulous getaway weekends to Vegas or whatever else we like to lie about. A narrative, it strikes me, has a broader reach and more intellectual possibility than a mere story. When we tell a story, that's a fine thing indeed, but when we write a narrative, that feels bigger somehow, even if it's really not.

So my amusing fifth-grade narrative establishes its context by making a series of statements: You're a naughty boy in fifth grade on Show and Tell Day. You're in the back of the room. You have a spit-wad blowgun made out of a Bic pen. Boy Genius has a ventriloquist's dummy named Dummy. And so on. You did not learn these things because I have shown you them. You have learned them because I have told you them. I have presented almost everything in my narra-tive in statement: "The Bald Eagle . . . looks like your grandpa. . . ." "The Bic Pen spit-wad blowgun is an extremely accurate weapon." "The dummy looks exactly like a small Boy Genius." I have only described in detail a couple of gestures and a couple of items per-taining to the passage of time—Boy Genius rises; Boy Genius takes a dummy from a bass clarinet case, yet you can easily visualize the physical situation and get a sense of the focal character's emotional situation. You have found yourself wandering into John Gardner's "vivid continuous dream," but I haven't dramatized anything either vividly or continuously.

Since we started taking serious English composition instruction, probably about the time we were in the fifth grade, our teachers have told us that good writing shows and does not tell. We are to use precise detail. We are to avoid abstractions and to write with good, old-fash-ioned concrete nouns and verbs. We are to avoid writing obvious, general statements. We are to find a way to demonstrate what we mean instead of coming out and expressing it directly. On a certain level, in basic English composition courses and beginning creative writing courses, this idea has some merit. Show and Don't Tell asks beginners to think more carefully about language and in turn about craft. Show and Don't Tell asks for specificity. Show and Don't Tell encourages beginners to write in image and in gesture and in a descriptive way that suggests moving forward in time, with the end result being literature that the reader can experience with both the senses and the intellect. I guess if we don't tell beginners this stuff, they won't know the ultimate goal of writing, because make no mistake about the goal: we want to engage our readership's senses and intellects; that's what serious creative writing is all about. Knowing the ultimate goal is a relatively easy thing compared to the path we take to get there.

For writers who have mastered the simple elements of craft, for writers who are no longer beginners, the concept of Show and Don't Tell has diminished importance because experienced writers know that writing itself is a continual process of telling. Even in image and in gesture, the writer is always telling the reader something. The writer communicates in language, in sentences, and a sentence's function in language is to transmit information from a writer to a reader. This information may be factual, emotional, sensorial, gestural, etc., but this information cannot appear on the page in any form other than statements that establish context and statements that elaborate or draw conclusions from an established context. The rich, real-life experience that Show and Don't Tell promises is not achieved through Show and Don't Tell but through the associations between numbers of contexts.

Even on a real-life elementary school Show and Tell Day, the children in class can see that the ventriloquist's dummy is a ventriloquist's dummy before the kid presenting the dummy tells the class what it is. Think back to your Show and Tell Day experiences. How often did a kid bring something to Show and Tell Day and the kids in class didn't already know what the thing was before the kid said a word about it?

I'm going to pick on my colleague Bonnie Jo Campbell here, because 1) she will be good-natured about it, and 2) she keeps a couple of pet donkeys in her yard back home in Michigan and likes to tell people about them. Now let's say that Bonnie brings a live donkey to Show and Tell Day; we may not know that donkey's name or anything about the donkey's storied history, but we know damned well, before Bonnie says a word, that she's standing there with a honest-to-goodness live donkey! We can see it.

When we write narratives, however, unlike on Show and Tell Day, if we don't first establish not only the existence of Bonnie's donkey but the place where she presents the donkey and maybe the time of day and maybe of year and maybe what she looks like and what her mood and demeanor might be, if we don't establish the specific world in which Show and Tell Day occurs and the specific objects and people within that world, then we will not have established the context in which we will learn the donkey's name. Without context, Bonnie might say, "This is my donkey named Quixote." And the reader will say, "What donkey? I don't see a donkey!" And if there is one absolute requirement in donkey narratives, it is this: We cannot write a donkey narrative without a donkey in it.

We have traditionally used the term *exposition* to describe the process of establishing context in narrative. In creative writing classes, if we hear about exposition at all—and let's be honest: we usually don't—we consider the idea of exposition as defined in the Freytag's Pyramid template, where it occurs as the first of the five necessary elements to a plot: exposition, rising action, climax, falling action, dénouement. Just like Show and Don't Tell, Freytag's Pyramid has significant merit for beginning creative writers. We need to know something about the place and the people (exposition), then some things have to happen, hopefully with some conflict and dramatic tension (rising action), then the conflict can come to a head (climax), then after that, we have a period of reflection and consequence (falling action), then we have a moment wherein one or more of the characters come to last realizations about the preceding events and then the narrative reaches a closure (dénouement).

But for more experienced writers, Freytag's Pyramid presents far more limitations than it does advantages. For one thing, not all plots follow Freytag's sequence; in fact, especially in modern literature, the likelihood of the Freytag sequence occurring in the plot is fairly low. For another thing, Freytag's Pyramid model assumes that plot, the overarching structure of the narrative, is more important to the narrative than its execution moment by moment. The biggest problem Freytag's Pyramid creates is the belief that exposition only belongs in the beginning of a narrative, when in fact this is never the case, not unless the entire narrative occurs in one location, one compressed time period, with no changes in mood or weather or posture. In narrative, we move from place to place and time to time and from one physical and emotional circumstance to the next; therefore, we need to write exposition throughout a narrative in order to orient our reader to each new segment of the narrative: a change in weather, in scene, in time, in feeling. This process is continual from the beginning to the end. We establish the first context to establish the next context, which is predicated upon the first context, then we establish the next context after that, which is predicated upon the context before that and the context before the context before that, and on and on, till we arrive at the end.

I once heard someone say that the best way to write exposition is to obscure it from the reader, to think of exposition as plumbing in a house, something that has a use but that nobody really wants to see. That probably is true—in a house. You probably don't want to see plumbing in a house. But in good, generous writing, the reader needs to see the obvious, which is the plumbing. Obvious statements of fact are what allow readers to interpret actions and images in a specific context, and from this interpretation the reader experiences metaphor and in turn reaches understanding. Obvious statements are the tenor for the vehicle that creates metaphor. In other words, if we hide the plumbing in a narrative, our narrative won't have running water.

Maybe a better way to think about exposition is to identify its rhetorical function. Exposition, as I have been suggesting, presents the obvious facts necessary for the moment-to-moment progression of a narrative. In rhetoric, we have another term for this, *prima facie*, which means "at first blush" or "at first glance." In order for an argument to proceed, we must know the simplest, most obvious elements of the argument, what anyone could plainly see at first glance. This is especially true of arguments requiring proof. For example, if you come home from work and see six empty mini-Snickers wrappers on the kitchen counter and then find your eight-year-old daughter in the living room watching TV with chocolate smeared on her cheeks, you will definitely accuse her of eating those candy bars. You will say, "Honey, there are wrappers on the kitchen counter; you have chocolate on your cheeks; you ate those candy bars!" She can deny it all she wants, but based on the *prima facie* evidence, she is guilty of the crime.

In a court of law, where I hope you won't find your eight-year-old daughter, *prima facie* evidence must be presented in each aspect of a case. This idea applies to all legal arguments wherein a burden of proof must be met, but since most of us spend more time watching TV than we do reading law books, let's frame this in *Law & Order* terms: We certify that the deceased is in fact dead, that the death was caused by such and such, that the accused was not only in position to commit the murder but had motivation to commit the murder, and look at this surveillance-camera video of the accused slapping the deceased upside the head with a canoe paddle! Of course, we could present our volumes of *prima facie* evidence and fail to prove our case beyond a reasonable doubt; structuring and maintaining an argument correctly doesn't ensure that the argument will be successful. Nevertheless, without presenting the *prima facie* evidence, we cannot make our case at all.

In a similar way, to prosecute a narrative, we perforce must present a series of *prima facie* elements—obvious things like time, place, weather, mood, gesture, health, circumstance, to name a few—and if we do not establish these elements, we cannot achieve the higher goals of narrative, which are emotional, sensorial, and intellectual, because we will not have established a context in which the higher goals of narrative can bear tangible, cerebral fruit.

This is all well and good, right? It is, as long as we keep in mind that *prima facie* elements of narrative cannot exist alone. *Prima facie* elements must adhere to enumerative material. *Enumerative*, as you probably know, derives from the rhetorical term *enumeratio*, which means to divide a subject into constituent parts or details and to list the details in such a way that supports the subject. In other words, first we have the evidence at first glance: "Timmy's right leg is in a cast." Then we have enumerative evidence that details a narrative consequence to the *prima facie* evidence: "He walks around on crutches, which makes his armpits hurt, and because he can't move his leg, because his leg is always stuck in straight position, he can't drive his car, which means when he goes on a date with his girlfriend, she has to drive." Essentially, adherence works as an analogy or as a series of analogies. Adherence could be concrete, as in the Timmy example I just used, or adherence could require the highest end of our analogic powers to decipher. Like this: "I like chicken. Will you marry me?" Chances are that a normal reading audience, an audience that wants its material on the one-to-one-correspondence nose, will not take the analogic leaps required to find the humor in the ideological wastelands between chicken and marriage. This does not mean the connections don't exist; this means that not everybody will be able to make them, which should not cause any of us to lose sleep. The range of adherences between *prima facie* evidence and enumerative material is as vast as the human spectrum of experience and intelligence.

This concept of items adhering to each other in an analogic way is known as a discourse. Michel Foucault, who has long been unnecessarily vilified in university creative writing circles, explains discourse as a two-part phenomenon: First, we have what he calls a *statement*, which is one idea, often general, that relates to other objects, subjects, and other statements. Second, we have the relationship between sequences of relations to objects, subjects, and other statements. A discourse, in Foucault's definition, is a conversation between texts and ideas. This is the same thing as saying we have *prima facie* evidence adhering to enumerative evidence. Or the same thing as saying we have exposition first, then we have material that develops that exposition. Or as saying that if the writer leaves out the easy parts, the reader will never understand the complicated parts.

Michel Foucault also expands his idea of discourse into *discursive formations* and *discursive fields*, both of which are ways in which the regularities of human thought produce discourses. Foucault uses the concept of discursive formation in relation to his analysis of large bodies of knowledge: political economy, religion, linguistics, psychology, music, medicine, natural history, science, mathematics, and so on. In creative writing, our discursive formations often center around the mysteries of human experience—love, loss, sadness, hate, joy, beauty, longing—but at the same time, because we are writing about the human experience, we connect with all possible discourses in the realm of humankind.

Discursive writing, therefore, is writing that produces a discourse. Discursive writing is the writing most of us want to be doing: to connect with as many discursive contexts as possible: emotional, spiritual, environmental, sociological, geographical, political, and on and on and on.

A perfect example of how this idea may manifest itself is the startling opening line of Joan Didion's masterpiece essay, "Slouching Towards Bethlehem": "The center was not holding."

So much happens in this first sentence. First, consider its profoundly general nature. The *center* could be anything. It could be the center of an egg. It could be the center of our minds. It could be the center of a baseball or of a dartboard or—to pick the obvious source of the line, to which the essay owes its title—the center could be an allusion to the William Butler Yeats poem "The Second Coming", but then again, not every reader will catch the allusion to Yeats, and even if readers do, the original line in the Yeats poem—"the centre cannot hold"—is also profoundly general and suggestive of metaphors that the reader comprehends through inference and analogy. The general nature of the opening line works to Didion's advantage because the line opens a vast range of ways in which this undefined term can adhere essentially to anything that follows.

Here's a rule of analogy: the more general an idea, the more specifics that can attach themselves to it. This same rule of analogy also holds true in essay and in narrative. As we recall from our days in English composition, a *thesis* is a general assertion that the specifics of an essay will support. Specifics attach to general assertions; general assertions attach to specifics.

Side note: Another tangential quality of *center* is that human perception itself tends to operate between polar opposites and in turn tends toward a center. We have right and left, right and wrong, forward and backward, good and evil, right leg and left leg, and so on, and our conscious minds operate between these opposites. Soren Kierkegaard, Martin Heidegger, Jean Paul Sartre, and a few other philosophers have taken this idea of a center of human perception, an existence between two opposites, and have expressed it in terms of a triangle, whereby human perception and thought constitute the constantly shifting apex between adjacent and opposite sides of a triangle's base. In any event, Didion casts a wide net in her opening sentence, or should we say she has circumscribed a large triangle?

Also of note in this sentence is the past progressive: *was holding*.

That's a compound verb, and compound verbs, especially in narrative, almost always serve to establish a context, a scene's beginning, a general state of being, etc., after which we shift to simple verbs within the established context. In other words, the verb form in the sentence helps to establish the context to which what follows will adhere. While we're at it, note that the *was* in *was holding* is not a *be* verb; *was* is an auxiliary in a compound verb; so when your friends tell you to avoid *be* verbs, you may ignore them when your verbs are compound and must take an auxiliary. In fact, whenever your friends tell you to avoid *be* verbs, you are in most instances wise to ignore them.

Again: "The center was not holding." Another element of that sentence that creates adherence with what follows is negation: *was not*. According to the writer/reader contract (and yes, there is one), whenever we write what something is *not*, our readers will expect us to write what that something *is*.

To summarize, then: This sentence presents a general notion that will require enumeration for it to obtain specific meaning. The compound verb form establishes a context that the following sentences will explore in detail. The negation in the sentence demands expression of its opposite. The next sentence of the essay, therefore, which begins "It was a country of . . ."—completes the reader's expectation and therefore adheres to the previous sentence. We know what something is not; now we will find out what something is. The structure *it was* is normally what we call the expletive or the existential *it*, meaning the pronoun does not take a specific antecedent and the phrase itself has no specific meaning and is only used as a way to fill the first syntactic slot of a sentence with a non-referential pronoun. We use this expletive construction routinely in speech: It's raining, it's snowing, it's five o'clock somewhere, and so on. We are wise, under normal writing circumstances, to avoid the existential *it* in our writing, but in this instance, *it* takes an antecedent—*center*—so the rest of the sentence, a series of predicate nominatives, adheres to the first sentence. The antecedent is the glue binding this sentence to its essay's thesis.

"The center was not holding."

Is all this making a mountain out of a five-word molehill? Maybe. Then again, if our opening line doesn't create a wide array of analogic possibilities, we probably aren't setting our sights high enough. We are here to build mountains, aren't we?

Now, to be open and honest about all this, I have to say that wide discrepancy exists concerning the meaning and the value of discursive writing. Some well-meaning scholars in English departments have suggested that the short story and the poem are not discursive, because they are forms so concentrated that they aren't capable of connections with wider discursive fields, and in turn, these well-meaning scholars have suggested that the novel is discursive because it is fluid and expansive and not abbreviated. This division based on size is false. Because a novel is *big* does not make it discursive. Likewise, because a short story or a poem is *small* does not prevent it from being discursive. The novels of Nora Roberts and Louis L'Amour, for instance, are not discursive, not even remotely. Similarly, a few words in a poem can often connect to so many human discursive fields that it would be impossible to enumerate them. Stevie Smith's poem "Not Waving but Drowning" comes to mind: "I was much farther out than you thought/ and not waving but drowning." Is there a limit to the discursive connections that line makes with the human experience? I think not.

When certain PhD Rhetoric/Composition types in English departments refer to discursive writing, they mean the term to be pejorative. Discursive writing, to them, is writing that skips almost randomly from one subject to another, that rambles, that digresses. According to these folks, creative writing, especially the type of creative writing that folks with MFAs produce, is discursive in this bad, rambling, digressive way—or if the Rhetoric/Composition people do secretly admire creative writing, they certainly won't trust a piece of creative writing alone in a room with one of their composition students.

Ironically, another group of PhD Lit-Crit-Theory types in English departments consider discursive writing to be writing that proceeds by reason and argument rather than by intuition, which is to say they feel *their* writing is discursive because of the great structural control required to produce it. According to these types, the majority of MFA creative writers write with all heart and no brain and are therefore incapable of writing discursive prose.

This is why Foucault has come to be vilified by people in the creative writing community—not because of Foucault himself but because numbers of his devotees in English departments take a dim or misinformed view of creative writers in the university. Lots of creative writers take a dim view of creative writers in the university, too, myself included, but this is something we keep in house as much as we can. Well, maybe this dim-view stuff has nothing to do with Foucault. Maybe the simple truth is there are a lot of assholes in English departments. I will admit to being one of them. I carry the card in my wallet, if you want to see proof. I also carry twenty bucks, if you'd like me to pay for lunch.

So yeah. We have more important work to do than worrying about nonsense that comes out of English Departments. Maybe the debate itself, as is true of many debates, constitutes various groups trying to come to grips with the same difficult question: How can we study and use language to improve our understanding of the human experience?

But for our purposes, discursive writing forms a conversation between ideas that we have set down on the page, and the elements of this conversation and the interactions between them are what generates meaningful narrative. Human life itself is a conversation. We want our work to reflect this. We want our work to generate a conversation with smart readers capable of seeing infinite possibility in what we have written. We want our work to generate a conversation within itself, with language that is continually clear yet continually surprising, with ideas that extend in wide arrays beyond the literal, obvious material at our writing's core. When we write with the goal of producing literature, we mean for our words to enter the broader discourse of humanity and to create both a discourse within a narrative and a discourse with the universe. Our success or failure at this endeavor, we can never quantify for certain, but that will never stop us from trying and keeping an open mind along the way.

The Poem of the Moment

If the poet can get us to believe about a small thing, we will be more likely to believe the poet about a big thing. One of the quickest ways to establish the reader's trust is through precise description of physical setting. More difficult are precise descriptions of emotional and spiritual conditions. All three mean giving us a combination of the familiar and unfamiliar, what we know with what we do not know. These three types of description are best communicated with the help of metaphor. And it is probably through the quality of metaphor that the poet most quickly achieves or loses the trust of the reader.

—Stephen Dobyns

THERE'S ALWAYS A POEM IN EVERY MOMENT

In every moment, there are elements that form a pattern, that coalesce to form a whole. Most of the time, though, we can't see it. We just see the separate objects, events, thoughts, and feelings. They exist in a kind of jumble, without pattern. To write a poem, you have to see (hear, feel, touch) the living moment, to get a glimpse of the order that exists within the chaos. Then you must express it in language.

In the 1950s when I was a child, there was a TV program called *The Andy Griffith Show*. Though it's long ago, I still remember one episode in which a film crew came to this very small town to shoot a movie. The director or cameraman was walking around with his hands in front of him, palms out and thumbs outstretched to make a frame he looked through. Opie, the curious little boy, followed him around and finally asked him what he was doing. When the cameraman explained he was framing shots, Opie began looking at everything around him through that frame his hands made, marveling that he never knew he had one. I think I've always remembered this because it was an early glimpse of composing the moment, looking for the arrangement of elements in ordinary life that reveals its shape—a process that tells us something about the nature of life itself.

There are poems everywhere all the time, but we can't see them. We're either moving too fast or we're fast asleep. Even when we try to go slower, to wake up and pay attention, still we miss most of what's happening. But there are sometimes occasions when we don't miss it, when we are acutely aware and can see the relationships, the connections in the swirl of all that surrounds us. As Wordsworth said, *We see into the life of things*.

I once had a student who said she'd been telling a friend how much she enjoyed the weekly writing class. "Are you doing a lot of writing?" he asked her. "No," she answered, "but I'm seeing every-thing differently."

THE STRUCTURE OF THE POEM OF THE MOMENT

As you know, there are many structures for poems—but one of the most basic is the poem of the moment. Other poems may cover a lot of ground. They can range far off in time and place. But the poem of a moment is rooted in one time and one place. It may scoop other thoughts, memories, events, into the moment, but it doesn't leave the scene never to return. The moment may last for just a few sec-onds or it may extend into some minutes. But it can't go into many hours or days without becoming a different kind of animal.

There are many reasons to recommend writing poems of the moment. Being rooted, grounded in just one time and place gives you and your reader a clear setting, a definite location. You're less likely to trail off into vagueness in this kind of poem and the clarity of the boundaries seems to engender clear language. The poem of the moment is, perhaps, the easiest kind of poem to write—though "easy" is a word that can't really be applied to poetry. But if you want to increase your odds of success as you start out to write a poem, this would be an excellent structure to choose. The poem of the moment has an innate dramatic tension. You're in a narrative, albeit one moment of that narrative, and we respond from our most primal self to story.

LOCATION

A poem that is set on the time-space continuum is particularly *rooted in this world.* As human beings, we live in time and space. We're born, grow up, live, and die *somewhere. Story* happens in time and space. Poems of the moment are necessarily rooted in a particular location.

At any moment, you're *somewhere*. You start out with a great advantage in writing a narrative poem that has a strong foundation in a specific landscape.

In his famous essay "The Triggering Town," Richard Hugo writes about the natural need of the poet to be situated in a specific geographical location, real or imagined: "If you ain't no place, you can't go nowhere" (7). And Stephen Dobyns, in *Best Words, Best Order,* says, "If the poet can get us to believe about a small thing, we will be more likely to believe the poet about a big thing. One of the quickest ways to establish the reader's trust is through precise description of physical setting" (139).

We can learn a great deal from fiction writers about place. The characters in a novel are shaped by where they live. They wouldn't be the same people anywhere else. Similarly the theme, events, and concerns of the poem arise out of the location of the poem. When you describe a place, you show how you feel about it (or how the character in a story or the speaker of the poem feels). For example, if you are describing a hospital, your description will be different if the speaker of the poem is entering the lobby with the expectation of seeing his first child born or if he's on his way to see his sister dying. Place affects everything. Ford Maddox Ford said he couldn't get a character into a room unless he knew the shape of the door knob.

GOING SLOW

Another reason, and perhaps this is the most compelling one, why poems of the moment have good odds of succeeding is that in order to write a poem of the moment, you have to stay in that moment for a while. You can't jump ahead. You can't skip on. You can't generalize and skate over a lifetime, never digging deeply into the texture of any experience.

The moment is intrinsically interesting if you inquire into any moment deeply enough because moments are where we actually live. We all know this intellectually. Be here now. Live in the moment. This is also the language of meditation, the practice of staying with each breath. But few, if any of us, are able to sink as deeply into the moment as the moment would allow—either in our lives or in poetry. Yet the poem of the moment invites us to do that, actually facilitates our doing that.

In contrast, one of the most difficult kinds of poems to write is what I call the grandmother poem. This is the poem where you try to include everything you know, feel, think, imagine, and have been told about your grandmother—or someone else—into one poem. This doesn't mean it's impossible. Carolyn Forche's "As Children Together" encompasses what is most essential about a friendship, beginning when she and her friend are girls and ending in the present. Carolyn Kizer's long poem, "Pro Femina," begins "From Sappho to myself, consider the fate of women" (113). That's no small chunk of time. But taking on an extended time span is difficult. It's like a beginning potter trying to throw a five-foot-tall vase. It's just hard to handle that much clay.

DISCOVERING THE MOMENT

Blake writes, "To see infinity in a grain of sand." An entire life or relationship can be shown through one moment of that relationship. So if you're thinking that you want to write about your beloved grandmother, your failed marriage, your complex relationship with your brother—you could start by trying to think of one moment. You could choose the most typical, iconic moment, the moment in which your brother was exactly himself. Or you could look for a moment in which he stepped out of character, the most surprising moment. Or perhaps the most dramatic moment, the most confusing moment, or the most ordinary moment.

Or you could make a list of a dozen possible moments that come to your mind. This brainstorming method is wonderfully freeing. Rather than trying to find the perfect moment, you make a list of a dozen or two dozen possible moments, without judging whether they will be the right ones for your poem. Brainstorming helps us to free ourselves up from restricted patterns of thought and to generate ideas that would stay hidden away in a more judgmental environment. In brainstorming, nothing is too strange or silly or disturbing to put on your list. Then, from that list, choose one moment that has some kind of resonance or draw for you. It may be an obviously significant moment or it may be on the surface a very mundane moment but one that packs a lot of emotion underneath. I once wrote a poem titled "The Moment I Knew I Shouldn't Have Married My Husband." That moment couldn't be more ordinary. I'm walking back to the car from the bathroom at a highway rest stop. But you don't need dramatic action to be hit with a life-shaking recognition.

As you begin writing the poem, you may not know immediately when the power of the moment in the narrative begins. But if you start with lines that are ultimately not needed, as you revise, you can always delete that "ramp" that got you into the poem. And if you don't include enough as you begin, you can go back and give us what the poem still needs.

The question of where to end can sometimes be challenging because every poem needs a discovery. If a poem from beginning to end is something you already knew before you began, you're still on the diving board. To tell a story you already know is a report, not a poem. Instead we want the experience to be enacted freshly in the poem. As Robert Frost said succinctly, "No surprise for the writer, no surprise for the reader."

The ending of any poem is crucial. Although no one will want to continue to read a poem that begins poorly, and problems in the middle of a poem are not desirable either, if the ending lands well, it's likely that you'll be able to work out the previous problems. And sometimes the reader will forgive some flaws if the ending of a poem is, as Stephen Dobyns advises, "both inevitable and surprising" (38). But if you don't have a satisfying ending, you don't yet have a poem. However, if you've written a strong poem of the moment all the way up to the end, then you have a solid foundation to work from.

A FEW TIPS

So, how do you approach a poem of the moment once you have chosen the moment? It bears repeating that the most basic and most helpful strategy is to go slowly. Of course this is essential in most poems, so practicing with the poem of the moment will help you develop your skills for any poetic structure. You want to slow down, stretch out the moment.

How do you do this? Detail and description. Bring us into the scene through our senses. Describe. Describe in detail. Use metaphors to describe. Sharon Olds says that in writing a poem, rather than trying to find the most interesting, vivid, best, etc., words, strive for *accuracy*. I've found this incredibly grounding and useful advice. So instead of looking for language that's impressive or lyrical or amazing or brilliant, if you focus on being accurate, you're likely to come up with precisely the right language because you're trying to be precise.

Beware of relying too heavily on abstractions or abstract language. Beware of overly explaining—too much talk *about* the event, rather than simply delivering the event to us so we can experience it for ourselves. You want the moment to take place on the page, to live on the page, rather than be a story about something that happened in the past.

Beware of psychological language—which I call *psychologese*. There are many kinds of diction that can be effective, but the language of self-help books won't make a poem, unless it's intentionally self-conscious or ironic.

LOOKING AT A POEM OF THE MOMENT

Let's trace how a poem stays with, moves through, diverges from and returns to, the moment.

Watch

Bad luck, bad history:
the right arm shriveled,
the hand curled
in on itself,
unusable,
the crippled gait

I try hard
not to stare at
when I see him
in the playground
I walk past
every day,

out on the court
alone, his good hand
hoisting the ball
up, banging the ball
on rim or backboard

so that it bounds
away and he has to
lumber after,
the gimped leg dragged
like a ball and chain
across the blacktop
over and over,

indefatigable,
his voice announcing
the last seconds

of the game forever
playing in his head
that he's always winning.

Genetic damage.
Damage of history,
of shame inside
the pleasure inside
the pity of
not being him,

of being white,
and then the panic
the day he calls me over,
saying, Hey man
can you help
a brother out?

Panic of borders
breached, of history
in the sour air
I'm breathing as I reach
into my pocket
for what he wants,

sour air of history
when he sighs,
and shakes his head,
and smiles at me
so wearily
without surprise

as if his days were
days of just
this kind of thing
to get through, to
put up with, saying,
Shit, man, I don't

want your money,
holding out to me
the wristwatch
he can't with one
hand, understand?
buckle to his wrist,

and could I do it?
and now I'm fumbling
with the frayed band
that I can't make
fit through the opening
of the metal clasp,

and so he talks me
through it, teaching
me how, the way
a father does,
teaching the child
something he better

learn, teaching it
patiently but
with a patience that
the tone says
isn't inexhaustible,
You got to slow

down, just ease it
through the slot
a little softer
like it wants
to go there on
its own, like that,

man, yeah, like that,
and it's done,
he's turned away,

> he's finished with my
> being anyone
> of use, I'm finished
>
> being useful,
> and again the cocked
> arm hurls the ball
> up toward the hoop
> and the fans go crazy
> as the announcer
> cries out three two one. (45)

—*Alan Shapiro*

So let's look at this poem and track the way Alan Shapiro moves us through time.

"Watch" combines a particular moment with more general remembrance. He begins by describing a man he sees regularly. This is ongoing time. We're not in the moment yet:

> Bad luck, bad history:
> the right arm shriveled,
> the hand curled
> in on itself,
> unusable,
> the crippled gait
>
> I try hard
> not to stare at
> when I see him
> in the playground
> I walk past
> every day,

Shapiro's language is spare. His clear observation and straightforward elegance is a worthy role model. We see this man described with a sharp eye, and although the speaker doesn't know anything about him beyond what he can see, the observations are detailed and his commentary sums it up in amazing brevity: "Bad luck, bad history." That opening line alone is a gem-like, impressive feat. The poem also brings the speaker in immediately, "I try hard not to stare at him . . ." so we're told this is going to be not only about the man, but about the speaker as well—about the relationship. The only metaphor he uses is a cliché ("ball and chain"), but it's so accurate, so physical, it gives new life to the old phrase and transcends cliché. We see the way this man drags his leg literally and vividly.

Then we come to the stanza where the emotion and the self-revelation ratchet up:

> Genetic damage.
> Damage of history,
> of shame inside
> the pleasure inside
> the pity of
> not being him,

This is a psychological/emotional exposure, but again it is so straightforward, so spare and astute, that it avoids psychological jargon or the feeling that we've fallen into explanation. And then this interesting stanza break:

> of being white,

So now we've gone beyond the disability, and Shapiro is bringing in the tension of race. This is a great example of how the poem can be grounded in this very specific situation, this one moment, *and* address major issues:

> and then the panic
> the day he calls me over,

This is where we shift into the *moment* of the poem of the moment.
Now we've gone from ongoing time to this one day, this one moment:

> saying. Hey man
> can you help
> a brother out?
>
> Panic of borders
> breached, of history
> in the sour air
> I'm breathing as I reach

Again, Shapiro is so spare in the way he tells us the whole story of
race: "borders breached . . . history in the sour air." And as he uses
the same syntax now for the third time, the same stark language, we
understand that this is the way he's going to address this huge and
inexhaustible subject:

> into my pocket
> for what he wants,
>
> sour air of history
> when he sighs,
> and shakes his head,
> and smiles at me
> so wearily
> without surprise

And now he shifts his view toward the man so that we can see somewhat into his experience. It's the speaker's interpretation of the man's
experience, but we feel he has gotten it right:

> as if his days were
> days of just
> this kind of thing

to get through, to
put up with, saying,
Shit, man, I don't

want your money,
holding out to me
the wristwatch
he can't with one
hand, understand?
buckle to his wrist,

and could I do it?

Now we see that the speaker had misunderstood, misinterpreted, because he carried so many assumptions, so many beliefs. The man's actual need and intentions are revealed.

and now I'm fumbling
with the frayed band
that I can't make
fit through the opening
of the metal clasp,

Here the camera is coming in closer, zeroing in on the wrist, the watch band, the clasp, and the frayed end of the band. Shapiro is giving us detail. He's slowing down because this is the moment when the two men connect, literally. He's moving in the camera. You can think of it like a movie camera. Your camera isn't bolted to the ground. You can move it in. You can pull it out:

and so he talks me
through it, teaching
me how, the way
a father does,
teaching the child
something he better

> learn, teaching it
> patiently but
> with a patience that
> the tone says
> isn't inexhaustible,

Here again is a commentary on what the speaker needs to learn about who he is and who this man is in their shared world. There is a whole essay in these few short lines about race, disability, human relationships—what we must learn from each other and the burden on the one who is doing the teaching. And then my favorite lines:

> You got to slow
>
> down, just ease it
> through the slot
> a little softer
> like it wants
> to go there on
> its own, like that,

We see here the sensitivity of this man who is physically damaged, mentally damaged, carrying the weight of how white people see him. And yet he understands something so tender and wise: "a little softer like it wants to go there on its own." Not just about buckling watches, of course, but about how to live:

> man, yeah, like that,
> and it's done,
> he's turned away,
> he's finished with my
> being anyone
> of use, I'm finished
>
> being useful,

Alan Shapiro just keeps on observing the relationship accurately. The man playing ball has a need and asks for simple human assistance. He has to persevere through the speaker's projections and fears and misunderstanding. He has to teach him. And then, when he does, there's no made-for-TV-movie ending. There isn't some kind of bond formed. The basketball player is done; he goes back to his game. No sentimentality. It is what it is:

> and again the cocked
> arm hurls the ball
> up toward the hoop
> and the fans go crazy
> as the announcer
> cries out three two one.

The ending is perfect. No amazing metaphors, no impressive and stunning word choices. Just exact observation and language that keeps us glued to the moment. This is a narrative so sharp in its observation of self and other that it's an unforgettable poem.

KWAME DAWES

Chameleon of Suffering

CALIBAN:
Be not afeard; the isle is full of noises,
Sounds and sweet airs, that give delight and hurt not.
Sometimes a thousand twangling instruments
Will hum about mine ears, and sometime voices
That, if I then had waked after long sleep,
Will make me sleep again: and then, in dreaming,
The clouds methought would open and show riches
Ready to drop upon me that, when I waked,
I cried to dream again.

—William Shakespeare

Parasite

I dress in secret, discarding my exile skin.
I constantly pat my pocket to feel the comfort
of my utility accent, exotic as a *slenteng* trenody,
talisman of my alien self, to stand out visible against
the ghostly horde of native sons, their hands slicing the air
in spastic language. I too am disappearing in the mist—a dear price
for feasting on the dead with their thick scent of history.

It is easy in this place to grow comfortable
with the equations that position the land,
the green of tobacco, the scent of magnolia,
the choke-hold, piss-yellow spread of kudzu, so heavy
it bends the chain link fence dividing 277;
the stench of wisteria crawling its pale purple
path through a dying swamp. I hear myself turning
heir to the generation that understood the smell
of burning flesh, the grammar of a stare, the flies
of the dead, undisturbed in an open field. My burden
is far easier, it's true. I have not acquired a taste for chitlins
and grits, but I wear well the livery of ageless anger and quiet
resolve like the chameleon of suffering I am.

The chameleon, we know, carries out a very basic technique for survival. It is an act of camouflage. By some remarkable chemistry, the creature is able to change its color in sympathy with the colors near to it. This way it can hide, it can insinuate itself into another environment that may even be hostile, and by disappearing it survives. There is, of course, a metaphor here. The metaphor may have little to do with the biology or evolutionary impulse of the act, but it works well for a poet seeking a way to understand the complexities of home, place, alienation, belonging, and most relevant to us—appropriation.

The chameleon can be seen as somewhat diabolic—a sneaky creature that allows its body to study the colors around it and then trans-
forms that body so it can become a part of that environment. Since
other creatures survive by discovering aliens in their midst, the
chameleon could well be said to be a threat—an alien threat, if you
will. But the chameleon can work as a metaphor for assimilation and
belonging. The chameleon, you see, does not stop being a lizard. It
does not alter its internal self, but it still manages to mutate into something quite different by the remarkable act of empathy—that is, the
capacity to absorb the nuances of the world outside of it and become
one with that world. Something changes in the chameleon, something
that goes beyond the superficial. The art of becoming is part of its
genius, and, as I have said, a function of its capacity to survive.

As one who has traveled to different places, I have long understood the importance of being oneself and yet being a part of the
space that has taken you in. Finding that balance may well be the
most critical skill that a poet or an artist can have.

The poet, you see, must be able to understand this idea of empathy. Empathy enacts a process of becoming, but that becoming is not
complete; it does not (and must not) occur with the total transformation of the person who is feeling or understanding. The act of
empathy entails being engaged and yet disengaged. Empathy allows
the individual to feel and yet not become so consumed by feeling
that he can't analyze, reflect, think, imagine, conceive of a way out,
remember what existed before, and conceive of what might exist
after a crisis. In other words, empathy allows us to be useful without
being clinical and cold—indeed, empathy ensures that being there
adds to the experience in ways that complete sympathy does not.
Ultimately, empathy ensures that the very value of having another
around is not lost completely.

The poet must also be there and be outside of there at the same
time. The poet must feel and yet be far away enough from feeling

to allow her to exercise form, the making of art at the same time. Here is how the poet differs from the average human being. The poet must both feel and not feel at the same time. The poet must not be so overwhelmed by what she sees that the ability to discover the art in the moment is lost. The poet must be both inside and outside of the world observed at the same time. As you can well imagine, one cannot *always* be a poet or something human could be lost. This is why I like to speak of the poetic instinct rather than simply declare that the poet must always be the poet.

The poet sees in experience, the potential for art. This is both our gift and our craft. It is best to simply exaggerate the sinful nature of this impulse so we can have a crude but helpful understanding of what it is about. The poet will steal your experience and use it to make poems. And while the poet may claim that the act of doing so is altruistic and represents some kind of homage to the subject, the poet is likely lying or simply working hard to assuage the sense of guilt for being a scavenger of sorts. The poet may say that by engaging the experiences of others, by stealing their stories and using them for art, she is in fact "giving voice to the voiceless" or enacting some kind of social work that will edify society in some profound way. First of all, the so-called voiceless hardly exist in reality. Most people have a voice and have been happily using it for all their lives. The problem is the listeners—nobody has been listening. At best, what the poet may do is be a mediator who manages to negotiate listening—that is to say, who manages to make those who have not been listening for various reasons start to listen to those who have not been heard. No doubt, if a poet pursues this act as a vocation, he should be lauded for it—it is a noble pursuit. But it does not change the fact that the poet is often pilfering to do so. So, put another way, while all of these good things may come out of this act of stealing, the impulse is not really about that.

The poet knows that writing poetry is a quest to delight. This, of course, is Dryden's construction, and it is one that many since have latched onto quite wisely. But we must not forget all of what Dryden proposed. "Delight" he says "is the chief, if not the only end of poetry: instruction can be admitted but in the second place." So Dryden does allow that poetry can instruct at some level and can do other quite sensible things.

I recently discovered an essay by my father, Neville Dawes, that he wrote when he was in his late twenties. He was reflecting on the value of verse and on Dryden. He proposed that "poetry begins in delight and ends in wisdom." A necessary proposition for him, a Marxist writer who would have worried about being a writer if the business of writing did not allow, even if only "in the second place" some opportunity for wisdom.

Having said this, though, I do think this business of delighting is sometimes misunderstood. There is often a feeling that art must not always delight. But that is because we believe that delight only pertains to loveliness, prettiness, lightness, and laughter. Once we get over this limiting understanding of delight, we can begin to see why the impulse to delight with language is as good a reason to live and to write as any. Delight has to do with the pleasure that we get (some might call it comfort, assurance, joy, awareness) from seeing something created from nothing, from discovering something beautiful in our world. Here beauty is the grace of our shared understanding of what is good and affirming about our world. The beauty is less in the content, the theme, the "meaning" of the work, but in the shape of the work, in the very existence of that shape.

So let's return to the chameleon. The chameleon is a freak. That is what it is. It enacts something quite freakish that, frankly, delights us. We are delighted by this alchemy of color that the chameleon manages to enact. It tells us something about this creature, about this creation. So we are delighted by the act of transformation. Yes, the colors that we witness are pleasurable or disgusting, but it is not this that delights us. Indeed, we may be repulsed by the color we see but remain delighted by the magical act of transformation achieved by the chameleon.

So yes, the making of poetry is something of a freak show. And what is beautiful about it is that we manage to turn experience into something beautiful, something that has a shape, and something that we can consume and understand, something, therefore, in which we can delight.

Which is why when a poet chooses to write about subjects that are weighty, to engage with human experience that is often dealt with by social sciences and political theorists, they do not become social scientists or political theorists, they do not become historians or sociologists, they do not become painters and musicians—no, they remain poets, because what they are doing is taking the subjects of these fields and pouring them into the rituals of poetry making. The poet is transformed, but the poet's transformation serves just one end: the making of something delightful called a *poem*.

I am seeking to explain something that has had to consume my time a lot lately. One of the presumptions about the work that I do is that I am actually trying to do some kind of sociological, historical, political, or grandly ideological work in the poetry I have written of late. I would like to take credit for these things because in many ways, it is the way that people understand our value as poets. It is harder for people to understand the more basic value of the poet as someone who brings delight. Here is what Shakespeare makes of delight:

> Be not afeard; the isle is full of noises,
> Sounds and sweet airs, that give delight and hurt not.
> Sometimes a thousand twangling instruments
> Will hum about mine ears, and sometime voices
> That, if I then had waked after long sleep,

Will make me sleep again: and then, in dreaming,
The clouds methought would open and show riches
Ready to drop upon me that, when I waked,
I cried to dream again.

Caliban is reassuring two drunks about the value of the island. You can hear in him such an appreciation of what Bob Marley called "the beauties." Yet Caliban is a slave; he is a man acutely aware of his enslavement and the need to break out of it. He is talking to two people who he hopes will conspire with him to take over the island. The creature is describing one of the critical motivations for his act of political usurpation. And yet, the "sweet airs" are the poetic space for him—the space that fills him with delight and tears. He cries so he can dream. The delight of poetry rests in the shape of poetry. And the shape of poetry is what allows us to turn experience into something quite beautiful, even as it is moving, compelling, transforming, and affective.

The writing I have done that has sought to engage experience has had to come with some key rules in place. I have had to first accept that I am not a slave to the facts. The facts represent the material that must consume the journalist and the historian. The facts do not consume the poet. Ours is a somewhat less reliable ideal. We are in search of the truth, which is often different from the facts. And the tyranny of truth is not enacted by the narrative, as is the case in journalism, but in the form itself—the shape of the thing called the poem. The poem has rules. It has structure, it has expectations, and those expectations are what make demands on the experience. And truth is part of that shape. The truth is emotional, and it is sentimental. It has to do with tone, mood, and feeling and that is not something we can walk away from or ignore. Truth also has to do with the shape of a thing, its pulse and feel. If what is produced does not delight, it has not achieved what the poem seeks to achieve. And so the poet who writes about experience must always be as doggedly committed to the poem as anyone else.

So that is the challenge. As I think of the way that many of these projects have unfolded, I realize that I am busy trying to experience the world through this act of empathy, which allows me to change color. But I remain me. I remain the core of these poems and I remain the manipulator of the experience to find something delightful as a result. Yes, people will be moved, people will be touched, people will feel as if they have learned something they did not know before. Yes, I may even serve as a historian of sorts and yes, I may give voice to the so-called voiceless. But what I am doing is rendering their voice in poetry. This is different from simply reproducing their voice. What I have at my disposal is more than just voice. I have more than just the limits of their language and their experience. I have at my disposal more than the limits of their consciousness. I have a wider palette. When my poem can show them things they did not even know about themselves, when it can reveal to them what they may have imagined but could not speak with delight, I know then that I have achieved art. I have become the chameleon of suffering.

The poet, I believe—and here, I remain stuck with simile and metaphor trying to describe that which I can't—is an antenna that is constantly catching sounds, feelings, ideas, colors, and moods that, in many ways, could be called key ingredients of verse.

As a young poet, I worried about this. I worried that I was using people. I worried that I was exploiting their lives. I worried that they would see themselves in my work and be upset. I worried this way because of my own sense of misguided hubris. I simply imagined that I *was* writing them. I was lost then. I did not know that I was not writing them. I was writing poems. There is a difference, an important one. I had to let go of my self-importance. That was the first task. And then I had to regard carefully how much I had misplaced by a sense of love, respect and deference for them, for these people I cared about. I had to stop confusing the act of making poems with the act of showing affection. What I have learned is that I am offering a gift to these people, but I have no ability to capture them in order to reproduce them in art. That is hubris. How could I? Instead, I am taking what they have given me and making poems—poems that give delight. But what has gone into these poems is not just them, not just their experience, but much more than that. I am an ordinary creature who has to turn experience into something that has shape and form. Their lives do not. What a poem is, is not what a person is. A poem sings its own song. Somewhere we will discover those we write about, but mostly we will discover them as transformed into art. There is an important difference.

So now, all I know is that I am trying to take the emotion and turn it into something that delights—the poem. You will start to see then that the real test of a poem's effectiveness has less to do with what its content is in that crass and crude sense of "what it is about" but in how it achieves its delight. The poem is about the shape of things, the beauty of the thing.

Put another way, and here one must accept the proposition that a blues song is in many ways as much of a poetic form as anything else, the quality of a great blues poem does not rest on the level of tragedy that it describes but on how well it describes whatever tragedy it tackles. Thus, the poem does not become more moving because a man has been cheated on ten times by his woman versus having been cheated on once by her. One need not overstate this analogy to make the point.

I have written several books of poems that have grown out of an engagement with various types of existing narratives and sources that could label my work "projects" and that could even challenge their poetic validity. I think that the history of literature has taught me that the test of such work is not whether the impulse to write on a subject is pure enough for poetry, but on the quality of the poetry itself—the genius, so to speak, of the chameleonic gesture of the poet of empathy.

"SPECIFICITY? YES. BUT ONLY IF IT'S RELEVANT."

Reflections on the Nuts and Bolts of Writing

STEVE AMICK

Intimacy, Realism, and Efficacy in the Battle of the POV: A Re-Introduction to 3rd Person

[T]he writer must believe that what he is doing is the most important thing in the world. And he must hold to this illusion even when he knows it is not true.

—John Steinbeck

I've lately reached a point, when it comes to this subject, where I now skip any attempt to appear polite and reasonable and balanced (in whatever way you want to define that word), so perhaps the subtitle for this should be "In Which Steve Steps on a Lot of Toes." Where I aim to get to is a richer understanding of the potential for what we call *close-limited third person* and some basic tricks for optimizing the sense of realism, empathy, engagement, and momentum in that mode. But first, we have to acknowledge the current landslide shift to the first-person side of the boat as well as address the corruption of that mode, the weird tinkering that's been happening as of late.

I should state clearly from the start that no, I don't hate first person point of view. When the story calls for it, I write in first person. When the story calls for it, I write in second person. But it's not an automatic, knee-jerk reaction. It's not based on my own style issues or what's hip. Point of view choice is not bellbottoms. First person has certain traits and utility—it's not a handlebar mustache in Brooklyn.

For the sake of focus, I want to limit this rant to POV in literary short stories, not in genre, not in novels. In short stories, every moving part serves a purpose—often, more than one purpose (what I think of as "using all the parts of the buffalo"). So we can best notice things like inefficiency or elements working at cross-purposes within the tight confines of a short story. And we'll only tackle first person and close-limited third, because both seem to me to often be selected out of similar impulses.

To start, given what's happened to first person, I believe we have to extensively re-establish what we're looking at:

A Possibly Insultingly Elementary Overview of 1ˢᵗ and 3ʳᵈ Person...

1ˢᵗ Person (participant or observer) (narrator = protagonist or narrator = observer)	**3ʳᵈ Person** (close-limited)
• Duality of story (story of the events + story of the telling) • Dramatic irony	• Character and actions observed from a distance & degree determined by YOU • Can speak both <u>about</u> and <u>for</u> protagonist

---

Here, on the left, is first person as it is ideally presented. I will resist calling this *traditional* first person and I'll explain why in a moment. We have both *Participant* and *Observer* forms—the narrator equals the protagonist or the narrator equals an observer to the events. Two major characteristics of this model come to mind for me. First, a *duality of story*—there's the story of the events as both the reader and the writer are meant to understand them, the "real" story, so to speak. And then there's another story layered onto this. There's perhaps the story of the *telling* of the events because, simply following human nature, we do not tell the world our crazy shit. We do not bare it all for no clearly defined reason. Back in the dark ages, when I was getting my MFA, in almost every workshop, the question was asked, usually, as I recall, by Richard Bausch: "Why is this speaker breaking the silence that normally exists between himself and the universe?"

The occasion could be crystallized in the form itself—more of a gimmick—an overt, stated occasion for the telling like, most famously, Holden Caulfield reporting to his shrink on the events leading up to his breakdown, or in epistolary form—narrative presented as letters. But even in less contrived forms, where the story isn't presented in this way, the story necessarily means something at least *slightly* different to the narrator/protagonist. In the extreme, this is the old unreliable narrator, out-and-out lying or crazy or deluded, but more commonly, the two stories may be incredibly similar in all but a few points, or there may be a certain focus or agenda to the narrator's story versus "your" story. We absorb both as readers, hence, the duality.

Second, because of this mismatch between what actually happened and what's on the page, we have *dramatic irony*. When there's a first-person narrator, dramatic irony must be present, and the less time that has elapsed between the telling of the events and the events themselves, the greater the dramatic irony.

Conversely, one could argue that the longer the time between the telling and the events, the more there's a cognitive distortion of memory. You may look way back to the summer of 1942 and say, "Boy, I was a scamp—I thought *this* way, I was doing *this* because of *this* . . ." and be very self-aware about that stuff—your motivation, the meaning of it all—but honestly, because of time and human memory, you'd experience some blurring and romanticizing of the specific details.

So we have distance between the two stories that stems from psychological/emotional guardedness or cognitive fallibility. A distortion.

First person, then, is a great choice if you want to make an already simple story more complex or layered, nuanced, or if you want to present something that's morally ambiguous or give more of a universal view of something. Stories that invest in the *feeling* or colorful multifacets of an event. Or stories in which the telling plays a key role in the story itself. What first person likely will *not* do—and this may seem counterintuitive—is simplify or streamline already complex stories or get at the indisputable truth of a matter or necessarily provide the most direct, concise conduit of insight into a character. First person has built-in flaws that are also its beauty marks in areas like truthfulness, memory, subjective bias, plot, momentum . . .

Now let's turn to that little, ignored square, if you will—the right side of the chart: 3rd Person (close-limited.)

This is not your great-granddaddy's third. We're not floating over the village, omniscient. (Which, I find, is what a lot of newer writers first think of when they hear the phrase *third person.* Don't worry: This is not that.)

With this choice, the first feature that comes to my mind is that character and actions are observed from a distance and degree (a depth) that's determined by *you,* the writer. Yes, it's close, but what's close? *You* decide, based on the needs of the story. And unlike first person, I see this as being on a dial. There's wiggle room. You can dial this up or down, fudge things a little one way or the other. It's forgiving and adjustable whereas I tend to see first person as more of a switch—either on or off. Like pregnant or not pregnant. You're either convincing in the role of this character or you're not. (You might doodle a little thermostat on the right side of this chart. Unless you're only borrowing this book.)

The second feature of close-limited third is also on a bit of a dial: you can speak both *about* and *for* the protagonist. Meaning both on behalf of the main character's internal consciousness plus stepping back slightly and describing or commenting on his or her situation. This gives you latitude to both go deep into her psyche and person-ality and voice, but also to make a comment on something that she might hesitate to state clearly, if required to speak for herself.

This ability to do both in close-limited third can save you from *pages* of meandering implication in first person. For example, in first person, inhabiting the character, I might have to hint around that I'm Asian American, of a certain age, then slip in some more small hints that I'm often claustrophobic, then some more hints that I'm from a certain region of the US . . . and on and on until the reader sleuths it out. So you can do that for seven or eight pages *or,* in close-limited third, you can just say, "He was born in a Japanese internment camp and so for, the rest of his life, was forever afraid of fences." Boom. Done. And I feel perfectly connected to that character. There's empathy and closeness there—we can go on to hear about his stomachache today or his loneliness or other internal issues—but this particular revelation may be something he would never just spit out like that himself. Not naturally. Not unless he's a narrowly-defined character of a very specific personality.

So what has it become lately? What am I griping about?

Currently, What We Often See...

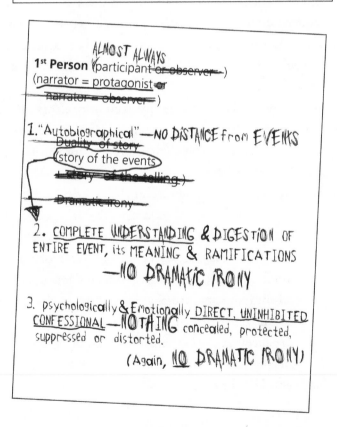

1st Person (participant ~~or observer~~) *ALMOST ALWAYS*
(narrator = protagonist ~~or~~
~~narrator = observer~~)

1. "Autobiographical"—NO DISTANCE from EVENTS
~~Duality of story~~
(story of the events)
~~(story of the telling)~~

~~Dramatic irony~~

2. COMPLETE UNDERSTANDING & DIGESTION OF ENTIRE EVENT, its MEANING & RAMIFICATIONS —NO DRAMATIC IRONY

3. psychologically & Emotionally DIRECT, UNINHIBITED CONFESSIONAL—NOTHING concealed, protected, suppressed or distorted.
(Again, NO DRAMATIC IRONY)

(aka "superhuman 1st person" / "bastardized 1st person" / "misused 1st person," etc.)

I hope you can still read it. I tried to make it look vandalized. I do feel that's what's happened to it. . . . (Note: The fonts here were selected to ironically illustrate the "rebelliousness" of this "revolutionary" mode. Feel free to insert your own Jolly Rogers and doodles of Che Guevara.) For the most part, these days, forget even *observer* form. We're seeing mostly a lot of narrator = the protagonist. So it's very autobiographical, if you will—not meaning that it's necessarily a true event but just that there's no real gap between actor and action. It's a lot of "this happened to me. I did this." *Thwunk.* (That last is the sound of unfiltered statements hitting the page.)

Second, the protagonist/narrator has an *astonishingly* complete and clear understanding and digestion of these events. The details, the ramifications, the greater meaning. . . . There's no dramatic irony—no mismatch between his or her understanding and ours. They're the same.

The third characteristic is this: From an emotional/psychological standpoint, it's a very direct, pure, uninhibited confessional. There are no protective barriers, no shielding, no reason for the narrator to pick and choose what's revealed.

Now, if you have the first and second characteristics, at the same time, even with zero psychological training—that is, you didn't take Psych 101—a layman might tell you that this seems improbable, if not impossible. Can a human be active in the center of important action and also understand and digest all the details and all the larger ramifications and meaning and present this purely, with the honest intention that it be taken as gospel? I say no.

So those two cancel each other out. They conflict and thus make for a gross artificiality. Coming directly from a human, they can't coexist. They can't both be true.

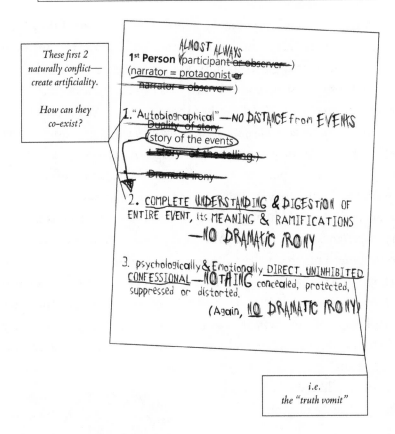

...And How That Begins to Break Down

These first 2 naturally conflict—create artificiality.

How can they co-exist?

ALMOST ALWAYS
1st Person (participant or observer)
(narrator = protagonist or
narrator = observer)

1. "Autobiographical"—NO DISTANCE from EVENTS
Duality of story
(story of the events)
(story of the telling)
Dramatic Irony

2. COMPLETE UNDERSTANDING & DIGESTION OF ENTIRE EVENT, its MEANING & RAMIFICATIONS
—NO DRAMATIC IRONY

3. psychologically & Emotionally DIRECT, UNINHIBITED CONFESSIONAL—NOTHING concealed, protected, suppressed or distorted.
(Again, NO DRAMATIC IRONY)

i.e.
the "truth vomit"

The only way the first and second element can coexist—or, more accurately, be presented on the page *as if* they're both true—is if the third one is not in place. If emotionally or psychologically there's something at play, there's something hinky going on. If it's not a pure, true confession. If there's *dramatic irony*. If we're supposed to understand that there's spin being put on the story.

Otherwise, they cancel each other out and the only thing you have is this third thing—the uninhibited pure confession. This is a stranger walking in and saying, "Boy, I just beat off in the swimming pool . . . Hey, how ya doing? Nice to meet you. . . ." What I call the *truth vomit*.

For the story to work, to feel natural, one of these three has to be distorted.

Now I'm not looking to make people feel defensive if they look at this and think, "Hey, that's what *I* do . . . ," but for the purposes of discussion, I struggle with how we can separate and label these two versions of first person. I hesitate to call my first outline *traditional first person*. *Traditional* implies there's an improved way to do it. It implies *customary, old-fashioned, based on habit*. And I don't think that's fair. I think of it more as "working" or "effective" or "real" first person. "First person, ideally." And this is some of where I step on toes, but I may call this recent version, above, *misused* first person or *bastardized* first person or *watered-down* first person. In a way, *superhuman* first person. And in the cases where we're talking about something that's driven purely by the desire to confess all, that only has that as its essence, I do think of that, frankly, as a truth vomit—even though it is, at its heart, entirely disingenuous and untruthful about the way it presents humans, both psychologically and cognitively: how we feel and how we think, how we process information.

You've likely seen this Venn diagram known as FAST, GOOD, CHEAP. It's lately been making the rounds online, but I recall things like this from my involvement in advertising years ago, and that is where this came from, from the design departments,

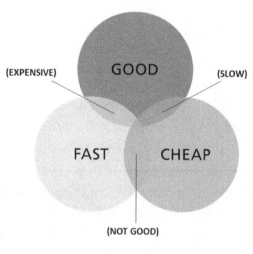

where they were grousing about the client's expectation for work

and the idea is the client can pick two, but they don't get the third one. The client can have the work good and fast but it won't be cheap, or cheap and fast but it won't be good, and around and around.

It's not an arbitrary rule—just to jerk around the client—it's a fact based on human limitations, spatial and time restrictions, logistics. . . . It reminds me a great deal of first person. I've taken a few stabs at making a direct one-to-one copy of this and had a little luck, but I suggest you try that yourself. It makes for a good exercise. You may find you can add even more circles but the outcome is the same—you can't have everything when humans are at the center of it. Something has to give.

First person, when it's working, is, by its nature, flawed. Beautifully flawed. Which is why first person also feels, to me, like the Venus de Milo. Technically, there's a flaw to this object because the arms are missing. But that flaw, I think, underscores just how perfect are the parts that *are* there. A first-person protagonist might exhibit great storytelling skills, let's say—they've got great structure, tension—and great language skills—crisp dialogue, realistic slang, vivid descriptions—but *man!—something is really wrong with his understanding of what just happened. He doesn't get that his best friend just slept with his wife.* . . . And that's moving and engaging and realistic. If the story were firing on all cylinders—if the narrator knows everything you know as a writer—if the story had all its limbs, so to speak, it wouldn't work nearly as well.

I also see a duality of story here. When we look at the Venus de Milo, we see at least two things. Our brain tells us this is a representation of a beautiful female torso, the perfection of anatomy, etc. But there's also a duality: We also see the story of the human attempt to express this. It becomes more beautiful because we see the struggle, the conflict in getting the expression out—carving the stone, something broke the limbs, it ended up in a field . . . the original intention was distorted.

It becomes more beautiful. The flaws frame the beauty. It puts human frailty at the center of the story. That's a working first-person story.

So the bastardized first person feels, to me, like someone has tried to Krazy Glue all the parts back onto the Venus de Milo.

A few years ago, I was bellyaching about the fact that something had mysteriously happened to first person while I wasn't closely watching and wanting a little backup to prove to my grad workshop at another university that I was not alone in this, I pretty much grabbed the first verification I could find online, just to show how widespread recognition of this problem was, beyond the insular world of their workshop. So I somewhat arbitrarily brought in an interview with the writer Cris Mazza in *The Rumpus*. I saw the sheer lack of digging I had to do to find allies as proof enough that I wasn't a crackpot, but what I found particularly interesting to note in Mazza's grumbling was what she says about distortion. She cites the lack of distortion in recent first-person stories as the reason she grew disenchanted with the form and quit writing those stories out of disgust. But then she eventually went back to the form, deciding to pile on the distortions. To not only allow a few human elements into the story—the "baggage" of lies, omissions, misunderstanding, lack of information, language limitations, memory failures, etc., but to heap them on to a character. Give 'em everything she had. It's a fun approach.

Now, Mazza also said something about beginning writers misguidedly assuming that because they're comfortable communicating in first person in real life, that must be the easiest way to produce a short story:

> Far too much fiction employs it for only surface reasons: it's "easy" for inexperienced writers to speak as themselves, it provides direct access to character thoughts, and of course it *is* a "voice" therefore the (erroneous) claim is that it's the only way for fiction to have a unique quirky or fresh "voice." But

these surface uses ignore and usually eliminate more interesting, complex, and I think *necessary* layers like irony, temporal distance, unreliability, and the nature of memory. (Frangello)

That's a good segue back to our first chart and let's reassess based on "ease":

So, When Deciding...(Bicycles and Swiss Army Knives)

1st Person (participant or observer) (narrator = protagonist or narrator = observer)	3rd Person (close-limited)
• Duality of story (story of the events + story of the telling) • Dramatic irony	• Character and actions observed from a distance & degree determined by YOU • Can speak both <u>about</u> and <u>for</u> protagonist

For simplicity of task, for a beginning writer, third person is learning to ride a two-wheeler, while first person is learning to ride a unicycle while simultaneously learning to juggle oranges. Or at least patting your head while rubbing your stomach. It's not a novelty item, certainly, but a puzzle, something everyone should try to tackle at some point. But every day, just starting out? That's some serious head-banging. It's an important tool to know and sometimes the only tool for a *particular* job, but it's never the only tool in the toolbox.

Close-limited third is more all-purpose, more of a Swiss army knife. Regardless of experience, if you're starting a new story and you don't yet know what it needs, close-limited third is a good default setting. You can start there and have easier access to all the information of the story and switch later, if needed. Starting in first is like saying, "I'm not sure what our plans are for the evening, so I'm going to slip into my tux and some scuba flippers." Odds are, you're going to need to change again.

Adding all this up with clear eyes, a close-limited, unwavering third person can be the most intimate, the most revealing, and the most useful POV available to you. It can be the fastest way in—and don't we supposedly now have the attention spans of fleas? Today, when we cut to the chase, when the conflict or tension has crept up and up, ever closer to the first page of a short story, how can we be flocking to first person, where the "baggage" of the telling should be slowing things down, getting in the way? That seems crazy. So by far, third person is the most efficient and the most general purpose. And when you opt for something else, that's fine, but you should realize the assets you're trading. It may be that the benefits of first person or second person do warrant the tradeoff, but you should try to understand what these attributes are and what they're best suited for and not just decide based on "Hey, that's my thing."

Now there *is* one downside to this close-limited third, with a little bit of a *"yeah but. . . ."* To get close to the protagonist's consciousness, you may have to dumb down a bit. You may find you're not writing at the same level of language and intelligence and humor as you're capable. I did this in my second book to the point where I questioned it in the editing, and my editor, to her great credit, had already been considering this and what she said was, "I know what you're saying and you are a better writer than these particular passages, but you're getting us really close to these characters and that's more important." And I think, looking back honestly, when I started writing, I was much more interested in shooting for sizzling language—great "grabber" sentences—than I was in the reality of the characters. So I'll take that tradeoff. Of course, when the dumb guy customer reviews on Amazon came out, it was a lot of "Jeezo, this guy don't write very fancy sentences. *I* can write fancier than that . . ."

But here's the "yeah, but. . . ." This downside—dumbing down your prose—that's *definitely* a factor in first person, too. You're stuck with exactly the prose skills and intelligence of your character; you have to use the *exact word* they'd use. So that's a washout. Tie. Even-steven. Leaving, I think, the tally marks favoring close-limited third.

Now in recognizing when you're in the "wrong" point of view, I don't know that there's any great golden rule, other than to get in the habit of asking yourself if this point of view *functions* in a way that's best for this story, and rather quickly, you'll start to develop personal shorthand for which kinds of things need what, and you'll get away from a gray sort of "it just feels comfy" approach, less of the "Hey, I'm just a first person kinda guy. That's how I roll. . . ."

For example, one little hint that I've noticed is that the things that are difficult to get to often thrive in third person. That may seem counterintuitive. Let me give you one of many examples I've seen: I was the thesis advisor for someone who was writing this wonderful collection of stories about post-Soviet Muscovites, and she contacted me with her latest installment and was frazzled. She had a story that was running to forty pages and just wasn't work-ing and she didn't get why. She really thought she had a handle on what the story was. So I had her send it to me and she was working from first person, attempting to approximate the charac-ter's real personality and all that good stuff—what I'd call "real" first person—and the narrator was a brilliant young surgeon who worked in the ER all day, then would come home to his apart-ment where he lived alone and try to deal with his very private problem. He seemed to have a sexual predilection (the Latin term escapes me) that was just a notch above or below—however you'd gauge that—from pedophilia. It was gross, but not illegal, basi-cally. He liked very young women. And he'd spend the evenings doing "research" online. But this character was so intelligent and had such good language skills and was so private and evasive, quite naturally, that we, as readers, just couldn't pin him down. What, exactly, was going on? The author tried to raise the stakes by bringing in a niece who was going to have to come to the city and move in with him to study ballet, and yet it still didn't force the problem out in the open. The mistake here was assuming that a very personal, intimate problem necessarily required first person—that first person would be the most revealing. Not from this guy. He was a dodgeball king, weaving and deflecting, parsing his words, bamboozling us, and so *this* guy was never going to drop his guard and tell us. Switching to close-limited third, she could keep all the basic intimate details, plus also tear down the barricade and reveal the real, shameful crux of the matter. So she could say something along the lines of—I'm paraphrasing here—"He would come home every evening with the full intention of doing research online, reading all the latest psychological studies in medical journals and trying to get to the bottom of what happened to him growing up, but invariably he would drift over to the adjacent porn sites and in the morning, feel worse about himself than he had before." So there we go. The hard to get to, here, thrives in close-limited third. As a side note, she not only had a better working story, but she also won a fellowship to the summer program in Prague. So . . . *that* worked. So some things, in true first person, the narrator hides from us, and others just don't register—just aren't processed the same.

Something more subtle that can trip us up is a false step that we might think of as *cognitive artificiality*, a misrepresentation of how we actually register cognitive processes. For example, this could easily slip past us in first person, if not closely examined: *I walked over to the window and looked out at the rain and I thought about a huge storm I experienced in my youth, remembering how it blew our shed away.* Really? More cognitively accurate is this string of thoughts: *It started raining out. When I was a kid, a huge storm blew our shed away.*

We don't naturally account for all this *looking* and *thinking* and *remembering* and *moving about*; instead, we report facts and stimuli. But when we work in first person, it can be easy to slip into this über-accounting that begins to play against what the internal experience *is* consciously acknowledging and, on the other hand, what simply . . . *is,* what's abstract.

It's interesting to me that my mother now has pretty rapidly advancing dementia and she sometimes has trouble eating because she forgets how to chew and swallow. She has to actively *think* about those acts. This is, quite clearly, the opposite of the norm. We don't normally take note of and record these actions: *"Walking to the window to look out, I was chewing a sandwich."* To do so would be cognitive artificiality, and if you're seeking more crisply defined details in a certain situation, first person may in fact be too abstract a vantage point for the story's needs.

I relate this phenomenon—and potential pitfall—to something I'd been doing in terms of dialogue since way back long ago before I developed my recent concerns about first person, and this is something that I now apply across the board, regardless of point of view. We all know the basic rule that, in dialogue, you sum up the unimportant stuff (the "hellos") and quote the important, but I take that a step further. Whether I'm in third or second or first, I make an effort to put the balance of the paraphrasing on the protagonist's half of the conversation, while giving more of the quotes to the supporting characters. My reasoning is that, for me, this distribution more closely approximates the cognitive process we go through during a real conversation and later, while recounting it. Just like you can't smell your own BO or don't recognize your own voice, we don't really hear what we're saying. We're too busy attempting to convey an idea, to communicate. We register how well we're doing, what sort of an impression we're making, and then we hear their response. So a real-life, spoken version of this, as example, would be something like, "Okay, I talked to her and I was real calm. I didn't go on and on and harangue her. I was real polite, but I told her the thing we talked about, about her moving out and she said, 'Oh, yeah, well what do you know about the real world, you big fat silver spoon guy.'" Quote, unquote for the other person. So the balance is sort of abstract perception close up/clarity at a distance. (I can't hammer this point enough—and so I do: Look for it again at the end as tip number three.)

BUT WAIT—WHY IS ALL THIS FIRST-PERSON STUFF HAPPENING?

In general, I think, whenever basic concepts fall through the cracks, we might have technology to blame, because a beginning writer can now work in isolation so much more than ever before. You could produce entire novel manuscripts and not even your wife would know. And that's wonderful—not that your wife doesn't know what you're doing, but that people can get started so easily these days. That's great. But they may miss some basic concepts that they would normally get by rote in more formal settings, with instruction and guidance, or even in casual writer's groups. And of course, there's also just a *ton* of bad information out there. I intentionally looked up a couple of spurious "how to write fiction" sites, just to further anger myself, and was amused to find, under the breakdown for the various points of view, this pearl: "FIRST PERSON—First person is the most intimate of points of view." Uh, no. I say no. Most *human-based*, maybe? So, a lot of basics are getting lost or blurred or simplified.

Now, the number one factor for the big push for first person these days has to be, obviously, the popularity of memoirs and blogs. For the first time ever, if you were to poll a fiction class, you'd likely find the majority of students are there almost in an ESL capacity. They find themselves in a fiction class, writing short stories, following an interest that was originally sparked, way back, by something other than fiction. In the past, a student would say, "In the eighth grade, I wrote something about the princess and the tiger. . . ." Now it's likely they started because they kept a journal or started a blog, or they read a memorable memoir. And that's great, but we should recognize that there's more of a *translation process* going on.

And quite naturally, if your ears have been filled with *I, I, I, me, me, me,* for years, *he* and *she* will of course feel like ye olde English. If unexamined, it will naturally just *"feel* wrong."

And a second factor: One reason first person is so often mishandled now in terms of character behavior *could* be the culture of reality shows and tabloid journalism that are numbing us to the idea of strangers just opening their big fat mouths and blabbing. This sort of thing could be why we get these pure confessionals, these truth vomits. We see too many people now who think all attention is good, infamy is fame; if the mikes are hot, start talking. And so we have to remind ourselves, in a sort of eureka, slap-your-forehead moment: "Oh, yeah. SHAME!" Right! Shame! Decorum! Privacy! Shyness! What about shyness?"

In the interview, Mazza feels that there's a circular trend, that the more this first person is published, the more a new generation of reader/writers unthinkingly jump on board and it goes round and round, feeding off itself. Maybe, but here's my thought on publishers' possible role in this. I've had a wide-*ish* range of experience with both small literary press publications and commercial publishing—and this may make me sound like a philistine, but comparing experiences, I can't get past the fact that by and large, the more in-depth, interrogative style of editing occurred in the big commercial places. They were not shy about asking, "Why is this here? Why this tense? What does this serve? Why is this in first person?" I'm not making a value judgment, but I have noticed a style difference, or maybe a policy difference, in editing from the small presses. The strongest pushback I've felt there has been along the lines of "Gee, you *may* want to take another look at your ending . . . if you *want*. If not, that's fine. It's *your* story." And the *least* intrusive was once receiving a little magazine in the mail and it was just my *manuscript*, basically just proofread, copyedited. ("Yeah, but—," I thought, "Aren't you going to ask me anything? Aren't we going to work on this?")

Again, I'm not trying to say that one approach is superior. I assume these gentler approaches are based on the idea that it's being respectful to the artist and that there may be a lengthy acceptance process, so if they take the story, it's already been thoroughly scrutinized. Perhaps. But if we get out of the habit of being directly asked to explain our choices, I think we get out of the habit of making *explainable* choices, and we just do things on a whim. If we're never asked "Why is this in first person, why is this in present tense, why is this here, do we need this passage. . . ?," we stop asking these questions ourselves.

WHY DO I CARE?

But why must I rant? Why don't I just do my own thing and not worry about everyone else? Well, I hate to see people put all their eggs in one basket, thinking they're making a stylistic choice, and do something that, down the line, may be snickered at much in the way that we now snicker at late nineteenth-century stage melodramas. You know: "I can't pay the rent!" "But you must pay the rent!' "Poor little orphan Dora!" "Out, onto the tundra with you and your small infant!" That kind of thing. And we now ask, "How could anyone ever have found this realistic?" I've said this and some friends have rolled their eyes at my take on it and suggested that I don't know anything and that maybe this style was popular just because it was campy and fun . . . and I've insisted, "No, this was *cutting-edge* stuff. They thought this was really *realistic*."

And then recently, without looking for it, I stumbled across this reprinting of a theatrical broadside from 1892:

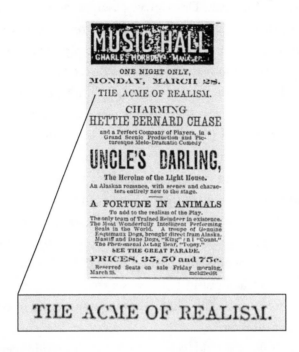

Look at that headline: The Acme of Realism. *So that* was what was driving this movement. And I personally wouldn't want to take a chance being part of something that might be dismissed in that way. Not that I'm deluded enough to think my own work will be around in a hundred years. Or a hundred days. But why take a chance? Finally, what my rants have been leading up to:

6 LITTLE CHEATS AND TRICKS
THAT CAN ADD UP TO A MORE INTIMATE 3RD PERSON

1. **All metaphors and turns of phrase**, though coming from the narrator, should be in keeping with the world and attitude of the protagonist. If he wouldn't have any understand-

ing of the thing, don't compare *his* thing to *that* thing. If your protagonist has never read a comic book in his life, then you shouldn't compare someone's whiskers to those of Uncle Scrooge McDuck. Descriptive passages, no matter how brilliant, that don't fit in the character's realm of reference can feel artificial—even if they're not coming directly out of that character's mouth as dialogue or a direct thought.

When I got to grad school, I didn't get this at all and my big thing was these really clever, Tom Robbins-style metaphors, and I was told to knock it off. But I didn't get it and didn't get it—I mean, the character himself wasn't saying these things—I was saying these things. . . . And I was told it doesn't matter that it's not coming out of his mouth: it pulls us away from the reality of this character's aura. It becomes more meta, focuses more on my writing and less on the bubble of empathy created around the character. When I finally got it, I got it, but it was a struggle to see. It's like an anachronism, really—like dropping a sports car into the Battle of Bull Run.

2. **Vocabulary** should be consistent with, or reminiscent of, the vocabulary known to, if not used by, the protagonist. Flavor all *narrative description* with the **diction, sentence structure, and rhythms of the protagonist** or *close* to it. This is one of the benefits of close-limited third person: We can cheat the language slightly. The narrator isn't *quite* as constrained as the protagonist might be. In first person, your character would use *this* word, word A, but you don't want to use word A, you want to use word B, only that word is much too foreign to his world. . . . In third person, you can use this other compromise word, word C. We're on that slightly adjustable dial.

I worked this angle heavily in my first novel where I had several major characters, each in their own chapters and sections, and I wanted to keep them clear and separate in the reader's mind at the start of each section without having to slap their names up at the top every time. So the "he" in one chapter is clearly the teenaged boy, based on the clipped sentences and the slang and the rhythms there, as opposed to the sections with the retired minister, which I intentionally wrote with a kind of King James Bible rhythm.

3. In dialogue, **shift the balance of the paraphrasing to the protagonist**. In the world of the protagonist, everything he or she says is of course brilliant and golden, but it registers more as a summary impression of what is said than an actual transcription. Save your pithy quotes for the supporting players. Again, this enhances the sense that we are cognitively processing the conversation the way the protagonist is. It places him or her in the center.

4. Once you've established the protagonist's name, use **pronouns**. We're often told that once you identify a character, rely on pronouns, slipping back into proper names only when you have to differentiate for clarity. But I believe in taking this general rule a step further: when I'm facing two "*he*"s in one sentence, for example, I choose to name the *non-protagonist,* the supporting character—Jimmy over there—and leave my protagonist with the plain pronoun. Because it's *him!* It's *her!* You know—*he! she!* The center of our universe! *That* guy. No nametags needed when you're walking around in their boots. . . .

If the name has some special meaning, congratulations—you're using all the parts of the buffalo. But symbolic character names don't become more symbolic by hammering them home. Endlessly repeating that his name is Frank or Newcomb or Medium Enis, just calls attention to the clever writing and distracts from the reality, and in this reality, he or she is the center of the world. In fact, each time you remind us his name is even something as unsymbolic as Joe, you're reintroducing us. Our intimacy takes one step back. Pronouns keep us on familiar terms, more connected with the character.

5. Don't be afraid to simply **tell the reader basic information**. We don't need to coax it out of you. *You* have nothing to be protective about—unlike, perhaps, your protagonist. "He was born in a Japanese internment camp. . . ."

6. **Stick with this one person's POV**—not multiple POV, not alternating, not nuanced shifts in perception like "little did he know. . ." or "meanwhile. . . ." The hardest part of this is resisting the urge to dip, just a teensy bit, into another's consciousness, to reveal some juicy tidbit of information or opinion. Just ask yourself: What little bit of information is worth popping the empathetic bubble I've carefully crafted around my protagonist?

   You've got a story about a guy with a mid-life crisis and we're with him when he buys a toupee and when he takes it home and you just want to tell us, just for a second, what his wife is secretly thinking when she sees it—resist that. Either find some other way to give us this information or do without. If you can't do without that information, you may be telling the wrong story. Maybe it's really her story.

True, these are small tweaks, but when done in concert, they do seem to add up to a significant effect. I must admit taking a certain perverse delight in the number of times readers have spoken to me about something I've written and incorrectly recalled it as being in first person when actually, if you go back and look, it was often in third. *Duped!*

Now, if it helps you to think of this as "HOW TO WRITE THIRD PERSON AS IF IT'S FIRST," that's fine. (Insert sigh here.) I think that *ignores* a lot of what I've been saying about the limitations and the true nature of first person . . . but all right, fine. I'll take it.

LAURA HENDRIE

Jaws of Life

Give up what you have to say, and you'll find something better.

—Richard Hugo

I write of the wish that comes true—
for some reason,
a terrifying concept.

—James M. Cain, The Butterfly

Ten years ago while finishing off a long letter to a friend, I decided to tack on a short anecdote about my father, who had been a professional gambler, but as soon as I started writing out this anecdote I realized I was telling it in my father's voice. I also realized that instead of a short and amusing anecdote to end a letter, this voice wanted to tell it as fiction. This voice was not going to let go. With the letter forgotten, I began to write as fast as I could, and a few hours later that same night I was rewarded with a second voice, one sounding somewhat like my mother's response to my father's gambling anecdotes, though not. Then a third voice, that of a child . . . then a fourth . . . and by the next morning I had a family of seven in Buffalo, Wyoming, in 1969 sitting on my desk, all of them waiting to tell their side of the story. I couldn't believe my luck. I knew the setting by heart, I had pivotal scenes already brewing, and my characters seemed loaded with intention. All I had to do was figure out which one would be the narrator and off we'd go.

And that was the problem. Every time I'd start the story rolling with one character, all the others would throw themselves flat on the page. They *all* wanted to go first. They all needed to be the narrator. And that old saw *show, don't tell*? They just wanted to tell. And tell and tell. They demanded to explain who they were and what they wanted and what they lacked and whom they loved. Interesting, maybe. But for momentum? It was as if we had bought our supplies and packed our bags and gassed up the car and squeezed in together to complete a long and arduous cross-country trip—but we were still sitting in the driveway arguing about who was going to drive.

I should mention this was not writer's block. I was writing flat out seven days a week, holidays included, and for a long, long time I was hopeful. I was sure the problem would sort itself out. All I had to do was hang in there and sooner or later these characters would get tired of talking so much. *Then* we could go somewhere.

Instead, four years and more than eight hundred pages later, I was half out of my mind. The narrative had changed focus so many times I couldn't remember what it was supposed to be about—and I still hadn't decided on a narrator. Every character I'd invented had talked his or her way out of the job. They had become too familiar to be interesting. Charles Baxter describes this phenomenon as "the crush of truth," and he's exactly right. In trying to clarify the nuanced complexity of these characters, I was slowly but surely crushing the mystery out of them, and instead of traveling through time in a novel, I felt as if I had created a car wreck with all my characters trapped inside screaming for help and me trying to get them out by banging on the windshield. With a thesaurus. I wasn't willing to give up—for better or worse, we'd become family—but I was beginning to sense a life-or-death situation inside that car, one requiring a rescue tool powerful enough to pry open the story and get some air in there.

Which was a tool I did not have.

When you're in graduate school, you've got all kinds of resources for solving writing problems: not just other writers and their reading lists, but workshops and lectures and peers with more expertise than you and books you've never read, never even heard of. If you want, you can suck the entire Western Canon up your nose and become a living resource yourself. Good idea. Do it. You won't be sorry. But *after* you graduate, when you find yourself stuck with a writing problem the likes of which you've never run into before, your only hope for survival will be books—and not just any books. I mean the first books, the main books, the books you love that encouraged you to start writing. These are the teachers you'll need, especially the ones still strong enough to grab you by the ear and make you sit up and listen. Some of these teachers you may have lost touch with over the years or outgrown. Others you've forgotten because there are so many other great teachers out there—but when you get tangled up in your prose, don't forget the books that first inspired you to write. Go looking through them for the heat source that, as Richard Hugo put it, can "ignite your need for words," and you may just discover the same source of heat missing from your own work.

So I turned to *Independent People* by Halldór Laxness. Nobody had ever mentioned this book in college or grad school, but it was my favorite book. It was also the book I'd re-read *just* before this family of seven from Wyoming had crashed into my life. So I read it a third time—but this time I read it like a writer searching for tools. I underlined. I took notes. I wrote commentaries tracing the structure, the pacing, the narrative arc, and so on—and I also tracked my own reactions. Every time I felt myself falling under the spell of the language, I stopped. Was it the characters? The action? The plot? What in this book seemed so seductive to me I couldn't stop reading it—and was it a tool I could somehow use in my own work?

Independent People is full of wonder, but as it turns out there's one guy I can't get enough of. His name is Bjartur and every time he appears on the page, I feel myself lean forward. Bjartur isn't just a well-drawn character. He's a larger-than-life phenomenon. Everything about him is magnified. His physical body is steel. His thoughts monumental. His dialogue astonishing. And when Bjartur goes into action? He not only hurls the story forward, he also bounces all the other characters around until they're just as electrifying as he is.

So after I realized how much Bjartur meant to me, I went looking through my bookcase for other examples of exaggerated characterization. I was stunned. Kurtz in *Heart of Darkness*. Cacciato in *Going after Cacciato*. Gatsby in *Great Gatsby*. Ahab in *Moby Dick*. The substitute teacher in Baxter's "Gryphon," Mrs. Shortly in Flannery O'Connor's "The Displaced Person," Bartleby the Scrivener in

Melville's story by the same name. More than half of the novels and stories I love are powered by exaggerated characters. And then I discovered that despite their uniqueness, these crazy larger-than-life characters share a set of unique properties realistic, life-sized characters seem to lack. Which to me meant that while they might prove bold enough to rescue my novel from internal collapse, they also might not be all that difficult to invent. And since I was entering the fifth year of work on my novel feeling I had not yet figured out how to begin it, they seemed worth a try.

★★★

Since *exaggeration* is a relative term, before we construct a larger-than-life character, we must know by comparison how to construct a *life-sized* character. Life-sized (i.e., realistic) characters, says Janet Burroway, are characters like you and me, people in whom we recognize—or at least *want* to recognize—some aspect of ourselves. Or as William Sloane said, the reader demands "Give me *me*" (36). You can invent a non-human character, of course—a talking dog, for example, as Chekhov did in the best dog story ever told, "Kashtanka"—but for your reader to care, that dog must exhibit some credible human—albeit, anthropomorphized—properties. Here's a quick review of those properties I culled from Burroway's book, *Writing Fiction: A Guide to Narrative Craft.*

  1. **Use Direct Characterization**. This means including specific, appropriate and carefully nuanced details of the character's physical appearance, thoughts, dialogue, and/or actions.

  2. **Choose the Right Point of View.** In order to deliver your carefully nuanced details, you must decide from what POV the story must be told. Should the narration shift from one character to another? Should it be confined to the main story teller? To a peripheral character? Would it be best to view the story omnisciently? It's

safe to say any POV can and will work as long as you pick the right one. If you don't, all those details of direct characterization you worked on won't be appropriate and you'll end up with a character who isn't credible.

3. **Place the Character in Time/Space.** Characters become credible when they're grounded in time and space. *Time* includes not only the present story-time, but historical details of backstory, and *space* includes not just letting us know the character's environment but showing us how he relates to it and how it affects her. As you know, fictional characters can exist in *any* time and in *any* space—including floating out there in gray matter in 3000 AD—but if you fail to mention *some* kind of time and space, the reader won't recognize them as credible. Which is precisely why Beckett *ignores* time and space—but that's another story. We're talking here about *realistic* characterization.

4. **Give the Character a Purpose.** Burroway defines purpose as "a desire which impels her or him to action" (124). This desire can be anything from wanting a glass of water to wanting five dollars to wanting a pretty face—but if you invent characters who have *no* purpose, they will have no reason for being in the story, and no matter how terrific *you* may think they are, your reader won't identify with them. Burroway says the purpose of most realistic characters is to find and fix themselves—and while I feel this is a simplistic notion, for the purpose of moving ahead toward the Jaws of Life, let's not argue.

5. **Give the Character Complexity**, or as Burroway puts it, "enough interior conflict that we recognize them as belonging to the contradictory human race" (124). This is important. Russell Banks once said, "The writer's only job is to tell the reader what the reader needs to know and the reader needs to know how to be human." Therefore, you can have fun creating all kinds of thrilling *external* conflicts for a character—a vicious landlord, an ex-spouse, starva-

tion, poverty, illness, rape, war, death—but your reader will be waiting for the internal struggle the character has when he faces the internal conflict with himself. Until you reveal that, we will not believe enough in his human credibility to actually care.

6. **Show the Character's Capacity for Change.** To be credible, realistic characters must show the capacity for dynamic change in understanding, commitment, values, and/or insights. Note: I am **not** saying characters must change—only that they must be *capable* of change. This may sound difficult, but if you've hard-wired the properties of **Purpose** and **Complexity**, your character will already automatically possess the capacity for dynamic change.

So there you have it. To create credible life-sized characters, all you have to do is include some nuanced details of their physical appearance, their thoughts, their dialogue, and their actions. Then choose the right POV, ground them firmly in time and space, and give them a purpose that propels them forward and an interior conflict that ensures they have the capacity for change. Easy, right?

Of course not. Creating credible realistic characters is a long and whimpering process, and as we all know, the devil is in the details. But then again, so is art.

★★★

Now on to an entirely different kind of fictional character. You could call it the *un*realistic character or the larger-than-life character or the exaggerated character, but these phrases aren't very interesting, and I certainly don't think they're powerful enough or fun enough to justify the kind of character we're here to talk about. So let's go with a metaphor instead. The Jaws of Life.

The Jaws of Life is a hydraulic tool invented for freeing people from car wrecks. It's shaped more or less like a pair of giant scissors. Here's how it works: You step up to the crushed car, you wedge the tip of the blades into a metal seam, you push a button, a hydraulic pump powers a piston, and with the force of several tons, the blades open, spreading the seam. Once the car is open, all you do is close the blades, unplug the hydraulics, and you're done. The Jaws of Life is a pretty amazing tool. Can you imagine how much manpower it took in the old days when firemen had to open crushed cars with crow bars and pick axes? Can you picture what it must have felt like to be trapped inside a vehicle the size of a bread box while a circular saw is screaming its way through the twisted metal right next to your ear? A Jaws of Life tool may be one of the most wondrous tools ever invented. All you do is push a button. Hydraulics do the rest. Simple, powerful, efficient, fast, and safe. And when you've got a group of beloved characters trapped inside a novel that's been crushed by your own clumsiness down to the size of a tinker's cup, a Jaws of Life character may be just what you need.

But who or what exactly are we talking about? Jaws of Life characters can be anyone—a pioneer, a millionaire, a substitute teacher, a farmwife, a doctor, a poet, a business man—but they arrive on the page in the same unique way a Jaws of Life tool arrives at a rescue scene: that is, *they arrive ready for action and they have no time to talk about it*. Listen to how one Jaws of Life introduces himself to a group of startled South American Indians:

> I was sent here. I'm not going to tell you who sent me or why. And I'm not going to tell you who I am or what I aim to do. That's just talk. I'm going to *show* you why I'm here. You go ahead and watch. And if you don't like what you see, you can kill me. (Theroux 136)

This is Allie Fox, the Jaws of Life character who runs the show in Paul Theroux's *The Mosquito Coast*, but every Jaws of Life character I studied would be willing to draw up the same contract. In blood, if necessary. Instead of *credible* characters in whom we recognize aspects of ourselves, these are *incredible* characters we want to watch. One-of-a-kind theatrical performers who step into the spotlight with such confidence that all eyes automatically turn to watch. That's why *only* one Jaws of Life can exist in a story. He must not only focus the reader on himself but focus the attention of all the other characters in his world. And if you're wondering why any writer in her right mind would want such a superego to step into a piece already too full of life-sized realistic characters, Allie Fox has the answer. With his usual modesty, he admits, "I'm much easier to remember than you are" (68). For this reason, Burroway's list of how to use details of appearance, thought, dialogue and action to create direct characterization can be completely reversed for a Jaws of Life. That may sound complicated, but it's not.

1. DIRECT CHARACTERIZATION.

Since you don't need to prove credibility anymore, a Jaws of Life character can jump straight out of your craziest imagination with no boundaries. Look at how Flannery O'Connor, for instance, uses details of appearance and action in the opening paragraph of her story "The Displaced Person" to introduce a Jaws of Life character we will never forget:

> Her arms were folded and as she mounted the prominence, she might have been the giant wife of the countryside, come out at some sign of danger to see what the trouble was. She stood on two tremendous legs, with the grand self-confidence of a mountain, and rose, up narrowing bulges of granite, to two icy blue points of light that pierced forward, surveying everything. (194)

A "giant wife of the countryside"? This is someone we've never seen before—and the narrator has the audacity to go further by *showing* us what, exactly, a giant wife looks like. Instead of just large legs or strong legs, she has "two tremendous legs," which, instead of walking up a hill, mount the prominence. Then a body rising up "narrowing bulges of granite" to her eyes, which are not merely organs of sight that can look at things but "two icy blue points of light that pierced forward, surveying everything." Mrs. Shortley is not just a large woman. She's not just larger than most. She is a geographical land mass. Nothing about her is half-hearted or subtle or nuanced. O'Connor super-sizes this creature with vibrant verbs ("mounting," "stood," "rose," "pierced"), pumped-up imagery, and magnified superlatives built to shock us awake. When this character steps up with "the grand self-confidence of a mountain," she may not seem believable—or even recognizable to us as a human being—but who can look away?

Why Mrs. Shortley, of course. While we're still gaping at her super-sized grandeur, she's already condemning the puniness of the human world down below her mound, which takes five indirect and wandering paragraphs to reveal themselves as "two negroes. . .hidden by a mulberry tree"(194), a priest who's "old" (195), Mrs. MacIntosh who's "small" (197) with "a nervous slide" (194), and the Displaced Person, who's "short" and "sway-backed" (195) with a wife "shaped like a peanut" and a child whose name sounds "like something you would name a bug" (195).

These similes and adjectives describe a world fraught with the human frailties we recognize all too well from our own lives. But note: Mrs. Shortley is *not* a part of that human mess. She's outside it, above it, superior to its messy imperfections, atop her mound. Her description allies more with the supernatural world than with anything that the ragtag realistic world down *there* can offer.

In less than a page then, Mrs. Shortley's magnified and singular appearance has not only caught our eye, but in disdainful opposition to the mournfully weak world of muddled characters below, she's focused the story hierarchically and kicked it into gear. Her steroidal presence demands action. Something's got to happen. We want to watch.

Because she is so utterly *in*credible in every way, she has started, focused, directed and *hurled* that story forward—a story which, without her, might have taken pages and pages to go anywhere.

It's important to note that not all Jaws of Life characters are physically enormous. Take Bartleby, the employee in Melville's "Bartleby, the Scrivener." He's got no meat on him at all, but as soon as his employer describes him as lacking any visible sign of *"anything ordinarily human,"* we know he's not going to be just another character. Melville has no intention of making him into someone we can recognize (2207). He's a Jaws of Life. He's going to be a complete change of pace from everyone else in the story. A mystery. A shock. Everything about him hypnotic and strange. Who *is* that guy?

Which brings up another reason for trying out a Jaws of Life character. You don't have to explain them. They are all-out bluffs. Instead of requiring a delicate blend of carefully nuanced details, you can slap them onto the page with a four-inch paintbrush in primary colors. Impossible metaphors, swollen superlatives, outrageous adjectives and all of it in unrestricted, authoritative language. A Jaws of Life character demands commitment to your wildest imagination, your boldest hyperbole and your most vivid daydreams.

Besides, they can be as fun to invent as anything you'll ever write.

So what kind of **thoughts** and **dialogue** can you invent for a Jaws of Life character? Not ordinary ones, that's for sure. Take Mrs. Shortley: While everybody else is fretting over money and talking about how to escape boredom and who's too lazy to work, she is seeing angels. She's sorting through the existence of evil as calmly as you might sort a box of colored chalk and proclaiming the Truth According to Her. All Jaws of Life characters do this. They don't have ordinary thoughts and they don't bother with ordinary dialogue. Their purpose is not to fit into the human world but to fix it—which is why in *Heart of Darkness*, the devotee of Kurtz says "You don't talk to that man—you listen to him" (127). For the writer who needs to clarify the moral themes of a story, a character who doesn't buckle under the truth is invaluable. Look at the opening of *The Mosquito Coast,* where the son of Allie Fox describes his father's conversation:

> We drove . . . the five miles into Northampton, Father talking the whole way about savages and the awfulness of America—how it got turned into a dope-smoking, door-locking, ulcerated danger-zone of rabid scavengers and criminal millionaires and moral sneaks. And look at the schools. And look at the politicians. And there wasn't a Harvard graduate who could change a flat-tire or do ten push-ups. And there were people in New York City who lived on pet food, who would kill you for a little loose change. Was that normal? If not, why did anyone put up with it?
>
> "I don't know," he said, replying to himself. "I'm just thinking out loud. . . ." (Theroux 3)

Note the rush and passion of the language. This man isn't chatting with his son. He isn't even teaching him. He's ranting. He's proclaiming the Truth—*his* truth—of what's wrong with the world and we sense it's not the first time. And when he suddenly ends his rant by dropping into the direct quotation "I don't know" and "I'm just thinking out loud," it's chilling. He's so focused on proclaiming what's gone wrong with the world, he isn't even aware that his son is listening.

On the other hand, just because a Jaws of Life has a vision of the truth doesn't mean he or she will do all the talking. Look at Bartleby in "Bartleby, the Scrivener." He has one answer for the business world: "I prefer not to"—and once he says it, he doesn't bother saying another word. In *The Great Gatsby,* Jay Gatsby arrives fully equipped with *his* answer as to how to fix *his* world—he's going to turn time backwards for Daisy—but he doesn't chat about it. He just *knows*. Like all Jaws of Life characters (and unlike most humans), he never bothers to question himself. That's what's so galvanizing about him. Epictetus said, "The world stands aside to let the man pass who knows where he's going" and whether it's a motor-mouth like Allie Fox, a religious prophet like Mrs. Shortley, an obsessed lover like Gatsby, a fanatic colonialist like Kurtz, or a living corpse like Bartleby, their obsessive belief in their own truth is what makes them so entertaining, not only for other characters within their stories but for readers as well.

So if a Jaws of Life arrives on the scene ready to fix the world, and if everything about him in appearance, dialogue, and thought is designed to make him *in*credible instead of credible, what will his actions be like? You guessed it. Freed from the gravitational pull of reality, this character moves like a dream. Watch Bjartur as he surveys his property:

> His movement was a response to the breeze, his gait in perfect harmony with the uneven land beneath his feet. . . . As soon as he halted, his dog came fawning . . . full of lice . . . starved of vitamins, for she stopped every now and again to eat grass. It was equally obvious she was wormy. And the man turned his face to the fresh wind of spring . . . savouring, in the submissiveness of his dog, the consciousness of his own power, the rapture of command, and sharing, for a second, in human nature's loftiest dream, like a general who looks over his troops and knows that with a word, he can send them into the charge. . . . (11)

Bjartur isn't just going for a walk here. His gait is in *perfect* harmony with nature. Vigorous, theatrical, and so commanding that his response to his poor little starved dog is to turn "his face to the fresh wind of spring." A terrific line, one telling us Bjartur is not only capable of ignoring suffering, he's impervious. This is not someone who's going to complain about blisters when he gets home or worry about his loved ones. He's free of all that. He's going to war against his world, and the confidence of his actions and gestures implies he may just have what it takes to win. If William Gass is right that "action *is* story," what better way to start out a novel than with a character who arrives on the scene not just prepared for action but already hurling himself headlong into it?

Imagination. That's what makes the Jaws of Life character so much fun. With a wild physical description to shock us awake, thoughts that are visionary instead of life-sized, dialogue that clarifies themes instead of trying to imitate human interaction, and actions that are magical instead of logical, this is one heck of a magician we're creating, one who can revitalize a story merely by stepping on stage.

2. CHOOSING THE RIGHT POINT OF VIEW

With realistic characters, choosing the right POV can be difficult, but when a Jaws of Life character steps on stage, the choice is easy. A Jaws of Life character can't tell his own story. He needs someone else to narrate the story for him, an exterior POV that can witness and applaud his performance without breaking the magical illusion of his supra-human power. This leaves only two choices. The first is *limited omniscience*, which O'Connor used to create Mrs. Shortley and Laxness used for Bjartur. But limited omniscience has problems. While it can jump inside a Jaws of Life character to reveal visionary thoughts, it *must* withdraw before any ordinary human thoughts crop up.

Most Jaws of Life stories, in fact, rely on a *peripheral narrator*—that is, a realistic character who can marvel at the performance but *not* get close enough to explain away the magic. Which leads to another tip: Peripheral narrators can't be just anybody. In terms of my car wreck metaphor, they have to be trapped inside the vehicle the Jaws of Life has arrived to fix. So the story of the obsessive Captain Ahab is narrated by a carefree Ishmael, the story of mad Kurtz by the very sane Marlow, and though Allie Fox in *The Mosquito Coast* is a non-stop ranter, it's his quiet son Charlie who tells the story. It's the peripheral character's desire for rescue that makes their narrative so compelling. Listen to the urgency with which the ordinary Nick Carraway describes the extraordinary Gatsby:

> He smiled understandingly—much more than understandingly. It was one of those rare smiles with a quality of eternal reassurance in it that you may come across four or five times in life. It faced—or seemed to face—the whole external world for an instant, and then concentrated on you with an irresistible prejudice in your favor. It understood you just as far as you wanted to be understood, believed in you as you would like to believe in yourself, and assured you that it had precisely the impression of you that, at your best, you hoped to convey. (48)

For Nick, this is no ordinary smile. Not only is it "much *more than* understandingly" but it offers "*eternal* reassurance." (Is there such a thing?) With dashes that sound like gasps, Nick tries to explain the magic of the smile away by saying "you *may* have seen it elsewhere," but no sooner has he regained his balance than he stumbles into "it faced," and then, gasping, "or *seemed* to face the whole external world." But how can a smile float free of its face to take in the *whole* external world? In desperation, Nick switches to an all-inclusive second-person "*you*" as if trying for consensus with his readers. But Nick's in a fix. He's never known anything like this smile—and when the power of it focuses in on him with that second italicized "*you,*" look at what happens to his language. His stumbling attempts to explain the magic disappear in a rolling unrestricted flood of belief. Nick can't explain it, but after that smile lands on him, he's not the same. He's been pulled out of his cramped realistic world and into a dream. This is a marvelous paragraph—and this change within the peripheral narrator is where a Jaws of Life character gets *really* fascinating and powerful—but more about that in a moment. For now, let's skim through the rest of Burroway's list of realistic characterization properties and see what a Jaws of Life character does with them.

3. PLACING THE CHARACTER IN TIME AND SPACE

When it comes to creating a Jaws of Life, you won't have to worry about his past. He doesn't have one. How he came to be is a mystery. That's why he's so easy to create quickly. He arrives with no baggage. He lives for the moment. You don't even have to think about inventing backstory for him.

The same goes for locating him in space. A Jaws of Life character may have to *live in* the realistic world, but he's not *of* it. He doesn't follow natural laws like everyone else. Which means a Jaws of Life does not need to eat. Or sleep. Or have sex. Or fear death. Attitudes, beliefs, and conventions that hold realistic characters back are nothing to a Jaws of Life. And unless he needs an assistant to accomplish his goals, intimacy and friendship are just not going to happen. Not for the Jaws of Life. Unfair as it might sound to call these characters hydraulic power tools, that's how they act. They're steel. They exist in a world all their own, and any connection they may have to reality (such as a husband, a wife, a child, a pet, or a basic biological need) does not concern them. In other words, just like the tool I named them after, these characters have no involvement with what's happening inside the car. Their only concern is fixing the car itself.[1]

GIVING THE CHARACTER PURPOSE, COMPLEXITY AND THE CAPACITY FOR DYNAMIC CHANGE

For a Jaws of Life character, Burroway's last three properties of characterization are more or less moot. Regarding **purpose,** realistic

---

1   This is the difference between a Jaws of Life character and what Flannery O'Connor defines as a *grotesque character*. Grotesques exist with other grotesques in a grotesque setting and their fight is against God. The Jaws of Life exists *alone* in a *realistic* setting with realistic characters and his fight is against the world. Thus, a Jaws of Life character may be grotesque, but not all grotesques can be a Jaws of Life. In fact, with the exception of Mrs. Shortley, very few are.

characters may need to find and fix themselves but a Jaws of Life character arrives to fix the world. Not himself. Rather than having what Burroway defines as "a desire that impels him to act," he *is* the desire (124). Nothing exists for him but his vision of the world as it should be, which means he has no interior conflicts. Instead of expanding inner **complexity,** all you have to do for a Jaws of Life is reveal inner *completeness.* There will be no self-doubt. No fear. No worry. Just a singular belief in the absolute correctness of his vision, and this—coupled with complete disregard for personal safety and human consequence—is what so galvanizes the story. Having arrived on the scene out of nowhere, having wedged himself into a messy and problematic and confused world that looks a lot like ours, against overwhelming odds, he's promising us the impossible: an escape from reality—and as his vision soars, we soar with him.

★★★

But wait a minute. If a Jaws of Life character doesn't need to find and fix himself, if he doesn't care about fitting into his world, if he lacks interior complexity so he never has any doubts or fears, what makes him so fascinating? And if he never questions the correctness of his own appearance, thoughts, speeches, or actions, how can he have Burroway's **capacity for dynamic change**? Well, I don't think he can—and when I first realized this, I was shocked. How could my man Bjartur be such a tool? If he can't change—if he's just as ridiculously bull-headed on the inside as he is on the outside—if he's steel all the way through and nothing is humanly recognizable about him, why should I care?

To answer that, I want to return to the POV narrator. As I said, a Jaws of Life character needs someone else to narrate the story and this narrator works best when he or she is a realistic character who has been swept up in the dream of being rescued from his own world by the Jaws of Life. He wants to explain it and so we listen—the same way we'd listen to someone whispering in our ear as we watch a performer on stage. But as we become aware that the performer is, for better or worse, not going to question himself and not going to change—*can't* change, no matter what—just as we're ready to turn to the peripheral narrator beside us to ask *who the hell is he?*—the Jaws of Life performs one spectacular grand finale. And this is what blew my mind.

He vanishes.

It may happen early on in the story, as in "The Displaced Person" where Mrs. Shortley is erased by a stroke, or it may happen nearer to the end, as in "Bartleby, the Scrivener" or the *Great Gatsby* or *Heart of Darkness* or dozens of other novels, where the Jaws of Life dies—but the amazing thing is, when the Jaws of Life dies, the story doesn't end. It gets handed off to someone else. And that someone is the peripheral narrator who's been telling us the story. Thus, the story of Bartleby becomes the story of the narrator who survives Bartleby. After Gatsby is gone, Nick is the story. After Kurtz dies in *Heart of Darkness,* Marlow becomes the story. And here is Charlie Fox, the long-suffering narrator in *The Mosquito Coast* taking over the story after his father has been killed. Charlie says:

> Once I had believed in Father, and the world had seemed very small and old. He was gone, and now I hardly believed in myself, and the world was limitless. A part of us had died with him, but the part of me that remained feared him more than ever, and still expected him, still heard his voice crying. (374)

A Jaws of Life character, in fact, cannot change himself—but *after* he's focused the story on himself, *after* he's jumpstarted the action, *after* he's upset all the other characters and fired up the imagination of the reader, just as his job as a literary endorphin is about to end for good, he hands the story back to the peripheral narrator, a realistic life-sized character who has gained enough credibility, perspective, and courage through the narrative to now tell the reader, at last, what it means to be human.

★★★

SAFETY MANUAL FOR THE JAWS OF LIFE

- Unless two Jaws of Life characters function as a unit, there can be only one Jaws of Life per story.
- They arrive fully assembled and prepared to act.
- They are incredible characters created through dramatic, theatrical, unpredictable, even absurd language, superlative metaphors, exaggerated details, no qualifiers, no nuance, and no hedging.
- They arrive saying NO to the natural laws of the realistic world.
- They do not doubt themselves.
- They do not act, speak, think, plan, or move half-heartedly.
- They do not admit to failure, weakness, or doubt.
- They do not reflect on their past.
- Instead of thoughts, they have visions.
- Instead of dialogue, they make prophesies that control the discourse of all others.
- They do not need to eat, sleep, have sex, worry, wonder, fear, fit in, or be intimate with others.
- They do not narrate their own story. Ever.
- They must leave before the story ends.
- After they leave, the story belongs to the realistic character who narrated it.

DAVID LONG

Nine Sentences

*Now we should consider the difficult question of how to be original.
You've doubtless been told there is nothing that hasn't been done
already—or, as Herman Melville, recalling Ecclesiastes, wrote in* Moby
Dick, *"Verily there is nothing new under the sun." Fortunately, there's
an unpretentious but strong idea that runs counter to this bleak pro-
nouncement. It was put most succinctly by a jazz musician who said,
"The way to be new is to be yourself."*

—Anna Held Audette

*Let me give you Dr. Don's Rule for Distinguished Writing. It's in the
voice . . . Do you want to wake up thirty years later facing a shelf of
voiceless grist with your name on the covers?*

—Donald Newlove

1.

I felt weak. I had to vomit in the corner—just a thimbleful of gray bile.

—Denis Johnson, "Work" in *Jesus' Son*

This is a Hall of Famer. The severely hung-over narrator is helping a friend salvage copper wire from a flood-ruined house. Consider how the moment plays without the last phrase—ordinary, vaguely squalid. Notice how deliciously out of place *thimbleful* is, the tension between it and *bile*. And yet, it's exactly the correct unit of measurement under the circumstances, and this last detail is what shakes loose our empathy—who hasn't found himself in such a state?

In Joyce Carol Oates' reworking of the events at Chappaquiddick (*Black Water*), after the unnamed Senator loses control of his car, the Mary Jo Kopechne character "heard, as the Toyota smashed into a guardrail that, rusted to lacework, appeared to give way without retarding the car's speed at all, The Senator's single startled expletive—'Hey!'" (11). It's *lacework,* as out of place as *thimbleful*, the very opposite of what we'd hope for in a guardrail. But haven't we seen iron rusted to a crumbly filigree? And doesn't this word, in its femininity, echo the violation of trust occurring in the larger story? Moments later, The Senator will kick the young staffer in the head as he wriggles free and swims, alone, to safety.

The presence or absence of a single word.

2.

It's hard to think of all the places and nights, Nicola's like a railway car, deep and gleaming, the crowd at the Un Deux Trois, Billy's. Unknown brilliant faces jammed at the bar. The dark, dramatic eye that blazes for a moment and disappears.

—James Salter, "American Express"

We always say too much. We use too many words, and we say things that no one needed us to say in the first place. Consider a hypothetical earlier draft of the above:

> It's hard to remember all those places we went back then, all those nights—for instance, Nicola's Bar, which was shaped like a railway car, deep and gleaming. I remember the crowds that used to collect at the Un Deux Trois, and at Billy's over on Second Avenue, the way brilliant faces I didn't recognize would be jammed along the bar, the way a dark, dramatic eye would blaze for a moment and disappear.

Seventy-four words. The final version has forty-four, more than a third fewer. So, your manuscript: Is it a 30-page story, or a 20-page story masquerading as a 30-page story—a 20-page story wearing a fat suit?

Now and then, we run into a writer whose style reduces expression to a stream of fragments—either to mimic the mind at work, or from the belief that the reader's ear will supply the missing words, or out of some other aesthetic preference. Here's Gulley Jimson narrating Joyce Cary's novel, *The Horse's Mouth*:

> No one in the bar but Coker. "Is it Willy again?" I asked her. Willy was Coker's young man. A warehouse clerk shaped like a soda water bottle. Face like a bird. All eyes and beak. Bass in the choir. Glider club. Sporty boy. A sparrowhawk. Terror to the girls. Coker was church, teetotal and no smoke. Willy her only weakness. (13)

And Annie Proulx in *The Shipping News*:

> The aunt let herself remember an October, the pond frozen, ice as colorless as a sadiron's plate, the clouds in thin rolls like pencils in a box. Crowberries encased in ice skins. The wind collapsed. Deepest silence, the vapor of her breath floated from her mouth. Distant soughing of waves. No dead grass trembled, no gull or turr flew. A pearl gray landscape. She was

eleven or twelve. Blue knit stockings, her mother's made-over dress. A boiled wool coat. English, tight under the arms, some castoff funneled through Pentecostal charity. (225)

Concision isn't the only virtue. Fullness, urgency, vividness—these all matter. Let me be clear: Stories shouldn't be under-imagined or faint of heart or too damn subtle for their own good. That said, each of us needs to come to terms with *paring down*. Two points, then: a) *no extra words*; b) as long as we're taking other chances, why not risk concision sometimes?

The Rings of Saturn, W.G. Sebald's book-length travelogue/novel/meditation on mortality, begins with a look at the life of Thomas Browne (1605-1682, physician, author of *Urn Burial*). For Browne, Sebald writes, there was "no antidote . . . against the opium of time" (24). Unfolding this idea, a few sentences later, he says: *Indeed, old families last not three oaks* (24).

That's what I'm talking about.

3.

I remember Sylvie walking through the house with a scarf tied around her hair, carrying a broom. Yet this was the time that leaves began to gather in the corners. They were leaves that had been through the winter, some of them worn to a net of veins. There were scraps of paper among them, crisp and strained from their mingling in the cold brown liquors of decay and regeneration. . . .

—Marilynne Robinson, *Housekeeping*

In 1066, so the story goes, the English, under newly crowned Harold II, lost the Battle of Hastings to William of Normandy, thereafter known as William the Conqueror. Before this intrusion, the Anglo-Saxons spoke what's called Old English, a mixed bag of words from German, Norse, Dutch, Celtic, and other sources (even Latin, from

Hadrian's time). Over the next four hundred years, Old English matured into Middle English, becoming recognizable as Modern English by the late 1400s. For a taste of this development, lay out pages of *Beowulf* (8th century), *The Canterbury Tales* (after 1387), and *Hamlet* (first printed 1603).

The lesson for us lies in what the Normans brought with them, namely French, one of the "romance" languages—that is, derived from Latin. For several hundred years, French was the language of the English court (many English surnames betray this derivation—for instance, *Spencer*, Lady Diana's family name, was originally *De Spencer*). The class of society with leisure to spend in reading and schooling, in discussing Big Ideas, used language derived from Latin. The people doing the day-to-day, hands-on work spoke Old English.

The Latin words surviving in contemporary English tend to be polysyllabic and abstract (*polysyllabic* and *abstract* are both Latinate). The Anglo-Saxon words tend to be, as the dictionary says, "plain and simple English, especially language that is blunt, monosyllabic, and often rude or vulgar."

I don't recommend being any more rude or vulgar than the situation calls for, but I do urge you to favor Anglo-Saxon words—they do their work quickly, they keep the writing physical and specific. Except, of course, when you need the nuance a Latinate word may give. Thus:

Latin: *implement, agriculture, architecture*
Anglo-Saxon: *rake, plow, seed, ax*

Latin: *animal, species*
Anglo-Saxon: *pig, dog, cow*

Latin: *locomotion, ambulate, pedestrian*
Anglo-Saxon: *walk, run, hop, creep, strut*

Latin: *oration, calculation, cogitate, premeditate*
Anglo-Saxon: *say, take stock, wonder, foresee*

Now look at the short passage from *Housekeeping* again (*house* and *keep* are Anglo-Saxon, by the way). Notice the short words, the preference for things, how sparingly Robinson uses words like *decay* and *regeneration*.

4.

The sap smell of the new boards mentholated the air.

—Deirdre McNamer, *One Sweet Quarrel*

William H. Gass (*Tests of Time*) puts it plainly: "Stories are strings of verbs" (11). Accurate verbs let us see (and hear, etc.) what's going on: "The deputy swung the rear of the skiff about and back-oared until the transom banged against the stone landing" (Cormac McCarthy, *Child of God*, 160). They call attention to *how* characters do things, because physical actions illuminate a character's nature—even small, humble ones. Their specificity lets us be in the moment with the character. Jack Driscoll's story "From Here to There," for instance, is told by a boy whose heartsick father has enlisted him to help paint enormous red numbers on the garage (so the mail can be delivered, including, possibly, a letter from the recently fled mother). We get a half-page of tight, getting-ready-to-paint detail putting us right there with the boy, observing: "Then he picked up a brush that was very stiff, and he bent the bristles back and forth until they softened some, and then he turned the brush handle down and slid it into his back pocket" (116).

Finally, verbs steeped in attitude can tell us how to *take* the information—literally, ironically, as bitter sarcasm, as wishful thinking or boast or as exuberant leap of imagination, as when Augie March blurts out: "A few days before I had been in Sicily where it was warm. Here it was freezing when I arrived; when I came out of the station the mountain stars were barking" (Saul Bellow, *The Adventures of Augie March*, 516). Barking stars!

It's possible to tart up your prose with too many geegaws, especially in the verb department. But we're not talking about window dressing, we're talking about getting it right. Deirdre McNamer's *mentholated* is almost too fussy yet isn't. First, she makes a stretch like this only when she needs to. Second, the pine boards belong to the just-built bleachers for the 1923 Dempsey-Gibbons prizefight, which the citizens of Shelby, Montana, have banked everything on. Calling attention to them is justified—entering, attendees *would* catch the scent of the wood, and the fact that most seats remain empty is an important detail. But beyond that, *mentholated* injects an odd note of cool, contrasting with the glaring midday heat, with the optimism of the city fathers—it's a note of premonition, a note from a minor scale.

Another point: We're often cautioned to stay away from the passive voice, and go light on the verb *to be*. Why? Passive verbs require no doers for their deeds—as in *Mistakes were made*. Who's responsible? We don't know; responsibility has been shirked. In addition, writing saturated with passiveness becomes, well, rather passive, rather inert, even turgid. The verb *to be* creates its own inertia. It says how things are but stops short of showing change. Since fiction is *about* change, it would make sense to emphasize the words that best portray it, to make the text rich in them. Furthermore, the verb *to be* is the bureaucrat's favorite. Everything in its cubbyhole, just *being*.

Years ago, I taught a class in technical writing, and our text contained this marvelous instruction: *Put the action in the verb*. I can even remember the sentence offered as example: *There are three components that this system relies upon*. Here's the concept: Every sentence contains a verb idea, but sometimes it's buried in, say, a dependent clause. The minds of English speakers are configured to receive information in a certain order—our basic sentence pattern is *subject, verb, object*. We can mess with this pattern all we want—messing with it can give the writing drama and pizzazz. Still, it's a good pattern. We shouldn't mess with it *needlessly*.

To recast our sentence, we find the real subject, then put the action in the verb: *This system relies on three components*. More direct, fewer words, no verb *to be*.

These days, as I revise, I routinely make this sort of change:

Draft: *The front door has a tendency to bang shut on its own.*
Rewrite: *The front door tends to bang shut on its own.*
Or: *The front door often bangs shut on its own.*

Draft: *Garberville is lacking in most ways when it comes to . . .*
Rewrite: *Garberville may lack . .*

Draft: *There was a row of young maples along the driveway.*
Rewrite: *Maple saplings lined the drive.*

But a final thought: verb forms exist because they fill a need. Sometimes we wish to emphasize that a thing or condition just *is*, so we call on the verb *to be*. Other times, receiving action is the point, or we don't need or want to get into who the doer is, so the passive voice is chosen.

Let me add that some writers, William Trevor, in particular, have a special affinity for the passive voice. Though the great majority of Trevor's sentences have active verbs, those in the passive sound quintessentially Trevorlike:

> "The cows were milked because no matter what the reason for Maureen's absence they had to be. The breakfast was placed on the kitchen table because no good would come of not taking food." ("Events at Drimaghleen" in *Family Sins & Other Stories*, 10)

> "Captain Gault thought it would be all right then: a lesson had been learnt." (*The Story of Lucy Gault*, 3)

"The old woman dies on the day before her hundredth birth-day. The stiffened body is taken from the bedroom, and the bedroom is empty now. An irony, the general opinion is, being taken at this particular time, but there it is." (*Felicia's Journey*, 202)

Similarly, we find a wonderful mastery of tone in Alice Munro's stories, resulting, in part, from her careful use of both *to be* and the passive voice:

There was a traditional belief in the family that Jimmy's grandmother was an excellent cook, and this might have been true at one time, but in recent years there had been a falling off. Economies were practiced beyond what there was any need for now. Jimmy's mother and his uncle made decent wages and his aunt Mary got a pension and the bicycle shop was fairly busy, but one egg was used instead of three and the meat loaf got an extra cup of oatmeal. There was an attempt to compensate by overdoing the Worcestershire sauce or sprin-kling too much nutmeg on the custard. ("The Love of a Good Woman" in *The Love of a Good Woman*, 28)

5.

She did understand, or at least she understood that she was supposed to understand. She understood, and said nothing about it, and prayed for the power to forgive, and did forgive. But he can't have found living with her forgiveness all that easy. Breakfast in a haze of forgiveness: coffee with forgive-ness, porridge with forgiveness, forgiveness on the buttered toast.

—Margaret Atwood, *The Blind Assassin*

Don't repeat yourself except on purpose, *for effect*. For common words or phrases, wait until the sound of the first use fades—a few lines. Truly uncommon words you may not be able to reuse in the same piece. I'm constantly circling words in student work, drawing lines to where the same word appears again unintentionally, clumsily. I do the same on my own drafts. A small thing, maybe. Yet writing gracefully involves getting the small things right. It's also a question of *credibility*. Writing should give the impression that *somebody's in charge*, that it's been examined line by line, that its parts communicate with each other.

But repeating words intentionally, gleefully, like Atwood's narrator, can be glorious. Very long sentences are often built on armatures of repeated words or phrases (see the bravura opening of Patrick Süskind's novel, *Perfume,* in Part 7, below) and, more generally, conscious repetition is one of the secrets behind writing rhythmic sentences. Hear the cadence of Pip's voice in the opening chapter of *Great Expectations*:

> A fearful man, all in coarse grey, with a great iron on his leg. A man with no hat, and with broken shoes, and with an old rag tied round his head. A man who had been soaked in water, and smothered in mud and lamed by stones, and cut by flints, and stung by nettles, and torn by briars, who limped and shivered, and glared and growled; and whose teeth chattered in his head as he seized me by the chin. (4)

And later in the book:

> It matters not what stranded ships repairing in dry docks I lost myself among, what old hulls of ships in course of being knocked to pieces, what ooze and slime and other dregs of tide, what yards of ship-builders and ship-breakers, what rusty anchors blindly biting into the ground though for years off duty, what mountainous country of accumulated casks and timber. . . . (360)

Listen to how the title phrase of Stuart Dybek's story, "We Didn't," becomes an incantation or refrain that links the images of an unconsummated love affair:

We didn't in the light; we didn't in darkness. We didn't in the fresh-cut summer grass or in the mounds of autumn leaves or on the snow where the moonlight threw down our shadows. We didn't in your room on the canopy bed you slept in, the bed you'd slept in as a child, or in the back seat of my father's rusted Rambler which smelled of the smoked chubs and kielbasa that he delivered on weekends from my Uncle Vincent's meat market. . . . At the dead end of our lovers' lane—a side street of abandoned factories—where I perfected the pinch that springs open a bra; behind the lilac bushes in Marquette Park where you first touched me through my jeans and your nipples, swollen against transparent cotton, seemed the shade of lilacs; in the balcony of the now defunct Clark Theater where I wiped popcorn salt from my palms and slid them up your thighs and you whispered, "I feel like Doris Day is watching us," we didn't. (233)

6.

It was as long a **night** as he could remember out of a great plenty of such **nights**. They lay on the wet **ground** by the side of the **road** under the **blanket**s with the **rain** rattling on the **tarp** and he held the boy and after a while the boy stopped shaking and after a while he **slept**. The thunder trundled away to the north and ceased and there was just the **rain**. He **slept** and woke and the **rain** slackened and after a while it stopped. He wondered if it was even midnight. He was **coughing**. . .

—Cormac McCarthy, *The Road*

But there's another reason to repeat words. Milan Kundera (*Testaments Betrayed*) puts it like this: "The rule: A word is repeated because it is important, because one wants its sound as well as its meaning to reverberate throughout a paragraph, a page" (114). Kundera believes that novels are built upon a base of *key words*. Comparing several translations of a passage from Kafka's *The Castle*, he decries the "synonymizing reflex." Where Kafka chose the same German words repeatedly, his translators try to "enrich" the vocabulary. "Richness of vocabulary," Kundera says, "is not a value in itself."

> The breadth of the vocabulary depends on the aesthetic intention governing the work. Carlos Fuentes's vocabulary is nearly dizzying in its richness. But Hemingway's is extremely narrow. The beauty of Fuentes' prose is bound up with the richness, the beauty of Hemingway's with the narrowness of vocabulary. (110)

Like Hemingway, Kafka restricted his vocabulary. The particular beauty of his prose depends, in part, on this fact. And now Kundera pushes his argument a step further. Whereas word choice should depend on "the author's personal style," translators often defer to "good English" (good French, good Icelandic, etc.), the conventional or textbook version of a language. That's the mistake, because, Kundera adds with a bold clarity: ". . . every author of some value transgresses against 'good style,' and in that transgression lies the originality (and hence the *raison d'être*) of his art" (110).

No novel I know better illustrates Kundera's point than Cormac McCarthy's post-apocalyptic masterpiece, *The Road*. As you'd expect, *road* is foremost among its key words. The others, drawn from a small reservoir of simple words, present the elemental conditions of the story: *cold, gray, ash, night, dark, rain, snow, water, fire, eat, jar/tin/can, sleep, ground, tarp, wrap, blanket, find, shiver, cough, gun/pistol, gone, nothing.* In one span of eight pages, for example, he chooses these words over 125 times. McCarthy is known for his love of arcane or archaic words (and there *are* a few in *The Road*), but his reliance on a straitened word pool seems utterly suited to the novel's charred landscape, to a world shorn of riches. McCarthy's "aesthetic intention," represented by these words, saturates *The Road*—every bit as much as attenuation saturates the sculptures of Giacometti, as human isolation saturates Edward Hopper's paintings, as shock and horror saturate Picasso's *Guernica*.

7.

In the period of which we speak, there reigned in the cities a stench barely conceivable to us modern men and women. The streets stank of manure, the courtyards of urine, the stairwells stank of moldering wood and rat droppings, the kitchens of spoiled cabbage and mutton fat; the unaired parlors stank of stale dust, the bed rooms of greasy sheets, damp feather-beds, and the pungently sweet aroma of chamberpots. The stench of sulphur rose from the chimneys, the stench of caustic lyes from the tanneries, and from the slaughterhouses came the stench of congealed blood. People stank of sweat and unwashed clothes; from their mouths came the stench of rotting teeth, from their bellies that of onions, and from their bodies, if they were no longer very young, came the stench of rancid cheese and sour milk and tumorous disease. The rivers stank, the marketplaces stank, the churches stank, it stank beneath the bridges and in the palaces. The peasant stank as did the priest, the apprentice as did his master's wife, the whole of the aristocracy stank, even the king himself stank, stank like a rank lion, and the queen like an old goat, summer and winter. For in the eighteenth century there was nothing to hinder bacteria busy at decomposition, and so there was no human activity, either constructive or deconstructive, no manifestation of germinating or decaying life that was not accompanied by stench.

—Patrick Süskind, *Perfume*

William Faulkner opens "Golden Land," a story about midlife debauchery, with a 258-word sentence. Rick Moody's novel, *Purple America,* begins:

Whosoever knows the latitudes of his mother's body, whoso-

ever has taken her into his arms and immersed her baptismally
in the first-floor tub, lifting one of her alabaster legs and then
the other over its lip, whosoever has bathed her with Wool-
worth's soaps in sample sizes, twisted the creaky taps and
tested the water on the inside of his wrist, and shovelled a couple tablespoons of rose bath salts under the billowing faucet,
marveling at their vermillion color, who has bent by hand her
sclerotic limbs, as if reassuring himself about the condition of
a hinge, and has kissed her on the part that separates the lobes
of her white hair, cooed her name while soaping underneath
the breast where he was once fed. . . . (4)

and churns along for several more pages, ending in "he shall never
die."

Colum McCann (*Let the Great World Spin*) presents Corrigan and
Jazzlyn's horrific van accident in one galloping 552-word sentence.
In Emily St. John Mandel's novel, *Last Night in Montreal,* we learn
that before he met Lilia, Eli had "never suffered, except insofar as
everyone does . . ." then the sentence morphs into a list of his lesser
sufferings that runs on another 315 words (10-11). Call this showing
off, but I prefer to think of it as the writer at play—in the sense that
baseball or soccer is played, or the blues. It's riffing, taking a solo.
You do it *once in a while.*

The long sentence gives you extra room to work, lets you unfold
meaning gradually, with a sense of drama, lets the words come at the
reader in waves, building toward a final note. Here's Tom McGuane
(*Nobody's Angel*):

In very early spring before the creeks flooded, before the first
bridges washed away and the big river turned dark, before the
snow was gone from the rugged shadows and the drowned
livestock tumbled up in the brushy banks, Patrick found the
airplane with his binoculars—a single ripped glimmer of fuse-
lage visible a matter of hours before the next flurry concealed
it for another month but not before Patrick had memorized

the deep-blue ultramontane declivity at the top of the fear-some mountain and begun speculating if in May he could get a horse through the last ten thousand yards of deadfall and look into the pilot's eyes. (5)

8.

I got the car and went home.

—William Faulkner, *The Sound and the Fury*

I had in mind juxtaposing some John Grisham sentences with sentences by literary writers. Singling out Grisham was a cheap shot, sour grapes on my part, owing to the ubiquity of his books on flights I took. Anyway, I expected to find one *The man walked down the street* sort of sentence after another. I was going to point out how slapdash and tin-eared and unsurprising they were. So I sat down at the branch library one morning and popped open Grishams and set about jotting down representative samples. But, really, the sentences I found weren't so bad. They got the job done, they stayed out of the story's way. In short, it felt wrong to complain about them. You find the same stuff among the greats:

> "He strolled out of the post office and turned to the right."
> (James Joyce, *Ulysses*, 73)

> "The large room was full of people."
> (F. Scott Fitzgerald, *The Great Gatsby*, 51)

> "Charles came into the parlor."
> (Gustave Flaubert, *Madame Bovary*, 134)

While we've taken an oath not to write dull sentences, many of our sentences are simple and straightforward. Workhorses. It's good to keep Occam's Razor in mind (the principle attributed to 14th-century logician William of Occam that says when trying to explain a phenomenon, "entities should not be multiplied beyond necessity.")

It's often paraphrased as "All other things being equal, the simplest solution is the best." For our purposes, we could say: Don't make your writing trickier, more complicated, more glammed up than it needs to be.

We could add that unadorned, even homely sentences, have a certain beauty. For instance, from Stewart O'Nan's short novel, *Last Night at the Lobster*: "With oven mitts he delivers the pots to Leron, who dumps them steaming into the gurgling InSinkErator" (128). We could observe, further, that a series of plain sentences often builds a context for one zinger, as in one of my new favorites, *Manhattan Transfer* (John Dos Passos): "She stood in the middle of the street waiting for the uptown car. An occasional taxi whizzed by her. From the river on the warm wind came the long moan of a steamboat whistle. In the pit inside her thousands of gnomes were building tall brittle glittering towers" (153-4).

9.

If it was true that there was no God, no Son, no Holy Mother, nor any of the lesser saints, what had happened to all my prayers? Were they perhaps circling in the empty heaven like a flock of birds whose nests had been destroyed by boys?

—Jerzy Kosiński, *The Painted Bird*

There's no way to know for certain which sentences are unique in the vast and checkered history of human utterance. Yet, every good reader knows the sensation of coming across a line or short passage that feels as though it's never been said before. Art critic Robert Hughes termed reaction to the seismic upheaval in the fine art world of the 1900s the "shock of the new." The sentences I'm referring to *do* sometimes shock, but more often they give us an odd shiver, a feeling of momentary displacement, or of being differently awake. Likewise, newness is vital, but it's a *by-product*, not the thing itself.

What I so much crave when I read, and recognize in these few amazing sentences, is the sound of someone's mind working at a peak of concentration. Originality is the *outcome* of that deep attention.

Sadly, most often we get only what we expect (or much *less*). Knee-jerk word combinations; bland, inoffensive tone; prepackaged figures of speech . . . a long checklist of pleasure-killers. Worse, I think, is the complacent state of mind that generates such writing, its docile agreement with the status quo.

A little epiphany from my long-ago stint in Montana's Writers-in-Schools Program: I was working with a middle-school class, trying to stir up conversation about a poem I'd brought in. A boy complained that it "didn't make sense." How I answered him is anyone's guess. But, later, it occurred to me that when we talk about "making sense," we really mean "conforming to an existing, agreed-upon sense," whereas the verb "to make" ordinarily implies *creating* something. In subsequent classes, I began talking about writers making *new sense*, where it hadn't exist before, out of whatever spare parts of language were at hand. Over time, this paradigm—*making regular sense vs. making sense anew*—became embedded in how I read and teach fiction.

Now, *The Painted Bird*. It's the story of a young boy abandoned in Eastern Europe during the Holocaust, a very grim, very tough novel, saturated with cruelty, mercilessness, disease, and abject superstition—if we didn't know better, we'd think we were adrift in the Dark Ages or in the darkest of fairy tales. It's tempting to think that Kosiński's fine writing renders the horrible parts tolerable—redeems them, so to speak. But that's not it at all. The writing is fine because of what I called, a moment ago, his "deep attention"; the horrible parts *aren't* tolerable, they're horrible.

Knowing no other life, the boy reports what he sees, what he lives through, what he imagines, without irony. *If the action is hot,* writers are often told, *let the language be cool.* And so Kosiński's narrator is most matter of fact when depicting atrocity. I hesitate to offer an example, but on page after page we find passages such as:

> . . .when [Ludmilla] was very young and innocent her parents ordered her to get married to the son of the village psalmist, notorious for his ugliness and cruelty. Ludmilla refused, infuriating her fiancé so much that he enticed her outside the village where an entire herd of drunken peasants raped the girl until she lost consciousness. (48)

And far worse. These accounts are essential to Kosiński's story, but the spaces between them are seeded with lines in a voice that feels truly unprecedented, the sound of a one-of-a-kind consciousness—for instance, the one heading this section, or the boy's stunning description of the old peasant woman who, briefly, shelters him:

> She looked like an old green-gray puffball, rotten through and waiting for a last gust of wind to blow out the black dry dust from inside. (5)

In the end, it's this making of new sense that sets *The Painted Bird* apart, that lodges it so tenaciously in our memories.

MARY HELEN STEFANIAK

Fiction in First Person: Narrators We Love— And Those We Love to Hate

Learning to write is a simple process: Read something, then write something; read something else, then write something else. And show in your writing what you have read.

—Marvin Bell

Flannery O'Connor once said that, as a fiction writer, "You can do anything you can get away with," which sounds like good news until she adds, "but nobody has ever gotten away with much." O'Connor apparently found first-person narrators so difficult to get away with that she avoided them completely, following advice she received as a young writer from novelist Caroline Gordon to make her (third-person) narrators all sound as articulate and objective as Samuel Johnson. I'm not sure if Gordon, who was the wife of influential critic Allen Tate, meant to say that *all* fictional narrators should sound like Samuel Johnson, or if her advice was tailored to O'Connor's fiction. Either way, Flannery took it to heart. The result, in story after story, is a dynamic contrast between the third-person narrative and the colorful dialogue of the characters, so many of them uneducated folks from O'Connor's version of the rural South. Here, for example, is a bit of scene from a story in her first collection, *A Good Man Is Hard to Find*. Mr. Head is about to take his grandson Nelson on a trip to the big city of Atlanta:

> "If you ain't been there in fifteen years, how you know you'll be able to find your way about?" Nelson had asked. "How you know it hasn't changed some?"
> "Have you ever," Mr. Head had asked, "seen me lost?"
> Nelson certainly had not but he was a child who was never satisfied until he had given an impudent answer and he replied, "It's nowhere around here to get lost at." (105)

If O'Connor let Nelson tell his own story, the first-person narrator would have to sound more like Huck Finn than Samuel Johnson. More to the point, the measured voice and omniscient perspective of her third-person narrator would not be there to give the reader a familiar position from which to observe these two headstrong but clueless and soon-to-be-chastened down-home Southern characters. Like Chekhov, who also avoided writing fiction in first person, O'Connor prefers to present her grotesques from a third-person narrative stance that seems "as objective as a chemist," as Chekhov once described his own approach. It's as though she can't trust them to win the reader over "in their own words"—a wise choice, perhaps, given the crew of self-satisfied racists, murderers, hypocrites, and busybodies who come in for a shot of redemption in her fiction.

By now you may be wondering why I have begun this discussion of "fiction in first person" by talking about two writers—O'Connor and Chekhov—who avoided using first-person point of view in their fiction. I have my reasons, the first of which is to emphasize that despite its widespread use by contemporary fiction writers, first-person narration is not a given, not the default mode, but a strategic choice. It's a choice that requires the writer not only to give up his or her authorial omniscience and hand over the reins of the story to one of the characters, but also (and here's the rub) to *create a voice that will win the reader over*—even if it's the voice of a narrow-minded busybody, an unschooled country boy, a megalomaniac, or a murderer. Like everything else in a work of fiction, a first-person narrator is something the writer has to get away with.

The best way to find out how to create a first-person narrator who will, despite all failings and limitations, succeed at winning the reader over is to follow William Faulkner's advice to "read everything, and ask yourself how they do it." I don't claim to have read everything—I only wish—but I have looked closely at fiction in the first person and asked myself how various first-person narrators have managed to win me over, or at least, to keep me reading. I plan to share what I've learned with you—but first, one more caveat.

This one comes from the work of a different O'Connor— Frank—an Irish writer who spent many years in New York and who did us the enormous favor of writing a story called "Repentance," which was published in Ireland in *Lovat Dickson's Magazine* in 1935, and then of rewriting it (as he was wont to do) for publication in the United States, where it appeared as "First Confession" in a collection

of his stories published by Knopf in 1951. Comparing these two versions of the same story is an invaluable lesson in revision: Summaries
are turned to scenes (and, less often, vice versa), material is omitted
or rearranged, the main character's name is changed from Micky to
Jackie, and—most important for our purposes here—the narrative
point of view makes a shift from third-person in the earlier "Repentance" to first-person narration in "First Confession."

The single most instructive thing about the revision is how the
shift from the third- to first-person point of view *increases* the distance between the reader and the action of the story—the opposite
of what we might expect. The increase is due, in principle, to the
fact that the narrator of "First Confession" is looking back at past
events, but the retrospective aspect of the narrative is something the
reader quickly forgets as we follow poor Micky or Jackie through the
travails of living with his grandmother and making his first confession. As you read these two passages, one from each version, consider
which one brings us closer, which one, in fact, immerses us in the
naked horror the boy feels toward his grandmother:

> As if that wasn't enough there was the sight of his grand-
> mother to upset him when he came home to dinner. His
> grandmother, his father's mother, had come to live with them
> and he hated her. He hated her wrinkled face and untidy grey
> hair; he hated her snuff-taking and the bare dirty feet on
> which she plodded about the kitchen; he hated the great meal
> of potatoes she cooked for herself morning and evening, the
> way she spread a potful on the table, peeled them with her
> fingers, dipped them in a heap of salt and then ate them. He
> hated her blind fumbling for things, and the way she produced
> snuff-box and purse and even sweets from her bosom, unpin-
> ning her blouse and shivering. ("Repentance," 71)

Compare that passage to this one, in first person:

> All the trouble began when my grandfather died and my

grandmother—my father's mother—came to live with us. Relations in the one house are a strain at the best of times, but, to make matters worse, my grandmother was a real old countrywoman and quite unsuited to the life in town. She had a fat, wrinkled old face, and, to Mother's great indignation, went around the house in bare feet—the boots had her crippled, she said. For dinner she had a jug of porter and a pot of potatoes with—sometimes—a bit of salt fish, and she poured out the potatoes on the table and ate them slowly, with great relish, using her fingers by way of a fork. ("First Confession," 79)

If your reason for using a first-person narrator is to bring the reader closer to that character's perspective, then compare these two passages and think again. The "psychic distance"—to use John Gardner's term—between the reader and the boy is nonexistent in "Repentance" with its third-person point of view. Not only are we *told* four times that "he hated her," but the word choice and details make her as distasteful to the reader as she is to the boy: she is fat, wrinkled, old, grey, snuff-taking; she has bare dirty feet, eats potatoes peeled with her fingers; she's given to blind fumbling, unbuttoning her blouse, and shivering. By contrast, the first-person narrator in "First Confession" handles the grandmother with a little humor and tolerance, if not compassion: she's "quite unsuited to the life in town," "the boots had her crippled," and she eats those potatoes "with great relish, using her fingers by way of a fork." Humor and tolerance require a kind of distance, a larger perspective that the boy in "Repentance" certainly does not share.

The fact is that a first-person narrator, being a solidly created character in his or her own right, tends to hold the reader at some distance, whether large or small, while a third-person narrator seems to "disappear" and thus can draw the reader as close to the characters and action as you the writer want them to be.

All right, now that I have, I hope, convinced you that narrating fiction in the first person should be a strategic choice—not a default mode—and one that does not necessarily close the distance between reader and character or action, let's look at a passage from a work of first-person fiction and ask ourselves how the writer created a voice that wins us over:

> She told me to pray every day, and whatever I asked for I would get it. But it warn't so. I tried it. Once I got a fish-line but no hooks. It warn't any good to me without hooks. I tried for the hooks three or four times, but somehow I couldn't make it work. By-and-by, one day, I asked Miss Watson to try for me, but she said I was a fool. She never told me why, and I couldn't make it out no way. . . .
>
> I set down, one time, back in the woods, and had a long think about it. I says to myself, if a body can get anything they pray for, why don't Deacon Winn get back the money he lost on pork? Why can't the widow get back her silver snuff-box that was stole? Why can't Miss Watson fat up? (15)

I expect that Mark Twain knew that getting away with a narrating voice like Huck's would be a challenge. How could he get his mostly middle-class readers to empathize and even identify with a boy unlike anyone they would choose to spend their time with under most circumstances? Huck is desperately poor and largely "uncivilized." He has no family, no formal education, and really very little in common, in terms of culture and experience, with the middle-class characters in the book, much less with readers like us. On top of all that, he talks funny—or at least, he "talks" in a way that looks funny on the page. It's almost as though Twain wanted to challenge himself by piling up as many obstacles as he could between Huck and the typical reader. Of course, the creation of a narrating character like Huckleberry Finn is a strategic move designed to a) put the reader in some unfamiliar shoes, and b) teach the reader some surprising lessons about what it means to be civilized. We all know that. But before Twain could accomplish those lofty goals, he had to create a narrative voice that would win the reader over.

How does he do it? By endowing Huck with a full slate of qualities that we find again and again in successful first-person narrators—the kind who keep us reading. As a narrator and as a character, Huck exhibits: 1) cluelessness, 2) vulnerability, 3) honesty, 4) humor, 5) exceptional powers of observation, and 6) a way with words—an often *irresistible* way with words.

Cluelessness—aka ignorance or innocence—is what we notice first in Huck's voice and character, but it's a cluelessness accompanied by exceptional powers of observation. By puzzling over things, Huck can point out the absurdities, large and small, and the necessary hypocrisy of "civilization" without coming across as a naysayer or a know-it-all. He is sincere (in a way that Holden Caulfield will claim to be a hundred years later). He's honest about his ignorance, even though it makes him all the more vulnerable to the machinations of the widow and Miss Watson and others whose intentions are much darker than theirs. Indeed, that vulnerability is put to excellent ironic use throughout the novel. Who can resist Huck's reasoning against the efficacy of prayer when it ends with the question "Why can't Miss Watson fat up?" The dialect that could set us apart from the narrator instead draws us in with its humor and surprises. He has a colorfully nonstandard way with words. Characteristics like these —cluelessness, vulnerability, humor, etc.—can overcome substantial potential resistance to your narrator. In fact, I've found that even *one* of these qualities can be enough to help you get away with a first-person point of view.

Let's consider another first-person narrator. This one—a 19-year-old supermarket cashier named Sammy—is from the early John Updike story, "A & P." The story starts this way:

> In walks these three girls in nothing but bathing suits. I'm in the third check-out slot, with my back to the door, so I don't see them until they're over by the bread. The one that caught my eye first was the one in the plaid green two-piece.

She was a chunky kid, with a good tan and a sweet broad soft-looking can with those two crescents of white just under it, where the sun never seems to hit, at the top of the backs of her legs. I stood there with my hand on a box of HiHo crackers trying to remember if I rang it up or not. I ring it up again and the customer starts giving me hell. She's one of these cash-register-watchers, a witch about fifty with rouge on her cheekbones and no eyebrows, and I know it made her day to trip me up. She'd been watching cash registers forty years and probably never seen a mistake before.

By the time I got her feathers smoothed and her goodies into a bag—she gives me a little snort in passing, if she'd been born at the right time they would have burned her over in Salem—by the time I get her on her way the girls had circled around the bread and were coming back, without a pushcart, back my way along the counters, in the aisle between the check-outs and the Special bins. They didn't even have shoes on. (227)

How does Updike get away with this one? The narrator's attitude toward women leaves a lot to be desired, but even readers who are understandably put off by his sexism have to admit that the kid has a way with words—plus, a penchant for details that makes him notice not only the girl's "sweet, broad, soft-looking can" but "those two crescents of white just under it, where the sun never seems to hit, at the top of the backs of her legs." A little later he describes the girl's breasts as "the two smoothest scoops of vanilla I had ever known there were," although all he has seen of them is the "shining rim" of pale skin at the top of her swimsuit. The kid's powers of observation, his reporting of this kind of detail, not only lets us see the girl in vivid and surprising ways but, more importantly, makes us see the world through the narrator's eyes and tells us a heap about him in the meantime. (I like the "hand on a box of HiHo crackers," too.) I don't have to subscribe to the narrator's (or Updike's) view of the world to empathize at the end of the story when Sammy's cluelessness about women and the world—and his limited place in it—leads him to make a quietly disastrous and irrevocable mistake.

For many years, Salinger's "For Esmé, with Love and Squalor" was my favorite short story in the world. A young American soldier about to be shipped out for the D-Day invasion has a certain claim on our sympathy to begin with, but his observation of details and his way with words are what make this character so effective—and affecting—as the narrator of the story. Through his eyes and in his words, Esmé and her little brother Charles are more vivid and memorable than any real-life children the reader will ever encounter in an English tearoom or anywhere else. Here's a glimpse, with the details and images I find most heart-breaking in italics (mine):

> She was about thirteen, with straight ash-blond hair of ear-lobe length, an exquisite forehead, and blasé eyes that, I thought, might very possibly have counted the house. Her voice was distinctly separate from the other children's voices, and not just because she was seated nearest me. It had the best upper register, the sweetest-sounding, the surest, and it automatically led the way. The young lady, however, seemed slightly bored with her own singing ability, or perhaps just with the time and place; twice, between verses, I saw her yawn. It was *a ladylike yawn, a closed-mouth yawn, but you couldn't miss it; her nostril wings gave her away.*
>
> . . . While I was still on my first cup of tea, the young lady I had been watching and listening to in the choir came into the tearoom. Her hair was soaking wet and the rims of both ears were showing. She was with a very small boy, unmistakably her brother, *whose cap she removed by lifting it off his head with two fingers, as if it were a laboratory specimen.* (90-1)

"For Esmé . . ." is well worth studying for the way Salinger keeps the narrator's—and thus the reader's—attention on Esmé and Charles, rather than focusing inwardly on his thoughts or feelings or fears. This outward focus is why I find the "I" of "For Esmé, With Love and Squalor" considerably more appealing than Holden Caulfield in *The Catcher in the Rye*, although Salinger gives Holden plenty of observations to report as well:

> I'm not going to tell you my whole goddam autobiography or anything. I'll just tell you about this madman stuff that happened to me around last Christmas just before I got pretty run-down and had to come out here and take it easy. I mean that's all I told D.B. about, and he's my *brother* and all. He's in Hollywood. That isn't too far from this crumby place, and he comes over and visits me practically every weekend. He's going to drive me home when I go home next month maybe. He just got a Jaguar. One of those little English jobs that can do around two hundred miles an hour. It cost him damn near four thousand bucks. He's got a lot of dough, now. He didn't *used* to. He used to be just a regular writer, when he was home. (1)

Salinger reveals Holden's vulnerability with just a mention of "this madman stuff that happened to me around last Christmas" and then makes him shift his gears and our gaze to his brother. A first-person narrator's vulnerability is best seen obliquely by the reader, rather than dwelt upon by the character. Here's the opening of the novel *Ellen Foster* by Kaye Gibbons. The eleven-year-old narrator does not dwell on her vulnerability; as a result, her situation hits us all the harder:

> When I was little I would think of ways to kill my daddy. I would figure out this or that way and run it down through my head until it got easy.
> The way I liked best was letting go a poisonous spider in his bed. It would bite him and he'd be dead and swollen up and I would shudder to find him so. Of course I would call the rescue squad and tell them to come quick something's the matter with my daddy. When they come in the house I'm all in a state of shock and just don't know how to act what with

two colored boys heaving my dead daddy onto a roller cot. I just stand in the door and look like I'm shaking all over.

But I did not kill my daddy. He drank his own self to death the year after the County moved me out. I heard how they found him shut up in the house dead and everything. Next thing I know he's in the ground and the house is rented out to a family of four. (1)

This little girl is not clueless, but she is a little girl, and we hate to think of what she might have gone through to make her "think up ways to kill my daddy." We might be glad that Ellen Foster doesn't live next door, but we're on her side, and we keep reading. Gibbons makes a wise choice, I think, in creating Ellen's voice—"But I did not kill my daddy. He drank his own self to death"—instead of handing the story over to a Samuel Johnson-type omniscient narrator, who might say, "But Ellen Foster did not kill her father. He drank himself to death the year after County welfare authorities had removed her from his custody.") That "my daddy" tugs at us, especially when it comes in the same breath as "kill."

And how does Nabokov get away with the mesmerizing voice of Humbert Humbert—pedophile, kidnapper, fraud? He starts with Humbert's love of—and way with—words, then moves quickly to his tragic love for "a certain initial girl-child" back when Humbert himself was a boy:

Lolita, light of my life, fire of my loins. My sin, my soul. Lo-lee-ta: the tip of the tongue taking a trip of three steps down the palate to tap, at three, on the teeth. Lo. Lee. Ta.

She was Lo, plain Lo, in the morning, standing four feet ten in one sock. She was Lola in slacks. She was Dolly at school. She was Dolores on the dotted line. But in my arms she was always Lolita.

Did she have a precursor? She did, indeed she did. In point of fact, there might have been no Lolita at all had I not loved, one summer, a certain initial girl-child. In a princedom by the sea. Oh when? About as many years before Lolita was born as my age was that summer. You can always count on a murderer for a fancy prose style.

Ladies and gentlemen of the jury, exhibit number one is what the seraphs, the misinformed, simple, noble-winged seraphs, envied. Look at this tangle of thorns. (11)

Throughout the novel, Nabokov makes us feel the helpless longing of middle-aged Humbert for the girl child Lolita, but this passage paints the old lecher as a boy, caught in the throes of a childhood crush:

At first, Annabel and I talked of peripheral affairs. She kept lifting handfuls of fine sand and letting it pour through her fingers. . . . The softness and fragility of baby animals caused us the same intense pain. She wanted to be a nurse in some famished Asiatic country; I wanted to be a famous spy.

All at once we were madly, clumsily, shamelessly, agonizingly in love with each other . . . the only privacy we were allowed was to be out of earshot but not out of sight on the populous part of the *plage*. There, on the soft sand, a few feet away from our elders, we would sprawl all morning, in a petrified paroxysm of desire, and take advantage of every blessed quirk in space and time to touch each other: her hand, half-hidden in the sand, would creep toward me, its slender brown fingers sleepwalking nearer and nearer; then, her opalescent knee would start on a long cautious journey; sometimes a chance rampart built by younger children granted us sufficient concealment to graze each other's salty lips . . . (14)

Whether we feel sorry for Humbert as a case of arrested development or simply recognize in the vivid recreation of his experience a paralyzing youthful crush of our own, Nabokov marshals Humbert's way with words, his powerful observation of detail, and a gift for sly humor—especially the humor inherent in unbridled alliteration—all of them handsome rewards that keep the reader reading. It's a very smart move on Nabokov's part. Pedophile and kidnapper Humbert may be, but there was a time when he was a pretty typical pre-adolescent boy who wanted to be a famous spy.

Suppose there was a rule that all first-person narrators must possess *at least* one of the aforementioned qualities: 1) vulnerability, 2) cluelessness, 3) honesty, 4) humor, 5) exceptional powers of observation, 6) an irresistible way with words. How do your favorite narrators measure up?

And why *these* qualities? The last three in the list explain themselves: They are qualities we appreciate for their own sake in all kinds of situations, not just in fiction. The value of the first three lies, perhaps, in the reader's own set of insecurities and desires. Admit it or not, we all feel vulnerable and clueless a great deal of the time. Maybe that's why we are likely to empathize with narrators who find themselves in tough spots, those who admit—to themselves and thus to the reader—that they are baffled by the world. Even a serial killer like Patrick Bateman can be made to seem, momentarily, almost human when he admits, as he does repeatedly in Bret Easton Ellis's *American Psycho:* "Something horrible was happening inside of me and yet I couldn't figure out why" (282).

The Brilliance of the Simple Line

My heart is moved by all I cannot save:
so much has been destroyed

I have to cast my lot with those
who age after age, perversely,

with no extraordinary power,
reconstitute the world.

—Adrienne Rich

After Listening to a Lecture on Form

I'm afraid of the mountains
in this thin glacial air,
of going to sleep in their shadow,
that the granite inside them
and the threads of bright metal
may not hold once the night comes.

I'm afraid of so many people talking,
the cat smile of the poetry scholar, his ridged skull.
When he spoke of measure
I could feel my wristwatch tighten,
remembered the payments coming due
on my daughter's tuition.

I went down by the horses.
Birds were walking in the hay
beside the feet of the Appaloosa.
He looked at me sideways
in the swaying dusk.
The wheels of his jawbones,
the great vein in his face.

Sometimes I can hardly breathe. (23)

—*Joseph Millar*

★★★

One thing I have always admired about my husband is that he can simply write a poem. Another way to say this is that he can write a poem without much "decoration," fanfare, or frill. No extra words, and every word counts. It's difficult to write a simple poem, a poem of precision, accuracy, depth, and breadth. One where each image is necessary to the whole, where the language both sings and means, makes and unmakes. After looking at the construction of this deceptively simple poem for years, I finally see how it works, how dependent it is on diction and word choice, the gravitas achieved through what I'll call *stately* language.

I find three categories of words in this poem: the stately, the elemental, and the vulnerable. Note the word choices in the opening stanza, words like *mountains, glacial, shadow, granite, metal;* they are all trochees, simple two-syllable words that have balance and heft, as a good knife handle has heft. Millar also uses words like *air, sleep, night, soft,* one-syllable words that imply the insubstantial world, as well as words such as *afraid, thin, threads, hold,* that imply the vulnerability and insignificance of the human in relation to the world. The word *shadow* could be placed in all three categories, depending on its usage: stately, elemental, vulnerable. Here, it's used as an image: The shadow belongs to the stately mountain, and so that shadow is seen in a more substantial context.

In the second stanza, we note the repetition of the word *afraid* and the reinforcement of the idea of the human as somewhat trivial, this time almost laughable: *people talking, cat smile, poetry scholar.* His *ridged skull* seems a nod to the great mountains overshadowing everything, but only in that it makes the poetry scholar seem a buffoon, a man trying to act like a mountain, and for at least this poet, failing. There is also the humor inherent in *measure* vs. *wrist watch, payments, tuition,* the diurnal and the eternal, set against the mundane.

In the third stanza, we feel the stark simplicity of the opening assertion as a counter to all that's been presented: "I went down by the horses." *Birds, hay, dusk,* are words and images that are elemental, eternal, real. And then the elevation of the horse and the movement toward the mythic, a position beyond mere mortals, diction and image taking over and making the moment as large as the mountain: *Appaloosa, wheels, jawbones, vein, face.* And then, one perfect word of action: *swaying*, and one carefully chosen adjective: *great*. Each word proceeding and unfolding as it should to the final *sentiment*, the slow flush of recognition: "Sometimes I can hardly breathe." The word *breathe* here is tied back to the *thin air* in the second line, so it is both literal as well as a figure that stands in for the emotion the speaker is feeling. I don't know now who said it, or if this is exactly right, but it was something like "there should be an invisible line at the end of every poem that says, 'And after that, everything changed.'" We now see the speaker, and ourselves, for who we are, small creatures in a vast landscape, looking for our rightful place, or maybe being reminded of our place in the grand scheme.

The poem balances on the premise of setting the mundane, even the silly, against the grandeur of nature and the human being's position in it, our natural awe and fear of what's more powerful than us: the mountains, the metal, the horses, as well as that on which we depend: the air, sleep, even the birds. Our daily concerns, our lofty intellectual exercises, are seen for what they are: transient. The true poet is in all of us who get up and leave the room, as Walt Whitman did in "When I Heard the Learn'd Astronomer," to simply look out at the stars, allowing the mystery to overwhelm and confound.

When I Heard the Learn'd Astronomer

When I heard the learn'd astronomer,
When the proofs, the figures, were ranged in columns before me,
When I was shown the charts and diagrams, to add, divide,
    and measure them,
When I sitting heard the astronomer where he lectured with
    much applause in the lecture-room,
How soon unaccountable I became tired and sick,
Till rising and gliding out I wander'd off by myself,
In the mystical moist night-air, and from time to time,
Look'd up in perfect silence at the stars. (34)

★★★

Whitman's poem is simple as well, not at all like his abundant, extravagant "Song of Myself." His simple repetition of *When, when, when* is set against the piling up mathematical language but stated simply: *proofs, figures, charts, diagrams, add, divide.* Whitman's two well-chosen verbs, as in Millar's poem, are notable: *rising* and *gliding.* Then his wonderful *wander'd,* which harkens back to the earlier *learn'd.* In the penultimate line, Whitman pulls out all the stops to give us the "mystical moist night-air," the first overtly poetic line in the poem, though he follows it up with the simplicity of a perfect, metrically balanced, ten-syllable line: "Look'd up in perfect silence at the stars." The "mystical moist night air" and the "perfect silence" seem more majestic and substantial than all that has come before.

The commonalities between these poems are evident in their dialectics: small stories set against a large landscape, what's known set against the unknown, and diction as the vehicle that gets us from there to here. To each poet, these moments were part of an ordinary day or night that somehow became emblematic of a certain kind of purity, things suddenly exactly as they should be, greatness aligned with a quiet joy and true astonishment, pure spirits moving through the world at the very pace they should be moving, like a horse walking, like the stars traveling through the night sky, the world presenting itself to be looked upon with fear and awe and a sense of supplication. In a word, holy, but a secular holiness, devoid of wrath or judgment, the kind of wordless purity essential to the human spirit.

Other writers who do this are James Wright, William Stafford, Jane Hirshfield, Lucille Clifton, Yusef Komunyakaa, Jack Gilbert and Linda Gregg, and the list goes on, but these are a few to look at who work in this vein: simplicity intensified through diction, syntax, pacing, and through the use, primarily, of nouns. Small poems that open up into mystery: Blake's grain of sand through which eternities are seen.

William Giraldi, speaking of H.L. Mencken, who implores us to be more demanding and exacting in our modern-day criticism, asked, "Why are aesthetic matters important? Because without the beauty of language and form, without the depth and dynamism of language, no one who has cultivated the diehard combo of intellect and taste will care a damn about what the writer wants to say." Yes, the beauty, depth, and dynamism of language is what elevates the poem, and without an understanding of how language works on us, the gloriously simple poem, the expansive poem, the poem we will remember, remains merely simple rather than a poem that is more than the sum of its parts.

I admire how these poets can make so much happen when working with so little. I'm not so good at it myself, and even after studying and imitating them, I have failed more often than succeeded. But it's worth the trying when the rewards can be so great.

★★★

One more detail. Until I mentioned the thematic similarities between Whitman's poem and Joe's, my husband hadn't noticed it. Though he was familiar with the poem, he hadn't actually read it for years. We are touched, as writers, by what we read. T.S. Eliot said "Good writers borrow. Great writers steal." And Joe's poem is an example of the best kind of "stealing," a hand reaching down from the unconscious, or stepping through the looking glass, and taking what it needs.

Here's another well-known example from Robert Hayden:

Those Winter Sundays

Sundays too my father got up early
and put his clothes on in the blueblack cold,
then with cracked hands that ached
from labor in the weekday weather made
banked fires blaze. No one ever thanked him.

I'd wake and hear the cold splintering, breaking.
When the rooms were warm, he'd call,
and slowly I would rise and dress,
fearing the chronic angers of that house,

Speaking indifferently to him,
who had driven out the cold
and polished my good shoes as well.
What did I know, what did I know
of love's austere and lonely offices? (41)

The diction in this poem is mostly simple, except for a few very well-chosen words: *blueblack*, *chronic*, *austere*, and *offices*. The stark line "No one ever thanked him" is similar in effect to Millar's "I went down by the horses." That kind of simplicity is hard won. We know the writer is capable of complexity, as evidenced in the music and tension in the lines that precede it: "with cracked hands that ached/ from labor in the weekday weather made/ banked fires blaze." And in Millar's poem, the lines: "the granite inside them/ and the threads of bright metal/ may not hold once the night comes." When complex lines are set against one stark line, simplicity sings and is weighted with intent.

DEBRA GWARTNEY

Specificity? Yes. But Only If It's Relevant

We are American writers, absorbing the American experience. We must absorb its heat, the recklessness and ruthlessness, the grotesqueries and cruelties. We must reflect the sprawl and smallness of America, its greedy optimism and dangerous sentimentality. . .We might have something then, worthy, necessary; a real literature instead of the Botox escapist lit told in the shiny prolix comedic style that has come to define us.

—Joy Williams

When I'm reading through manuscripts of nonfiction prose, it surprises me to frequently run into detail not yet earning its keep. I don't mean the images aren't vivid or gruesome or pretty (the color of the sky at midnight, the chicken bone stuck in a father's throat, the purring motor of your first car). They may be all those and more. But when detail comes off as simply gratuitous, as is too often the case, the reader doesn't know where to invest, and the specificity ends up doing more harm than good to the narrative.

Unless a reader senses that it is pointing her or him toward a depth of meaning, revealing critical motivation or emotion, detail serves primarily as decoration. Maybe a writer has pulled in certain sensory images, for instance, to make a scene feel "real," which is a worthwhile aim except that veracity for veracity's sake isn't enough to make a piece of prose matter to the reader.

So what is enough?

As he often does, John Gardner says it best in *The Art of Fiction*: "In addition to watching the rhythm of a scene—the tempo or pace—the writer pays close attention in constructing the scene to the relationship, in each of its elements, of emphasis and function. By emphasis we mean the amount of time spent on a particular detail; by function we mean the work done by that detail within the scene and the story as a whole" (59).

The problem is that instead of what Gardner suggests—a few select details emphasized in just the right way—we readers too often get buried under a dump of specificity, where every detail gets the same weight, and few are used to reveal the inner life of the character.

★★★

My teachers often scrawled the same note in the margin of papers I wrote in high school and college: *be specific*. Yes, specificity is critical. Specificity is what engages the reader when abstraction can distract or confound the reader. "The air smells good," for instance, is a so-what line. A mile away, you can tell that sentence is flat and uninspired. A more concise, evocative image is what we're after, for both concision and precision allow the reader to pick up the scent, too. "It's a radiant fall Sunday in 1970, and the air smells like fallen apples after rain," Mira Bartók writes in *The Memory Palace* (86).

Still—and here's my argument about pushing beyond the gratuitous—even if the detail is as vivid as air that smells like fallen apples, it must *also* be highly relevant to the emotional complexities of the characters as well as whatever psychological dilemma the reader is confronting in the narrative. Again, as Gardner points out, it's not the details themselves but how certain details are elevated, shaped. It's the way the writer directs the scene, beginning to end. In other words, the skilled writer is one who uses detail to teach a reader how to read the work, what to take in, what to hold as important.

In aggregate, relevant detail can be used to create an atmosphere that sends a signal to the reader—you know she is there and that she has a capacity for an emotional life no different from yours. As Janet Burroway puts it, "If you refuse to direct our judgment [through the selection and shaping of specific detail], you may be inviting our indifference" (58).

Here's an exercise I use in workshops to address this idea about the weight and function of detail: Let's say your character has received a call telling her she's won a big writing prize. Even before she hangs up, she experiences a rush of conflicting emotions. Jubilation, and yet troubling questions are seeping in already: *Will I get a second call telling me it was a mistake? Will people expect too much of me after this?* Let's say that happiness swells larger than doubts, floating her from the kitchen to the living room to report the news to a loved one who's reading in a chair. When she steps into that room, in this state of exhilaration, her doubts tamped down, what does she notice? Light coming in the window? The textures of art on the wall, the rugs, the curve of the overstuffed chair? The colors, the smells, the sound of the clock ticking—what gets through the filter of this particular person in this particular emotional state in this particular moment? This is narrowed perception. One's emotional state dictates what gets noticed and what fades to the sidelines.

Thinking about this idea of being sensitized by experience, let's complicate the scenario: The character walks into the room to share her terrific news and sees her loved one with a cigarette even though she's asked him a million times not to smoke in the house and there he is dropping ash on her favorite chair—suddenly she shuts down, won't talk, won't tell about the happiest of happy announcements because, well, *to hell with this guy who doesn't respect her wishes.* On the way back to the kitchen, an anger burns in the character, an anger she hardly understands. She's in emotional chaos.

For the writer to convey a complicated state of mind, every detail on the page must point to human ambivalence and contradiction, the confusion of emotion that can, for instance, lead to inexplicable rage. That is, vulnerability shifts because of what you experience and the state you're in when you experience it. It's a remarkable thing when a writer is able to tap into the heart of such human complexity.

When you sit down to write a scene, don't give us a laundry list of details from your current state of mind. To do so creates that flat, uninspired prose. Predictable prose. Instead, rediscover the churning mix of emotion back when the event occurred, and ask yourself: Of all the details in the room, which are the ones I noticed when I felt like x?

★★★

Most anyone who's been in a writing workshop has learned about the uses of detail:

- Details reveal character.

- Details create a sense of space, which is different from naming place.
- Details intensify the action, up the ante.

Here are three related notions that may help refine the idea of *relevant* detail:

1. Specificity can be used to acknowledge to the reader that you live in the same world she does. You are not the authority, but the reader's companion.
2. Specificity can signal to the reader that you are aware that life is not all about cause and effect.
3. Specificity is not unassailable. All you can offer is suggestion, and embrace the contradiction and ambivalence inherent in life experience.

Stop-Time, Frank Conroy's memoir, is one I can't help but bring up at this point—the book has been around a long time now, I realize, published in 1967, but I return to the scenes in *Stop-Time* again and again to remember what makes them so potent: relevant detail.

Conroy's is a coming-of-age memoir about many things—one of those is Frank's "divided self." According to personal narrative masters such as Vivian Gornick and Sven Birkerts, this is a prime facet of memoir, the way we delude ourselves, hide from ourselves, claim to want one thing when we actually desire another. For instance, young Frank (as recalled by adult Frank) lets everyone know he's an independent spirit, he needs no one, he can make it just fine on his own. He despises any hint of authority and runs from it as fast as he can, even if the result is self-sabotage. Conroy's masterful scenes, though—and the highly relevant detail he employs—show a longing in the boy to be *known*. To be protected and cared for by an adult. This is his secret desire, his tender heart. He needs much more than he can admit to himself. It's a dynamic he sets up early in the book and then complicates and recomplicates throughout the chapters of *Stop-Time*.

For instance, in this early scene, we're still getting to know the intricate mind games young Frank plays with himself to keep buried (from those around him, and himself) his fears and doubts. No matter how afraid or alone he feels, it's not worth the risk to disclose weakness.

Frank's mother and stepfather are working in a mental hospital on the weekends—they stay in a nearby cabin, rudimentary to say the least—and they leave Frank in the shelter at night while they work. His job is to keep the stove burning so that the cabin will be warm when the parents return.

> Every Friday the cheap padlock was opened, every Friday I stepped inside. A room so dim my blood turned gray, so cold I knew no human heart had ever beaten there—every line, every article of furniture, every scrap of paper on the floor, every burned-out match in a saucer filling me with desolation, depopulating me . . . all these objects had been watched by me in a state of advanced terror, watched so many long nights that even in the daytime they seemed to be whispering bad messages. (45)

Note that Conroy does not describe the exact pieces of furniture. Note that it's not a grocery receipt and a candy bar wrapper on the floor, but instead "every scrap of paper." Conroy wants these items to get only a certain amount of attention, so that the most relevant language gets the weight. The most important word in the graph is "depopulate" and he's not going to allow too much detail to take away the power of that word. In these early pages, Conroy is painting a picture of a boy who has absolutely no one to turn to, and so he teaches himself—to a fault—to manage that which is clearly beyond him.

After he watches his parents leave for work through the snow and in this "depopulated" state of mind, Frank is alone:

> I dried the dishes slowly and put them away, attempting to do the whole job without making a sound. Occasionally, a floorboard creaked under my weight, sending a long, lingering charge up my spine, a white thrill at once delicious and

ominous. I approached the stove nervously. The coal rattled and the cast-iron grate banged despite my precautions. I had to do it quickly, holding my breath, or I wouldn't do it at all. Once finished I checked the window latches. There was nothing to be done about the door; it couldn't be locked from the inside and mother refused to lock it from the outside because of the danger of my getting trapped in a fire.

By the yellow light of the kerosene lamp I sat on the edge of the bed and removed my shoes, placing them on the floor. The Big Ben alarm clock ticked off the seconds on a shelf above my head, and every now and then a puff of coal gas popped in the stove as the fuel shifted. I got under the covers fully clothed and surveyed the stillness of the room, trying to slow my breathing. For an hour or more I lay motionless in a self-induced trance, my eyes open but seldom moving, my ears listening to the sounds of the house and the faint, inexplicable, continuous noises from outside. (In this state my ears seemed rather far away. I was burrowed somewhere deep in my skull, my ears advance outposts sending back reports to headquarters.) As I remember it the trance must have been close to the real thing. It was an attempt to reach an equipoise of fear, a state in which the incoming fear signals balanced with some internal process of dissimulation. At best it worked only temporarily, since fear held a slight edge. But for an hour or two I avoided what I hated most, the great noisy swings up and down. The panic and the hilarity. (48-49)

While the boy claims to hate "the panic and the hilarity," that's just the state young Frank creates again and again in the book, with ever-increasing negative consequences. He says he wants a state of equipoise, and yet every time balance is offered, he squanders it, spoils it, runs from it. He's so familiar with tumult and fear that he keeps conjuring both. Conroy never directly explains this is what's going on in the interior of young Frank—instead, he shows the boy's jumbled state brilliantly through relevant detail.

Each scene is also shaped to let us in on Frank's relationship with Dagmar, his mother, and Jean, the step-father. This particular triangle runs through the whole book. Jean, cocky and yet mostly weak and ineffective. Dagmar, who simply refuses to know her son—she is incapable of seeing any situation from his vantage.

As a prelude to the scene above, we find out that young Frank is not allowed to stay home with his teenaged sister because Dagmar/Jean want to return to a warm cabin. He's their worker bee. They set the alarm so Frank will get up and put more coal in the stove in anticipation of their return, a task he despises. On the night of this scene, the alarm clock goes off just moments after he's finally fallen asleep and he cannot rouse himself out of hard-won slumber to do the job. Dagmar and Jean come back to the cabin to find the place cold—Frank, despite his night of anguish, has failed them.

The boy is told to get out of the bed so they can get in. He's to stay inside and be absolutely quiet for seven hours so they can sleep. But before she closes her eyes, Dagmar turns to her son: "'It's not very much to ask you to keep the fire going,' my mother said. 'I never ask you to do anything'" (51).

The entire scene, every detail, is shaped and presented so that Dagmar's indictment, when it arrives, hits us like a fist in the throat. Because of the way the writer has prepared us, we know, as adult Frank knows, that she has asked the boy for *everything*, and he's done his best to give it.

As writers, we must constantly ask ourselves: what gets elevated, what gets emphasized, and to what effect? Whatever is generalized in this scene from *Stop-Time*—fear, for example—is inflated by specificity, and ordinary specificity is used in extraordinary ways. The creak of the floor triggers the imagination. The popping of the fuel in the stove triggers the imagination: the coal is described as a beast, but he doesn't mention the stove's color. We know it's black. Why say what's already in the reader's mind? Conroy has brought no unfamiliar element into the scene; he uses only familiar details (weight and function) to take us deep into the boy's psychological dilemma.

Perhaps the most effective detail comes in the parenthetical statement: "(In this state my ears seemed rather far away. I was burrowed somewhere deep in my skull, my ears advance outposts sending back reports to headquarters.)" (49).

Immediately preceding these lines we don't find concrete details, but again, details just precise enough: "my ears listening to the sounds of the house and the faint, inexplicable, continuous noises from outside" (49). A lesser writer would give us a list. A tree branch rubbing the window. A loose door banging against the frame. A deer thumping by. But here's where Conroy recognizes that life is not cause and effect. It's not: Deer is outside + deer makes noise = I get scared. It doesn't matter what the noises are. What matters is how he responds to any and all noises. What gets emphasized: young Frank fooling himself into thinking he's protected because he's sent his ears out to listen for strange sounds.

Conroy teaches us that instead of always going for what we've been trained to write—the photographic image—we might think instead about the idea of atmosphere. Go for the deeply human, which is quite often the nonlogical. Ears that seemed far away. Advanced outposts. This is Conroy's way of letting the reader know he is well aware of the nature of fear and how fear can reshape reality—and he knows you are aware, too.

WORKS CITED

Alcosser

Epigraph: Ueda, Makoto. *Matsuo Basho.* New York: Twayne Publishers, 1970.

Berg, Stephen. *With Akhmatova at the Black Gates: Variations.* Urbana-Champaign: University of Illinois Press, 1981.

Hirshfield, Jane. *Come, Thief.* New York: Alfred A. Knopf, 2013.

Hirshfield, Jane. "Skipping Stones" in *My Business is Circumference: Poets on Influence and Mastery.* Edited by Stephen Berg. Philadelphia: Paul Dry Books, 2001.

Merwin, W.S. "Little Soul" [translation of Hadrian] in *The Shadow of Sirius*, 31. Port Townsend: Copper Canyon Press, 2008.

Merwin, W.S. "Translator's Notes: Little Soul." *Poetry* (April 2006).

Niedecker, Lorine. *Collected Works.* Berkeley: University of California Press, 2002.

Oliver, Mary. "Pen and Paper and a Breath of Air" in *Blue Pastures*, 45-60. New York: Harcourt Brace, 2005.

"Patricia Goedicke Robinson." *Missoulian* (Missoula, MT), Jul. 23, 2006.

Pound, Ezra. *Gaudier-Brzeska: A Memoir.* London: John Lane, 1916.

Quinn, Alice. "In the Beforelife: Franz Wright." *The New Yorker*, Jul. 9, 2001.

Roub, Gail. "Getting to Know Lorine Niedecker." *Wisconsin Academy Review* 32, no. 3 (1986): 37-41.

Tadić, Novica. *Night Mail*. Translated by Charles Simic. Oberlin: Oberlin College Press, 1992.

Tsvetaeva, Marina. *Tsvetaeva: Art in the Light of Conscience*. Translated by Angela Livingstone. London: Bristol Classical Press, 1992.

Ueda, Makoto. *Matsuo Basho*. New York: Twayne Publishers, 1970.

Waley, Arthur. *The Way and Its Power: Lao Tzu's Tao Te Ching and Its Place in Chinese Thought*. New York: Grove Press, 1958.

Wheelwright, Philip Ellis. *Metaphor and Reality*. Bloomington, Indiana University Press, 1962.

Yourcenar, Marguerite. *Memoirs of Hadrian*. New York: Farrar, Straus and Giroux, 2005.

Zagajewski, Adam. *Without End*. Translated by Clare Cavanagh, Benjamin Ivry, Renata Gorczynski. New York: Farrar, Straus and Giroux, 2002.

Amick

Epigraph: Steinbeck, John. "The Art of Fiction No. 45" [interviewed by Nathaniel Benchley]. *The Paris Review* 48 (Fall 1969).

Frangello, Gina. "The Rumpus Interview with Cris Mazza." *The Rumpus.net*. n.p., accessed October 3, 2012. http://therumpus.net/2011/05/the-rumpus-interview-with-cris-mazza/

"Uncle's Darling, The Heroine of the Light House." [Advertisement] *Lewiston Saturday Journal* (Lewiston, ME), Mar. 26, 1892, 11. Google News Archive. Reprinted in: Roycraft, Philip. "Queen of the Opera House." *Michigan History Magazine* (2012): 28.

Bass

Epigraph: Dobyns, Stephen. *Best Words, Best Order: Essays on Poetry*. New York: St. Martin's Press, 1996.

Dobyns, Stephen. *Best Words, Best Order: Essays on Poetry.* New York: St. Martin's Press, 1996.

Hugo, Richard. *The Triggering Town.* New York: Norton, 1992.

Kizer, Carolyn. "Pro Femina" in *Cool, Calm & Collected: Poems 1960-2000.* Port Townsend, WA: Copper Canyon, 2001.

Shapiro, Alan. "Watch" in *Old War.* New York: Houghton Mifflin, 2008.

Bell

Epigraph: Mill, John Stuart. *The Collected Works of John Stuart Mill, Volume I: Autobiography and Literary Essays.* Edited by John M. Robson & Jack Stillinger. Toronto: University Of Toronto Press, 1981, 140.

Coman

Epigraph: Kidder, Tracy. *Mountains Beyond Mountains: The Quest of Dr. Paul Farmer, A Man Who Would Cure the World.* New York: Random House, 2009, 294.

Davis

Epigraph: Personal communication with William Kittredge.

Butler, Robert Olen. *Tabloid Dreams.* New York: Henry Holt, 1996.

Dybek, Stuart. *I Sailed with Magellan.* New York: Picador, 2003.

Heidegger, Martin. *Poetry, Language, Thought.* New York: Harper-Collins, 1971.

Hemingway, Ernest. *The Old Man and the Sea.* New York: Scribner, 1952.

Lahiri, Jhumpa. *Interpreter of Maladies.* New York: Houghton Mifflin Harcourt, 1999.

Roth, Philip. *Portnoy's Complaint.* New York: Random House, 1967.

Udall, Brady. *Letting Loose the Hounds*. New York: Simon & Schuster, 1997.

Dawes

Epigraph: Shakespeare, William. *The Tempest*. 1623. Act 3, Scene 2.

Dawes, Kwame. "Parasite" in *Midland: Poems*. Athens, Ohio: Ohio University Press, 2001.
Dryden, John. *A Defence of an Essay of Dramatic Poesy*. 1668.
Shakespeare, William. *The Tempest*. 1623.

Gwartney

Epigraph: Williams, Joy. "The Art of Fiction No. 223" [interviewed by Paul Winner]. *The Paris Review* 209 (Summer 2014).

Bartók, Mira. *The Memory Palace*. New York: Free Press, 2011.
Burroway, Janet. *Writing Fiction: A Guide to Narrative Craft*. New York: Little, Brown, 1982.
Conroy, Frank. *Stop-Time*. New York: Penguin Books, 1977.
Gardner, John. *The Art of Fiction: Notes on Craft for Young Writers*. New York: Vintage, 1991.

Hendrie

Epigraph: Hugo, Richard. *The Triggering Town*. New York: W.W. Norton, 1979, 31.

Burroway, Janet. *Writing Fiction: A Guide to Narrative Craft*. 6th ed. New York: Longman, 2003.
Cain, James M. *The Butterfly*. New York: Alfred A. Knopf, 1947.
Conrad, Joseph. *Heart of Darkness*. New York: New American Library, 1910.

Fitzgerald, F. Scott. *The Great Gatsby*. New York: Collier, 1986.

Laxness, Halldór. *Independent People*. New York: Random House, 1997.

Melville, Herman. "Bartleby the Scrivener." *Norton Anthology of American Literature*. 2nd ed. Edited by Nina Baym. New York: Norton, 1985.

O'Connor, Flannery. *The Complete Stories*. New York: Farrar, Straus and Giroux, 1985.

Sloane, William. *The Craft of Writing*. New York: Norton, 1983.

Theroux, Paul. *The Mosquito Coast*. New York: Houghton Mifflin, 2006.

Houston

Epigraph: James, Henry. "The Art of Fiction." *Longman's Magazine* 4 (September 1884).

Korb

Epigraph: McPhee, John. "The Art of Nonfiction No. 3" [interviewed by Peter Hessler]. *The Paris Review* 192 (Spring 2010).

Didion, Joan. *Slouching Towards Bethlehem*. New York: Farrar, Straus and Giroux, 1968.

—. *The Year of Magical Thinking*. New York: Knopf, 2005.

Hurston, Zora Neale. *Mules and Men*. 1935. New York: Harper Perennial Modern Classics, 2008.

Jamison, Leslie. *The Empathy Exams*. Minneapolis: Graywolf, 2014.

Prose, Francine. "Untitled" in *Radiant Truths: Essential Dispatches, Reports, Confessions, & Other Essays on American Belief*. Edited by Jeff Sharlet. New Haven, CT: Yale University Press, 2014.

Robinson, Marilynne. *When I Was a Child I Read Books*. New York: Farrar, Straus and Giroux, 2012.

Skloot, Rebecca. *The Immortal Life of Henrietta Lacks*. New York: Crown, 2010.

Smith, Zadie. "Elegy for a Country's Seasons." *New York Review of Books*. April 3, 2014. http://www.nybooks.com/articles/archives/2014/apr/03/elegy-countrys-seasons/

—. "Man vs. Corpse." *New York Review of Books*. December 5, 2013. http://www.nybooks.com/articles/archives/2013/dec/05/zadie-smith-man-vs-corpse/

Sparks, Stephen. "The Faltering Sense of Self: An Interview with Leslie Jamison." *Tin House*'s "The Open Bar" blog. April 21, 2014. http://www.tinhouse.com/blog/34467/34467.html

Strayed, Cheryl. *Wild: From Lost to Found on the Pacific Coast Trail*. New York: Knopf, 2012.

Laken

Epigraph: Solnit, Rebecca. "Apricots" in *The Faraway Nearby*. New York: Viking, 2013, 3-4.

Abrams, J. J. Quoted in "A Long Time Ago, in a Universe More Analog," by Logan Hill. *The New York Times,* October 28, 2013.

Barbash, Tom. "Mysterious Key Sends Boy Sifting through His Life's Wreckage after 9/11." *The San Francisco Chronicle,* April 3, 2005.

Barton, Emily. "Typographical Terror." *The Village Voice,* April 11, 2000.

Beaumont, Peter. "A Haunting House." *The Guardian: The Observer,* July 8 2000.

Bellafante, Ginia. "Map Quest." *The New York Times Sunday Book Review,* June 19, 2009.

Campbell, Bonnie Jo. "The Yard Man" in *American Salvage*. New York: Norton, 2009.

Cunningham, Michael. *A Home at the End of the World*. New York: Picador, 1998.

Faber, Michel. "A Tower of Babel." *The Guardian*. June 3, 2005.

Ginsberg, Alan. "Howl" in *Howl and Other Poems*. 1955. Reprint, San Francisco: City Lights Publishers, 2001.

Hemingway, Ernest. *A Farewell to Arms*. 1929. Reprint, New York: Scribner, 1995.

Kakutani, Michiko. "A Boy's Epic Quest, Burrough by Burrough." *The New York Times,* March 22, 2005.

Lupton, Ellen. *Thinking with Type*. 2nd ed. Princeton, NJ: Princeton Architectural Press, 2010.

Marcus, Ben. "The Genre Artist." *The Believer*. July 2003.

McInerney, Jay. "The Remains of the Dog." *The New York Times,* June 15, 2003.

Nabokov, Vladimir. *Lolita*. 1955. Reprint, New York: Vintage, 1989.

Smith, Zadie. *White Teeth*. New York: Vintage, 2001.

Swift, Graham. "Words per Minute." *The New York Times Sunday Book Review,* June 10, 2012.

Updike, John. "Mixed Messages." *The New Yorker,* March 14, 2005.

Wolff, Tobias. *The Night in Question: Stories*. New York: Vintage, 1997.

Woolf, Virginia. *A Room of One's Own*. 1929. Reprint, Mansfield Centre, CT: Martino Fine Books, 2012.

Laux

Epigraph: Rich, Adrienne. "Natural Resources," in *Dream of a Common Language*. New York: W.W. Norton, 1978, 67.

Giraldi, William. "On Joseph Epstein." *The New Criterion* (May 2014): 14-19.

Hayden, Robert. "Those Winter Sundays" in *Collected Poems*. Edited by Frederick Glaysher. 1997. New York: Liveright Publishing.

Millar, Joseph. "After Listening to a Lecture on Form" in *Overtime*. Carnegie Mellon University Press, 2013.

Whitman, Walt. "When I Heard the Learn'd Astronomer" in *Leaves of Grass*. 1855. Dover Thrift Editions, 2007.

Long

Epigraph: Audette, Anna Held. *The Blank Canvas: Inviting the Muse.* Boston: Shambhala Publications, 1993, 50. // Newlove, Donald. *First Paragraphs: Inspired Openings for Writers and Readers.* New York: St. Martin's Press, 1992.

Atwood, Margaret. *The Blind Assassin.* New York: Anchor Books, 2001.

Bellow, Saul. *The Adventures of Augie March.* 1953. New York: Viking Press, 1962.

Cary, Joyce. *The Horse's Mouth.* 1944. New York: Harper, 1990.

Dickens, Charles. *Great Expectations.* 1861. New York: Fine Communications, 2005.

Dos Passos, John. *Manhattan Transfer.* New York: Houghton Mifflin, 1925.

Driscoll, Jack. "From Here to There" in *Wanting Only to Be Heard.* Amherst: University of Massachusetts Press, 1992.

Dybek, Stuart. "We Didn't" in *I Sailed with Magellan.* New York: Farrar, Straus and Giroux, 2003.

Faulkner, William. "Golden Land" in *Collected Stories of William Faulkner.* 1950. New York: Vintage Books, 1977.

—. *The Sound and the Fury.* 1929. New York: Vintage Books, 1954.

Fitzgerald, F. Scott. *The Great Gatsby.* 1925. New York: Scribner, 1953.

Flaubert, Gustave. *Madame Bovary.* 1857. New York: New American Library, 1979.

Gass, William H. "The Nature of Narrative and its Philosophical Implications" in *Tests of Time: Essays.* New York: Knopf, 2002.

Johnson, Denis. "Work" in *Jesus' Son.* New York: Farrar, Straus and Giroux, 1992.

Joyce, James. *Ulysses.* 1922. New York: Vintage International, 1990.

Kafka, Franz. *The Castle.* 1926. New York: Everyman's Library, 1992.

Kosiński, Jerzy. *The Painted Bird.* 1965. New York: Grove, 1995.

Kundera, Milan. *The Art of the Novel.* 1986. New York: HarperCollins, 1993.

—. *Testaments Betrayed*. 1993. New York: HarperCollins, 1995.

Mandel, Emily St. John. *Last Night in Montreal*. Lakewood, CO: Unbridled Books, 2009.

McCann, Colum. *Let the Great World Spin*. New York: Random House, 2009.

McCarthy, Cormac. *Child of God*. 1973. New York: Vintage International, 1993.

—. *The Road*. New York: Knopf, 2006.

McGuane, Thomas. *Nobody's Angel*. New York: Random House, 1982.

McNamer, Deirdre. *One Sweet Quarrel*. New York: Harper Collins, 1994.

Moody, Rick. *Purple America*. New York: Back Bay Books, 1998.

Munro, Alice. "The Love of a Good Woman" in *The Love of a Good Woman*. New York: Knopf, 1998.

Oates, Joyce Carol. *Black Water*. New York: Dutton, 1992.

O'Nan, Stewart. *Last Night at the Lobster*. New York: Penguin, 2007.

Proulx, E. Annie. *The Shipping News*. 1993. New York: Touchstone, 1994.

Robinson, Marilynne. *Housekeeping*. 1981. New York: Picador, 2015.

Salter, James. *Dusk and Other Stories*. 1988. New York: Modern Library, 2010.

Sebald, W. G. *The Rings of Saturn*. 1995. New York: New Directions, 1998.

Süskind, Patrick. *Perfume*. 1976. New York: Vintage International, 2001.

Trevor, William. *Family Sins and Other Stories*. New York: Viking, 1990.

—. *Felicia's Journey*. New York: Viking, 1995.

—. *The Story of Lucy Gault*. New York: Viking, 2002.

Magnuson

Epigraph: Used by Dale Ray Phillips in teaching. See "Dale Ray Phillips" faculty profile page at http://www.murraystate.edu

Didion, Joan. "Slouching Towards Bethlehem" in *Slouching Towards Bethlehem*, 84-130. New York: Farrar, Straus & Giroux, 1968.

Foucault, Michel. *The Archaeology of Knowledge*. Translated by Alan Sheridan. New York: Pantheon Books, 1972.

Freytag, Gustav. *Technique of the Drama*. Translated by Elias J. MacEwan. Chicago: Scott, Foresman and Company, 1900.

Smith, Stevie. "Not Waving but Drowning" in *New Selected Poems of Stevie Smith*, 67. New York: New Directions Publishing, 1988.

Yeats, William Butler. *Michael Robartes and the Dancer*. Churchtown, Dundrum, Ireland: The Cuala Press, 1920.

McNally

Epigraph: Carlson, Ron. Personal communication quoted in John McNally, *The Creative Writer's Survival Guide: Advice from an Unrepentant Novelist*. Iowa City: University of Iowa Press, 2010, 224.

Percy

Epigraph: Crews, Harry. *Getting Naked with Harry Crews: Interviews*. Gainesville: University Press of Florida, 1999.

Atwood, Margaret. *The Handmaid's Tale*. Toronto: McClelland and Stewart, 1985.

Ferris, Joshua. *Then We Came to the End*. New York: Little, Brown, 2007.

Houston, Pam. *A Rough Guide to the Heart*. London: Virago, 2000.

Kirn, Walter. *Up in the Air*. New York: Doubleday, 2001.

Levin, Philip. "You Can Have It" in *New Selected Poems*. New York: Alfred A. Knopf, 1991.

Magnuson, Mike. *The Right Man for the Job*. New York: HarperCollins Publishers, 1997.

McIlroy, Kevin. "The People Who Own Pianos" in *The Complete History of New Mexico: Stories*. Minneapolis: Graywolf, 2005.

Orlean, Susan. *The Orchid Thief*. New York: Random House, 1998.

Turner, Brian. "At Lowe's Home Improvement Center" in *Phantom Noise*. Farmington, ME: Alice James Books, 2010.

Wolfe, Tom. *The Right Stuff*. New York: Farrar, Straus and Giroux, 1979.

Stefaniak

Epigraph: Bell, Marvin. "32 Statements about Writing Poetry" in *We Wanted To Be Writers*. Edited by Eric Olsen & Glenn Schaeffer. New York: Skyhorse Publishing, 2011, 87.

Ellis, Bret Easton. *American Psycho*. New York: Vintage Books, 1991.

Gibbons, Kaye. *Ellen Foster*. 1987. Reprint, Chapel Hill: Algonquin Books, 2012.

Nabokov, Vladimir. *Lolita*. New York: G. P. Putnam's Sons, 1955.

O'Connor, Flannery. *A Good Man Is Hard to Find and Other Stories*. New York: Harcourt, 1955, 1976.

O'Connor, Frank. "First Confession" in *Twice Told Tales: An Anthology of Short Fiction*. Edited by Gerard A. Barker. Boston: Houghton Mifflin, 1979.

—. "Repentance" in *Twice Told Tales: An Anthology of Short Fiction*. Edited by Gerard A. Barker. Boston: Houghton Mifflin, 1979.

Salinger, J. D. *The Catcher in the Rye*. New York: Little, Brown, 1951.

—. "For Esmé, With Love and Squalor" in *Nine Stories*. 1953. New York: Little, Brown, 1981.

Twain, Mark. *The Adventures of Huckleberry Finn*. New York: Harper, 1918.

Updike, John. "A & P" in *Single Scene Short Stories*. Edited by Margaret Bishop. Layton, UT: Gibbs Smith, 2007.

ABOUT THE AUTHORS

SANDRA ALCOSSER's poems have appeared in *The New Yorker, The New York Times, Paris Review, Ploughshares, Poetry* and the *Pushcart Prize Anthology*. Her books of poetry, *A Fish to Feed All Hunger* (University of Virginia Press, 1986) and *Except by Nature* (Graywolf, 1999), received the highest honors from the National Poetry Series, the Academy of American Poets, and Associated Writing Programs. She received two individual artist fellowships from NEA and served as National Endowment for the Arts' Conservation Poet for the Wildlife Conservation Society and Poets House, New York, as well as Montana's first poet laureate and recipient of the Merriam Award for Distinguished Contribution to Montana Literature. She founded and directs San Diego State University's MFA program each fall and teaches in Pacific University's MFA program.

STEVE AMICK has published two novels with Pantheon: *Nothing But a Smile* and *The Lake, the River & the Other Lake*, which was a Book Sense Pick and a *Washington Post* Book of the Year, and was cited in the *Encyclopedia Britannica's Britannica Book of the Year* as one of three "standout" debuts of 2005. Both books received the Michigan Notable Book Award. Venues for his shorter work include *McSweeney's, Zoetrope:All-Story, Playboy, Story, Southern Review, Cincinnati Review, Michigan Quarterly Review, The New York Times*, NPR's "The Sound of Writing," and various anthologies. He has had plays produced in Chicago and—somewhat inexplicably—won a Clio for work in advertising. He received an MFA in fiction from George Mason University in 1991 and lives in Ann Arbor.

ELLEN BASS' poetry books include *Like a Beggar* (Copper Canyon Press, 2014), which was a finalist for the Paterson Poetry Prize and the Northern California Book Award; *The Human Line* (Copper Canyon Press, 2007); and *Mules of Love* (BOA Editions, 2002), which won the Lambda Literary Award. Bass co-edited the groundbreaking book, *No More Masks! An Anthology of Poems by Women* and has published several nonfiction books, including *The Courage to Heal: A Guide for Women Survivors of Child Sexual Abuse* (HarperCollins 1988, 2008) and *Free Your Mind: The Book for Gay, Lesbian and Bisexual Youth* (HarperPerennial, 1996). Her awards include an NEA Fellowship, two Pushcart Prizes, the Elliston Book Award, the Pablo Neruda Prize, the Larry Levis Prize, *New Letters* Poetry Prize, Greensboro Poetry Prize, and the Glenna Luschei *Prairie Schooner* Award. Her work has appeared in *The New Yorker, New York Times Magazine, American Poetry Review,* and many other journals.

MARVIN BELL has been called "an insider who thinks like an outsider," and his writing has been called "ambitious without pretension." Bell was for many years Flannery O'Connor Professor of Letters at the Iowa Writers' Workshop. He served two terms as the state of Iowa's first Poet Laureate. He has collaborated with composers, musicians, dancers, and other writers, and is the originator of a form known as the "Dead Man" poem. His 24 books include *Vertigo: The Living Dead Man Poems* (Copper Canyon Press, 2011); *Whiteout* (Lodima Press, 2011), a collaboration with photographer Nathan Lyons; and *After the Fact: Scripts & Postscripts* (White Pine Press, 2016), a collaboration with writer Christopher Merrill. His literary honors include awards from the Academy of American Poets, the American Academy of Arts and Letters and *The American Poetry Review*, Guggenheim and NEA fellowships, and Senior Fulbright appointments to Yugoslavia and Australia.

CAROLYN COMAN's books for children and young adults include *The Memory Bank* (Arthur A. Levine, 2010), a graphic story book created in collaboration with artist Rob Shepperson; *What Jamie Saw* (Front Street, 1995; National Book Award finalist and Newbery Honor book); *Many Stones* (Front Street, 2000; National

Book Award finalist and Printz Honor book); *Bee & Jacky* (Front Street, 1998), *The Big House* (Front Street, 2004), and *Sneaking Suspicions* (Front Street, 2007). She is also the author of *Writing Stories* (Stenhouse, 2011), a professional book for classroom teachers. She has taught at Vermont College and Hamline University, in their MFA programs in Writing for Children and Young Adults, and at Pacific University's MFA in Writing program. She has recently completed an adult novel based on the life and writings of Etty Hillesum.

CLAIRE DAVIS' first novel *Winter Range* (Picador, 2000) was listed among the best books of 2000 by the *Washington Post, Chicago Sun Times, Denver Post, Seattle Post, The Oregonian,* and *The Christian Science Monitor,* and it was the first book to receive both the PNBA and MPBA awards for best fiction. Her second novel, *Season of the Snake* (St. Martin's, 2005), and her short story collection, *Labors of the Heart* (Picador, 2007), were both released to wide critical acclaim. The short story "Labors of the Heart" was recorded for NPR's *Selected Shorts* on stage in New York's Symphony Space. She is co-editor of the anthology *Kiss Tomorrow Hello: Notes from the Midlife Underground by Twenty-Five Women over Forty* (Doubleday, 2008). Her stories and essays have appeared in numerous literary magazines such as *The Gettysburg Review, Shenandoah, Southern Review, The Pushcart Prize Anthology,* and *Best American Short Stories.* She lives in Lewiston, Idaho, where she teaches creative writing at Lewis-Clark State College.

KWAME DAWES is the author of nineteen books of poetry and numerous other books of fiction, criticism, and essays. He has edited over a dozen anthologies. His most recent collection, *City of Bones: A Testament* (Northwestern University Press) will appear in 2016 along with *Speak from Here to There* (Peepal Tree Press), co-written with Australian poet John Kinsella; and *A Bloom of Stones: A Tri-lingual Anthology of Haitian Poetry Written After the Earthquake* (Peepal Tree Press), which he edited. A Spanish-language collection of his poems, titled *Vuelo,* will appear in Mexico in 2016. His awards include an Emmy Award, a Webby, the Forward First Book Prize for Poetry, the Hollis Summers Prize, several Pushcart Prizes, Best

American Poetry selections, the Hurston/Wright Legacy Award, the *Poets and Writers* Barnes and Noble Writers for Writers Award, and a Guggenheim Foundation fellowship. In 2004 he received the Musgrave Silver Medal for contribution to the Arts in Jamaica and in 2008 the Elizabeth O'Neill Verner Governor's Award for the Arts in South Carolina. Dawes is currently the Glenna Luschei Editor of *Prairie Schooner* and Chancellor's Professor of English at the University of Nebraska. The co-founder and director of the Calabash International Literary Festival, he is founder and Director of the African Poetry Book Fund.

DEBRA GWARTNEY is the author of a memoir, *Live Through This*, (Houghton Mifflin Harcourt, 2009), a finalist for the National Book Critics Circle Award and the National Books for a Better Life Award. Her book was named one of the best books of the year by *The Oregonian* and the Pacific Northwest Booksellers' Association. Gwartney has published in many magazines and newspapers, as well as literary journals including *Tin House, The Normal School, Creative Nonfiction, Prairie Schooner, Washington Square Review, Kenyon Review, Salon,* and *Triquarterly Review.* She is a contributing editor at *Poets & Writers* magazine and in 2015 won the *Crab Orchard Review* prize for nonfiction. Gwartney was co-editor, along with Barry Lopez, of *Home Ground: Language for an American Landscape* (Trinity University Press, 2006).

LAURA HENDRIE's first book, *Stygo* (MacMurray & Beck, 1994), won the American Academy of Arts and Letters Rosenthal Award in 1995, the Mountains & Plains Booksellers Fiction Award, and a finalist citation for the PEN/Hemingway Award. Her novel, *Remember Me* (Henry Holt & Co., 1999), was a Book Sense selection, a Barnes & Noble Discover New Writers selection, and a finalist for the Mountains & Plains Booksellers Award. Her fiction has been aired on NPR and published in many anthologies including *Missouri Review, Colorado Review, Best of the West, Writers Forum,* and *Going Green*; her nonfiction has appeared in magazines such as *Outside, Boston Review, LIFE,* and *Chicago Tribune.* She has taught at Lighthouse Writers in Denver, Colorado, and at Warren Wilson College in Asheville, North Carolina. She currently lives in Salida, Colorado, and has just finished a novel, *The Year We Won a Firebird*.

PAM HOUSTON's most recent book is *Contents May Have Shifted* (W.W. Norton, 2012). She is also the author of two collections of linked short stories, *Cowboys Are My Weakness* and *Waltzing the Cat*; the novel, *Sight Hound*; and a collection of essays, *A Little More About Me*, all published by W.W. Norton. Her stories have been selected for volumes of *Best American Short Stories*, *The O. Henry Awards*, *The 2013 Pushcart Prize*, and *Best American Short Stories of the Century*. She is the winner of the Western States Book Award, the WILLA award for contemporary fiction, The Evil Companions Literary Award, and multiple teaching awards. She is professor of English at the University of California at Davis, directs the literary nonprofit Writing by Writers, and has taught in the Pacific University low-residency MFA program and at writers' conferences around the country and the world. She lives on a ranch at 9,000 feet in Colorado near the headwaters of the Rio Grande.

SCOTT KORB's books include *The Faith Between Us* (Bloomsbury, 2007), a collection of personal essays presented as a conversation with Jewish writer Peter Bebergal; *Life in Year One* (Riverhead, 2010), a popular history of first-century Palestine; and *Light Without Fire* (Beacon Press, 2013), an intimate portrait of the first year at America's first Muslim liberal arts college. He is associate editor of *The Harriet Jacobs Family Papers* (UNC Press, 2008), which was awarded the American Historical Association's 2009 J. Franklin Jameson Prize. With Robert Bolger, he edited a collection of essays about David Foster Wallace and philosophy, *Gesturing Toward Reality* (Bloomsbury, 2014). Scott teaches writing at New York University's Gallatin School of Individualized Study and Eugene Lang College at The New School. He lives with his family in New York City.

VALERIE LAKEN is the author of a story collection, *Separate Kingdoms* (Harper Perennial, 2011), and a novel, *Dream House* (Harper Perennial, 2010). Her work has received a Pushcart Prize and has been long-listed for the Story Prize, the Frank O'Connor Award, and *Best American Short Stories*. She holds an MFA from the University of Michigan and teaches at Pacific University's MFA program and at the University of Wisconsin–Milwaukee. She is at work on a graphic novel.

DORIANNE LAUX is author of several poetry collections, most recently *The Book of Men* (W.W. Norton, 2012). The recipient of national grants and awards, including fellowships from the Guggenheim Foundation and the National Endowment for the Arts, Laux lives in Raleigh where she teaches for the MFA program at North Carolina State University. She is also a founding faculty member for Pacific University's low-residency MFA in Writing program.

DAVID LONG's short stories have appeared in *The New Yorker, GQ, Granta,* and many anthologies. He has three short story collections, including *Blue Spruce* (Scribner, 1995), and three novels, *The Falling Boy* (Scribner, 1997), *The Daughters of Simon Lamoreaux* (Scribner, 2000), and *The Inhabited World* (Mariner, 2006). He is at work on a book of short fiction and a sequel to *The Falling Boy*. Since 1999, Long has lived in Tacoma, Washington.

MIKE MAGNUSON is the author of two novels, *The Right Man for the Job* (HarperCollins, 1997) and *The Fire Gospels* (HarperCollins, 1998), and three books of nonfiction, *Lummox: The Evolution of a Man* (HarperCollins, 2002), *Heft on Wheels: A Field Guide to Doing a 180* (Harmony Books, 2004), and *Bike Tribes: A Field Guide to North American Cyclists* (Rodale, 2012). His short fiction and nonfiction have appeared in *Esquire, Gentleman's Quarterly, The Massachusetts Review, Men's Health, Popular Mechanics, Backpacker*, and other publications, and he is a longtime contributing writer with *Bicycling* magazine. His piece "Whatever Happened to Greg LeMond"—originally published in *Bicycling*—has been reprinted in *Best American Sports Writing 2010* and in *The Best of Bicycling Magazine*. He lives in Appleton, Wisconsin, where he is finishing a novel about the Belgian Resistance in World War II. Whenever he gets the chance, he rides bicycles or plays the drums.

JOHN MCNALLY is the author of three novels, *The Book of Ralph* (Free Press, 2004), *America's Report Card* (Free Press, 2006), and *After the Workshop* (Counterpoint, 2010); two story collections, *Troublemakers* (University of Iowa Press, 2000) and *Ghosts of Chicago* (Jefferson Press, 2008); two nonfiction books, *Vivid and Continuous: Essays and Exercises for Writing Fiction* (University of Iowa Press, 2013) and *The Creative Writer's Survival Guide: Advice from an Unrepentant Novelist* (University of Iowa Press, 2010); and a Young Adult novel, *Lord of the Ralphs* (Lacewing Books, 2015). He has edited seven anthologies. His work has appeared in more than 100 publications, including *The Washington Post, The Sun, Virginia Quarterly Review*, and several anthologies, including *Shadow Show: All-New Stories in Celebration of Ray Bradbury* (William Morrow, 2012), *New Sudden Fiction: Short-Short Stories from America and Beyond* (W.W. Norton, 2007), and *Don't You Forget About Me: Contemporary Writers on the Films of John Hughes* (Simon & Schuster, 2007). He has been the recipient of fellowships from Paramount Pictures (Chesterfield Writer's Film Project), the University of Iowa (James Michener Award), George Washington University (Jenny McKean Moore Fellowship), and the University of Wisconsin-Madison (Djerassi Fellowship). McNally lives in Louisiana, where he is professor and writer-in-residence at the University of Louisiana at Lafayette.

BENJAMIN PERCY is the author of three novels—*The Dead Lands* (Grand Central, 2016), *Red Moon* (Grand Central, 2013), and *The Wilding* (Graywolf, 2010)—as well as two books of short fiction, *Refresh, Refresh* (Graywolf, 2007) and *The Language of Elk* (Grand Central, 2013). He writes the Green Arrow series for DC Comics. His fiction and nonfiction have been published by *Esquire*, where he is a contributing editor, *GQ, Time, Men's Journal*, the *Wall Street Journal, Poets & Writers*, the *Paris Review, Glimmer Train, Ploughshares, McSweeney's*, and *Tin House*. His honors include the Whiting Writers' Award, an NEA fellowship, the Plimpton Prize, two Pushcart Prizes, and inclusion in *Best American Short Stories* and *Best American Comics*.

MARY HELEN STEFANIAK is the author of *Self Storage and Other Stories* (New Rivers Press, 1997), and two novels: *The Turk and My Mother* (W.W. Norton, 2006), which has been translated into seven languages, and *The Cailiffs of Baghdad, Georgia* (W.W. Norton, 2011), an Indie Next Great Read and winner of the 2011 Anisfield-Wolf Book Award for Fiction. Her fiction has appeared in many periodicals and anthologies, including *New Stories from the South,* and her short essays can be found online at www.iowasource.com. She lives in Iowa City and Omaha, where she teaches at Creighton University.

INDEX